AutoCAD®
PROGRAMMING

Computer Graphics Technology and Management Series

Series Consulting Editor: Carl Machover
Edited by: David M. Gauthier

AutoCAD: Methods and Macros

by Jeff Guenther, Ed Ocoboc,
and Anne Wayman

VersaCAD Tutorial: A Practical Approach to Computer-Aided Design

by Carol Buehrens, CADD Specialist
CR/CADD, a division of
Consolidated Reprographics

DataCAD for the Architect

by Carol Buehrens

AutoCAD®
PROGRAMMING

Dennis N. Jump

TAB Professional and Reference Books

Division of TAB BOOKS Inc.
Blue Ridge Summit, PA

FIRST EDITION
FIRST PRINTING

Copyright © 1989 by TAB BOOKS Inc.
Printed in the United States of America

Library of Congress Cataloging-in-Publication Data

Jump, Dennis.
    AutoCAD programming / by Dennis N. Jump.
        p.   cm.
    Includes index.
    ISBN 0-8306-9093-X   ISBN 0-8306-9393-9 (pbk.)
    1. AutoCAD (Computer program)   I. Title.
T385.J86   1989
620′.00425′02855369—dc19   88-32991
                                                       CIP

TAB BOOKS Inc. offers software for sale. For information and a
catalog, please contact TAB Software Department, Blue Ridge
Summit, PA 17294-0850.

Questions regarding the content of this book
should be addressed to:

    Reader Inquiry Branch
    TAB BOOKS Inc.
    Blue Ridge Summit, PA 17294-0214

Larry Hager: Acquisitions Editor
David M. Gauthier: Technical Editor

Contents

Acknowledgments

There are two ways to avoid failure:

1. Don't start.
2. Don't stop.

There are a number of people who have thanks (or damnations) coming to them for getting me started on this project. And there are the saints that didn't let me stop. I'll name them all in one place so that the catagories aren't too obvious.

Larry Hager.

Ron Powers.

My family.

Renzo Spanhoff (Toot Toot!).

The Staff of The Great SoftWestern Company (Bill, Diana, Susan and Terri).

To Gwynn, Shelly, and Hilary,
mostly for their patience.

P.S.
For those of you who still wonder what I do for a living, this explains it a little better.

Introduction

The reasons for the acceptance of using CAD systems on personal computers are many. The reasons for the success of AutoCAD embodies most of the characteristics of this acceptance. Forgive me if I miss the majority of the reasons, but here goes:

Very wide command set.
Good mixture of simple and complex functions.
Intuitive use.
Wide selection of peripheral devices and options.
Available in several languages.
Reasonably priced.
User can modify tablet menus and screen menus.
Internal programming language.
Well documented.
A large number of third-party applications.

It is this last reason — isn't it clever how it worked out like that? — with which this book deals. We are going to take a look at how you can write application programs that use AutoCAD as a companion. AutoCAD can provide data to an application, and AutoCAD can display drawings produced by your application.

Now, don't expect this book to write your application for you. It can't. It will show you how to get data from AutoCAD for use in an analysis program. You provide the analyzer. It will show you how to prepare data acceptable to AutoCAD. You provide the numbers.

I've divided the discussions about application programming into five sections. Each section contains two chapters covering the subject matter. These sections are:

Programming Techniques
Setting the AutoCAD Scene
AutoCAD, The Driver
AutoCAD is a registered trademark of AutoDesk Inc.

In the *Programming Techniques* section (Chapters 1 and 2), you will find a discussion of various techniques used throughout the remainder of the book. The topics are somewhat general in nature in order to bring everyone to a common starting point when the CAD programming starts. There are explanations and plenty of examples of binary tree structures, string manipulations, and the heavily used finite-state machines.

Of all of the sections, the Setting the AutoCAD Scene section (Chapters 3 and 4) is the lightweight. This section is full of definitions and AutoCAD basics. Users of AutoCAD can spend a career using the program without seeing some of the patterns and nuances of it. This section points out command structures, MS-DOS interfaces, and AutoCAD files.

The next section, *AutoCAD, The Driver,* focuses on the interpretation of the output files, which you can use as a source of drawing information for programs. There are two files of interest here.

Chapter 5 deals with the Drawing Exchange Format (DXF) file. This file format is now the standard format for the exchange of drawing information between CAD systems on personal computers. Whether you use AutoCAD or another system, this chapter is important. This chapter contains some rough passages. I hope that I have smoothed them out for you.

Chapter 6 covers the attribute system. There are two ways that attributes can be extracted from a drawing. These are through the ATTEXT command and the TXT file, and through the DXF file. I cover both methods. Naturally there are numerous program listings to guide you.

AutoCAD can drive your application. Conversely, your application can drive Auto-CAD. The section, *AutoCAD, The Driven,* covers the ways in which you can get graphic data into AutoCAD.

Chapter 7 discusses several aspects of the AutoCAD script file. The script file allows the redirection of commands away from the keyboard and to a file. Program-generated commands have a direct path to the drawing command processor of AutoCAD. You don't plunge right into generating script files. I let you get your feet wet first. There are several small script files in this chapter that are convenient for everyday use. I even show my method for generating AutoCAD script files for the foreign (to me) language versions of AutoCAD.

Chapter 8 gets pretty thick, but it isn't as rough as Chapter 5. This chapter covers the generation of DXF and DXB (a binary form of DXF) from an external program. This chapter looks at all parts of the DXF file with suggestions for creating the necessary records. There are several variations in the examples. This is to show that there are any number of ways to generate this data. Most of the examples are real code that I borrowed from work (It's okay, I own the company.). They didn't all come from the same program, so the styles and techniques may not always match.

One of the things that I want to show in these chapters is the similarity in the preparation of the data before writing it to the files. Although you may have to hold your mouse a little differently from file format to file format, you should be able to change only the output routines to make a program change for script output to DXF or DXB output. The required data remains the same from one output format to the next; only the innards change.

The appendices contain large tables and listings which, although necessary for serious application development, are too bulky for inclusion in the normal text.

As this book goes to publication, AutoDesk has released AutoCAD Release 10. This release contains the long-awaited 3-D constructs for more sophisticated mechanical and architectural renderings. I have had a chance to use this product with some of our commercial software, which use the algorithms in this book. I have not run into any compatibility problems. The algorithms in this book skip over the newer elements of Release 10. I'm looking forward to another book with more detail on Release 10, Auto-LISP, and other aspects of AutoCAD application programming.

Please enjoy.

1

Data Structures and Techniques

WELCOME TO THE WORLD OF **CAD** PROGRAMMING! I'VE GOT GOOD NEWS FOR YOU. IT'S A small world and there's room for more good application programs for the **CAD** packages out there (as long as you're not competition. Competitors should not buy this book.).

We're going to take a trip through the programming techniques that you can use to make AutoCAD a software companion. We're going to start with an up-close look at several general programming conventions and encapsulate them into routines that we can use throughout all of the **CAD** related topics.

Soon enough, we'll get into interfacing programs to AutoCAD. We'll look at methods of extracting drawing information from AutoCAD **DXF** and attribute files. Turning the tables, we'll continue with the preparation of drawing data in several formats that Auto-CAD understands. We'll be driving AutoCAD with our own instructions. Finally, we'll look at application programming from within AutoCAD with Auto**LISP**.

I don't know about you, but I don't care for lengthy introductions any more than lengthy good-byes. Let's get started with some programming.

DATA STRUCTURES

Although the production of good software seems to stress the development of algorithms, in reality, the efficient use and storage of information can turn algorithm development into an almost minor task. In these next two chapters, we'll look at some general techniques in data storage and manipulation.

The main concern of this chapter is to explore, explain and develop elementary data structures and algorithms. These topics form the backbone of the techniques used throughout the discussions that follow.

Chapter Two covers slightly more advanced topics with emphasis on combining algorithms to form more complex processes. Once we can get a bunch of the puzzle pieces on the table, we can start to put the puzzle together. Therefore, some of these topics will be continuations of topics started in this chapter.

At all times the primary thing that you will see in these chapters is the collection of meaningful information from AutoCAD data files. This collecting process will not only give us data to organize and store; but it will give directions that guide your program's operation—a data-driven environment instead of a process-driven one.

The topics covered in this chapter are:
Organization of lines and points
Binary trees
Decorating the binary tree
String storage
Symbol table

ORGANIZATION OF LINES AND POINTS

Since the primary element in the **CAD** system is the line, the first structure with which we will deal is a means of saving and organizing collected lines. Since the connectivity and continuity of lines can be an important aspect in some drawings and application programs, the emphasis of this section will be towards constructing a structure that builds and preserves the relationships of the line information.

Let's start by looking at the simplest case of defining and storing a line. And, to do that, we'll need to begin with the definition of a point. Figure 1-1 shows a point in three dimensional space. I wish that this could be a hologram, but we'll have to make do with a two dimension representation. A point has no size, yet it occupies a location in space. In three dimensional space, we note the location of a point by its distance along the three perpendicular axes, X, Y, and Z. The units of measurement are arbitrary.

In this discussion we identify a line by selecting two points on that line. In formal geometry, a line is of infinite length and merely passes through the two selected points. Figure 1-2 shows a line passing through some points. However, in a **CAD** system, we

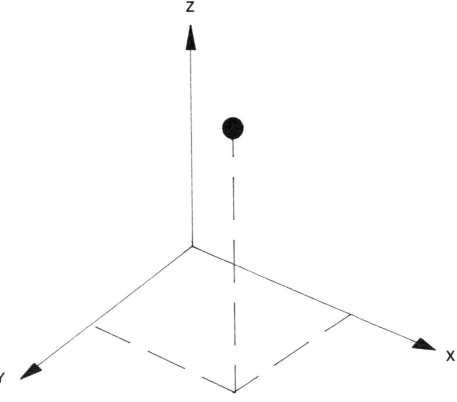

Fig. 1-1. A point in 3-D space.

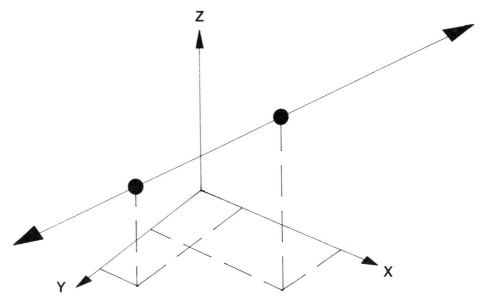

Fig. 1-2. A line in space.

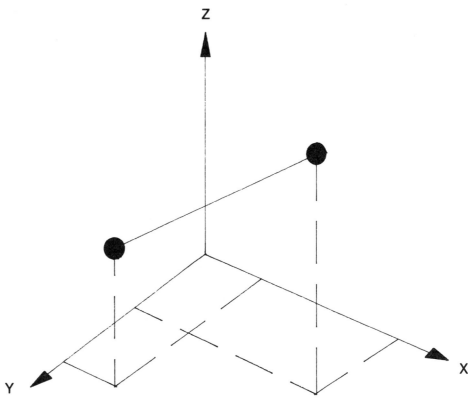

Fig. 1-3. Endpoints of a line segment.

```
double          from_x;
double          from_y;
double          from_z;
double          to_x;
double          to_y;
double          to_z;
```
Listing 1-1. Simple variables to hold coordinates.

actually deal with line segments. These are everyday lines that have definite beginning and ending points. In this case, the two points that identify the line are its end points. In a two dimension drawing points are identified by their X and Y coordinates. We add a Z coordinate for drawings in three dimensions. Figure 1-3 shows the identifying end points of a typical line segment. For the remainder of our discussion, the term "line" refers to a line segment.

In the programming arena, use simple variables to hold the values of the end point coordinates for identifying simple lines or in a situation where you want to retain information for a short time. Looking at a simple line with its X, Y, and Z coordinates for the two end points, you could employ the following variables. Listing 1-1 is a good example of defining a group of variables for storing a line.

This scheme works nicely when the programming situation is not very complicated. There are enough circumstances in which this form of organization is usable that it should not be cast aside as too elementary. Most commonly, primitive subroutines use this arrangement. Take, for example, the task of finding the length of a line. Listing 1-2 is the code for the distance function. In this case, the discrete variables appear as parameters to the distance function. The function sees the values as simple variables. When the end points of a line are passed to the distance function, it calculates the distance between the points. The units of measurement are arbitrary.

The extra variables in the example make the code easier to read. In real life and in a real program, the x, y, and z local variables are not used. You would write the entire routine in a single line.

```
double    sqrt(); /* for usage definition */
double    distance(from_x,from_y,from_z,to_x,to_y,to_z)
double        from_x;
double        from_y;
double        from_z;
double        to_x;
double        to_y;
double        to_z;
{
double        x;
double        y;
double        z;

    x = to_x - from_x;
    y = to_y - from_y;
    z = to_z - from_z;
    return sqrt (x*x + y*y + z*z);
}
```
Listing 1-2. The distance function.

```
typedef
  struct
  {
    double       x;
    double       y;
    double       z;
  }              coord;
```
Listing 1-3. The basic coord structure.

Once again, coding with simple variables to hold point coordinates is not a wrong thing to do. However, there comes a time when the program becomes so overwhelmed with coordinate variables that it becomes difficult to figure out which one holds which coordinate. Grouping the x, y, and z coordinates together to organize our program is the next step.

In a logical sense, the coordinates of the end points are a single entity. To completely identify a unique point, all three values (in a 3-D system) must be present. So, the next development is to group the coordinate values into a record style structure. This record structure becomes the starting point for our data structure evolution. You can be sure that we'll twist it around a bit, but you'll see a continuity of it throughout the book. Let's start with a simple definition for coordinates. Listing 1-3 is the type definition of our basic *coord* data structure.

Two points define a line. And, we have just defined a point, a location in space with X, Y and Z coordinates. The structure for defining a line would then be a record structure that identified the line's two end points. Listing 1-4 is the simple brute force definition of a line.

```
typedef
  struct
  {
    double       fx;      /* from */
    double       fy;
    double       fz;
    double       tx;      /*  to  */
    double       ty;
    double       tz;
  }              line;
```
Listing 1-4. A first attempt at organizing a line.

If the job of finding independent line segments interests you, this data structure could prove useful. Listing 1-5 shows the declaration of an array of these line types holding many line segments.

```
line                lines[200];
line                *next_line = lines;
```
Listing 1-5. Structure for holding several line values.

As a program recognizes and saves lines, it increments a counter to show the next available space. In this example, the counter is an address pointer to the next line storage element. It can be incremented also. The name of this variable is next_line. Its initial value is set to the beginning of the line structure.

Using this brute force organization, searching for and finding line connectivity (strings of connected line segments) may be a slow process. The major reason for this is that you must provide extra data or processing steps to determine connectivity. You must search and find the corresponding line definition that shares an end point from the collected list of line segments. Knowing the "to" coordinates of the from-to pair of one line, you search the active list for a matching "from" value. On the average, you will have to look at half of the entries. The search ends when the "from" coordinates for a line segment match the known "to" coordinates. With this match, you know that the individual links are connected.

However, when modeling a large network of lines with hundreds or thousands of line segments, there are methods which improve both memory use and search time.

Let's tackle memory use first. The section on binary trees will cover the search problem. Using the brute force structure shown earlier, when processing connected line segments, the program saves a coordinate's value twice in the line structure. Once as the "to" value and again as the next "from" value. End points are the exception, being recorded only once apiece. With eight bytes being used for every double precision floating point value, you don't need to be doubling up the coordinates if conserving memory area interests you. Figure 1-4 illustrates the brute force method of coordinate management.

Suppose that we leave the coordinates in the coord structure and let a line structure simply reference or point to the two coordinates that defined the line. Figure 1-5 shows a small step toward a better method of handling coordinates. Listing 1-6 is the new definition of the line record.

I've added a reference to some, so far, undefined layering reference. Since **CAD** layers can carry significant information, I've added the reference to show how easy it is to add extra data to the line structure. You might add a reference to **LINETYPE** so you could distinguish between continuous, dotted or dashed lines. Line width would be another candidate for this structure. Of course, the application decides what is appropriate and what is not.

From			To	
1.234	0.0		2.345	1.200
2.345	1.200		2.345	2.431
2.345	2.431		2.500	3.125
2.500	3.125		3.000	3.500
0.000	0.000		1.000	1.000
1.000	1.000		0.000	0.500
0.000	0.500		0.000	2.500

Fig. 1-4. Brute force line management.

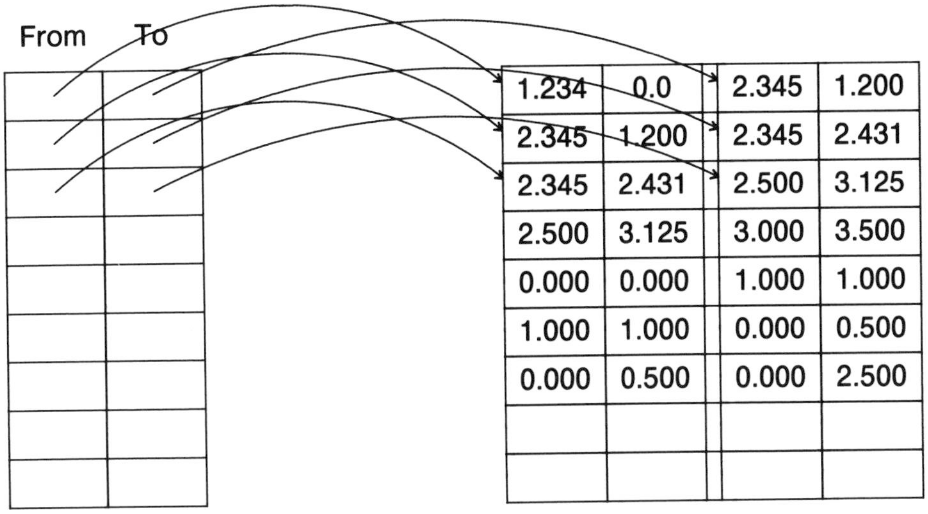

Fig. 1-5. Referencing endpoints for lines.

Figure 1-6 shows a compressed form of the line and coordinate relationship. The end point reference pointers in the line values share common coordinates. This significantly decreases the amount of room required to store lists of coordinates.

We could produce a smaller line definition if we stored the coordinates of the end points in an array. Instead of keeping a pointer address in the line structure which needs two to four bytes (depending upon the memory model that you are using), you could keep the integer (two bytes) index of the coordinates in the line value. This produces a more compact structure. However, this forces the program to calculate the address of the

```
typedef
  struct        line
    {
      coord     from;
      coord     to;
    }           line;

line            lines[100];
int             num_lines = 0;
int             i;
double          fx;
double          fy;
double          tx;
double          ty;

for(i=0;i<num_lines;i++)
  {
    fx = lines[i].from.x;
    fy = lines[i].from.y;
    tx = lines[i].to.x;
    ty = lines[i].to.y;
  }
```

Listing 1-6. Reorganized line definition.

7

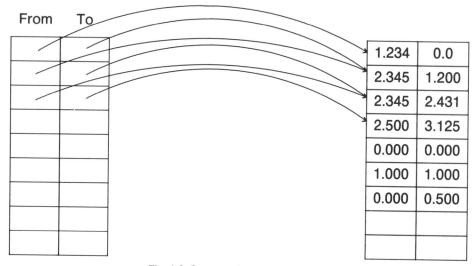

1.234	0.0
2.345	1.200
2.345	2.431
2.500	3.125
0.000	0.000
1.000	1.000
0.000	0.500

Fig. 1-6. Compressing the references.

coordinates for each retrieval. This can take extra computing time and more program space for the conversion instructions. You don't write this code yourself. The compiler generates it at every array and index use. Use of the method depends upon your comfort level with addresses and pointers. Listing 1-7 shows the details for using integer indexes.

```
coord           lines[100];
int             next_line = 0;
int             from_ref[100];
int             to_ref[100];
int             i;

for(i=0;i<next_line;i++)
  {
   fx = lines[from_ref[i]].x;
   fy = lines[from_ref[i]].y;
   tx = lines[to_ref[i]].x;
   ty = lines[to_ref[i]].y;
  }
```

Listing 1-7. The line definition with array indexes.

I tend to stick with pointers. They allow the flexibility of referencing predefined data, array structures, stack, and heap without being tied to any one of them. A single pointer variable reaches all of these memory areas.

For the moment, let's step back and review coordinates and lines by building a set of small arrays and functions for dealing with lines. This will give you an idea of the relations involved. Listing 1-8 is the data declaration section of our review code.

The extra variables, next_line and next_coord, assign the next available position to new lines and coordinates. When they reach a maximum value, the structure is full and cannot allow anymore entries.

You build an active list in the array of lines and end points with functions like insert_line. This is not a function that I would normally employ. It is too simple for efficient

```
typedef
  struct
   {
    double          x;
    double          y;
    double          z;
   }              coord;

typedef
  struct
   {
    coord          *from;
    coord          *to;
   }              line;

line              lines[100];
line              *next_line = lines;
coord             points[170];
coord             *next_coord = points;
```
Listing 1-8. A typical set of data declarations.

```
coord *find_coord(x,y,z)
double     x;
double     y;
double     z;
{
coord      *c;
/* * * * * * * * * * * * * * * * * * * * * * */
/*  This function finds and returns the      */
/*  address of the coordinate structure      */
/*  containing the passed values             */
/*  It will add the values to the POINTS     */
/*  array if they are not found              */
/* * * * * * * * * * * * * * * * * * * * * * */

   c = points;
   while (c < next_coord)  /* for all valid coords */
    {
     if ((c->x == x) && (c->y == y) && (c->z == z))
       return c; c++;
      /* well, it wasn't that one -- try next  */
    } /* coordinates not found in table -- add them */
   c = next_coord++;
   /* set values */
   c->x = x;
   c->y = y;
   c->z = z;
   return c;  /* send back address of added values */
}
```
Listing 1-9. The find_coord function.

```
line *insert_line (fx,fy,fz,tx,ty,tz)
double      fx;
double      fy;
double      fz;
double      tx;
double      ty;
double      tz;
{
line        *l;
/* * * * * * * * * * * * * * * * * * * */
/*  This function adds a new line which is */
/*  defined by the passed parameters       */
/*  It will use the FIND_COORD function     */
/*  to avoid duplication of coordinates     */
/* * * * * * * * * * * * * * * * * * * */

    l = next_line++;  /* get next available line */
    l->from = find_coord (fx,fy,fz);
    l->to = find_coord (tx,ty,tz);
    return l;
}
```

Listing 1-10. The insert_line function.

processing of complex drawings. It does give you an idea of what can be done. Listing 1-9 is the secondary find_coord function.

Listing 1-10 is primary function, insert_line. I tag these functions as primary and secondary because the main program would use the insert_line function. The find_coord function gets used by only the insert_line function.

So as not to clutter the code, the functions lack suitable checks for signaling when they reach the end of the arrays. The checks would involve testing the next_coord and next_line variables to see if they were greater than the address of the last element in the array. If this happens, the program gives an appropriate message and returns a pointer value of **NULL**.

To insert a line, your program would call the insert_line function with the end points of the line as parameters. It does not search for duplicate lines. However, the find_coord function, called by insert_line, does search the list of coordinates so that duplicate coordinates are not recorded. It appears first in the listings, as it would in your program, so the insert_line will know that it returns the address of a coordinate group instead of the C default assumption of integer.

One of the weak points of this arrangement is the linear search of the coordinates table. As mentioned earlier, this is a slow way to do things. The search finds if a set of coordinates have already been stored. If the coordinates are in the table, there is no need to add the coordinates again. The function returns the address of the found coordinates.

Granted, the code is simple and very little can go wrong with it. This can be a real selling point for this search method. It is a quick way to prove whether an idea is right or wrong. However, without getting involved in mathematical analysis of the search time, let's just say that it is one of the slowest search methods available. Everything has a tradeoff. If the code and structure is easy, the payoff in speed is not very good. Faster processing relies on more complex structures.

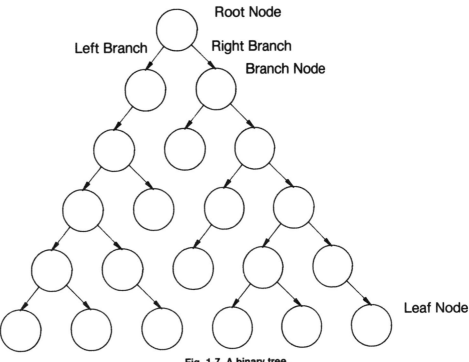

Fig. 1-7. A binary tree.

BINARY TREES

To increase the search speed for coordinates, we'll use a binary tree. Actually drawing one of these things (Figure 1-7) produces an upside down tree (at least as nature treats a tree). The top element (or node) is the root. This is the anchoring node for the entire tree.

Branches (or branch nodes) grow from the root and other branches. Branches that are anchored to other branches are sub-trees.

At the ends of the branches are leaves. Leaves are nodes without further sub-trees. They are terminals. They can become branches when we attach leaves or branches to them.

Notice that each node can support up to two sub-trees. This is where the binary designation comes in. See Figure 1-8. There can be one sub-tree on the left side (the left branch) and one sub-tree on the right.

It is up to the program to build the tree by attaching nodes to the left or right side of a given node. We'll get to that. You may pick any scheme that you wish in determining node attachment. However, the normal method is to attach nodes according to the value of the data within the node. Nodes of lesser value attach to the left side and nodes of greater value attach to the right. Figure 1-9 is a binary tree constructed to sort a group of numbers. The numbers arrived in this order: 18, 22, 10, 15, 25, 3, 12, 16. Can you see the reason why the tree grew to this shape?

This makes the search fairly simple to describe. Try the following algorithm on the Figure 1-9 with the value of 12. Start at the root node.

If you find the target value in a node, you have finished the search. If the target value is less than the value in the node, you continue the search in the left sub-tree. Otherwise, you search the right sub-tree. At the new search node, the root of the new sub-tree, you find yourself in the same situation as before: Is the value in this node, or do I search left or

11

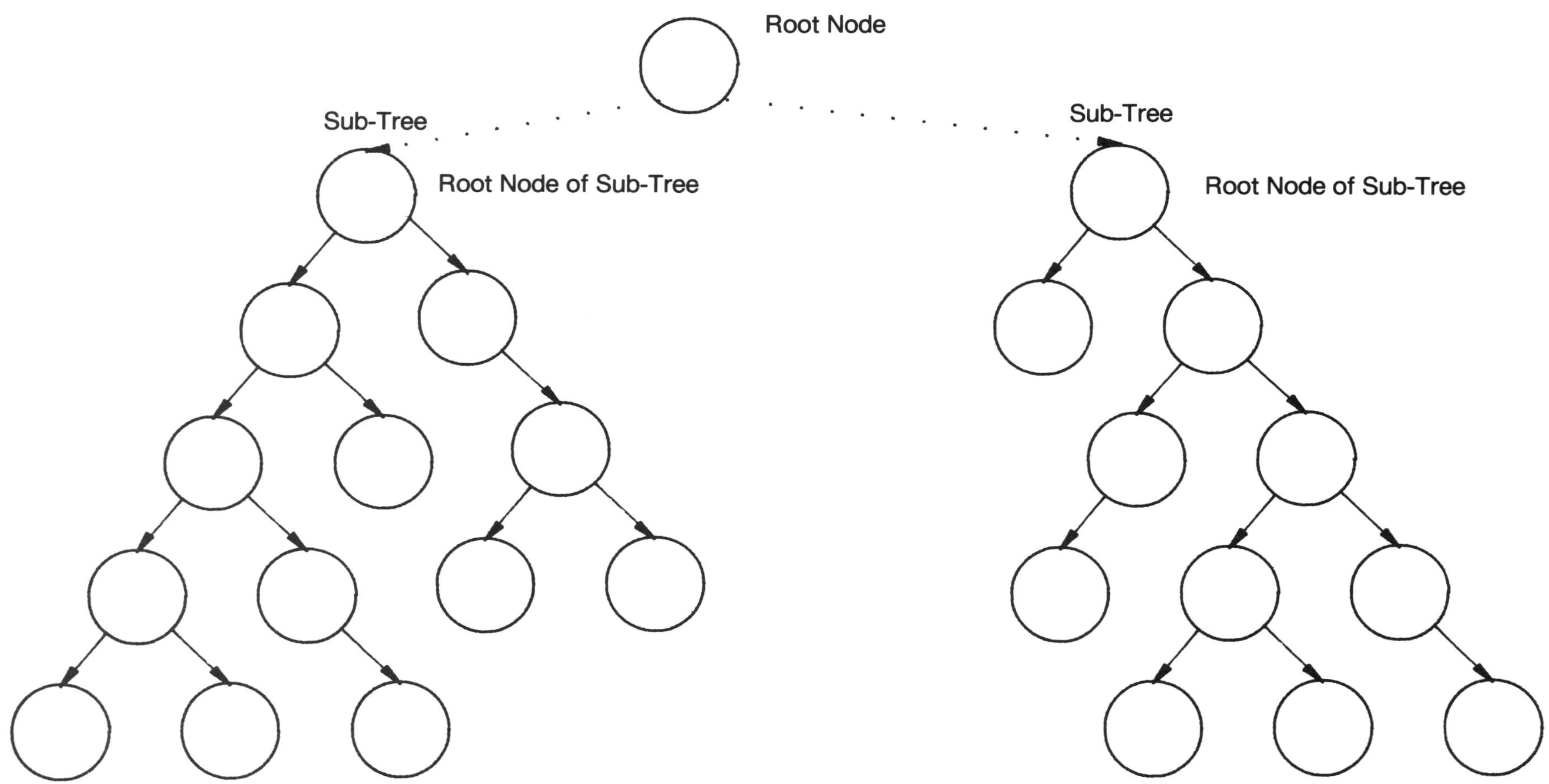

Root Node

Sub-Tree

Root Node of Sub-Tree

Sub-Tree

Root Node of Sub-Tree

Fig. 1-8. Sub-trees in the binary tree.

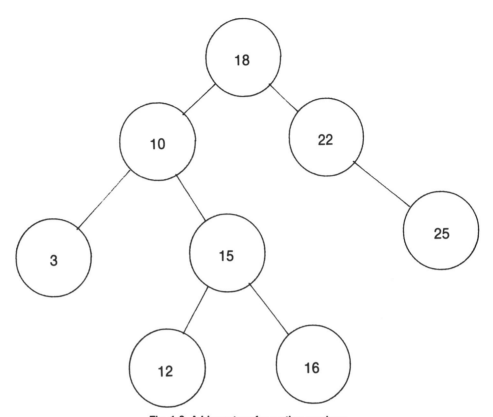

Fig. 1-9. A binary tree for sorting numbers.

right? You can fashion this repeating aspect of the algorithm as either a loop or recursive routine. But, maybe not so simple to program.

Before we get into the programming example of building a binary tree of coordinates, let's update the coord data structure. The structure of the coord record changes somewhat. We add left and right address pointers so the program can find the sub-trees. Listing 1-11 is the structure definition that we will use in the binary tree program examples.

The next group of listings are support utilities for the find_coord function. Listing 1-12 is the comp_coord (compare two coordinates) function. Given two coordinates (x, y and z), this function decides whether the first set of values is less than, equal to or greater than the second. To indicate its decision, it returns -1 to indicate less than, 0 for equal values, and +1 when the first is greater than the second. It entails more than simply

```
typedef
  struct a
  {
    double     x;
    double     y;
    double     z;
    struct a   *left;
    struct a   *right;
  }          coord;
```

Listing 1-11. The coord structure adapted for the binary tree.

```
int comp_coord(x1,y1,z1,x2,y2,z2)
double        x1;
double        y1;
double        z1;
double        x2;
double        y2;
double        z2;
{
/* this function compares two sets of coordinates */
/* the results are:                               */
/*                    0 -- coords equal           */
/*                   -1 -- first < second         */
/*                    1 -- first > second         */
/* get rid of the easy -- wanted case first       */

    if ((x1 == x2) && (y1 == y2) && (z1 == z2))
      return 0;

  /* check all possibilities of first less than second */

    if (x1 < x2) return -1;
    if ((x1 == x2) && (y1 < y2)) return -1;
    if ((x1 == x2) && (y1 == y2) && (z1 < z2))
      return -1;

  /* first must be greater than second */

    return 1;
}
```

Listing 1-12. The comp_coord function.

comparing two numbers since there are six values with an implied x, y and z ordering involved.

The new_coord function (Listing 1-13) handles the basic maneuvers in creating a new binary tree node. It fetches a node from heap space, initializes some values, and stuffs coordinates into others. It returns the address of the new node. Other functions will attach the node to the tree.

If we go back to the earlier find_coord and insert_line functions, we have to change only the find_coord function. The insert_line function still receives a pointer to the coord group and has no interest in the origin of the pointer. Listings 1-14 and 1-15 show two ways to write the find_coord function. They are identical in function, but some C short cuts appear in Listing 1-15. All of the other listings (1-11 through 1-13) are straight forward enough for me to resist tinkering with them. This algorithm leaves us with the structure shown in Figure 1-10.

DECORATING THE BINARY TREE

If we hang bits and pieces on our tree (Can you see where this is leading us?), we are decorating the tree.

So far, we have shown lines as our means of finding coordinates. Let's approach this from another angle. Imagine tying lines to points instead of points to lines. So far we have

```
coord *new_coord(x,y,z)
double     x;
double     y;
double     z;
{
coord          c;
/* this function gets a new coord node from heap    */
/* it then fills the record fields with coord data */
  c = (coord *)malloc(sizeof(coord));
  c->x = x;
  c->y = y;
  c->z = z;
  c->left = NULL;
  c->right = NULL;
  return c;
}
```

Listing 1-13. The new_coord function.

been saying that a line is defined by two particular end points. Suppose we turn it around and say that a point uses a particular line. We could identify a line by its coordinates instead of identifying coordinates of a line.

The approach is, having a point, identify the lines that use that point. Bear in mind that nobody has ever said that a point couldn't serve as the intersection of several lines.

```
coord *find_coord(n,x,y,z)
coord          *n;
double     x;
double     y;
double     z;
{
/* this function compares coords with value in    */
/* current node (see notes in comp_coord)         */
/* tree search continues if there is a sub-tree   */
/* search ends when match is made or a leaf is    */
/* added for new coords                           */

    switch(comp_coord(x,y,z,n->x,n->y,n->z))
      {
      case -1 : if (n->left) return find_coord(n->left,x,y,z);
                n->left = new_coord(x,y,z);
                return n->left;
      case  0 : return n;
      case  1 : if (n->right) return find_coord(n->right,x,y,z);
                n->right = new_coord(x,y,z);
                return n->right;
      }
    return NULL;
}
```

Listing 1-14. The find_coord function for binary trees.

```
coord *find_coord(n,x,y,z)
coord      *n;
double     x;
double     y;
double     z;
{
   switch(comp_coord(x,y,z,n->x,n->y,n->z))
    {
     case -1 : return ((n->left) ?  find_coord(n->left,x,y,z) :
                                    (n->left = new_coord(x,y,z));
     case 0 : return n;
     case  1 : return ((n->right) ?  find_coord(n->right,x,y,z) :
                                    (n->right = new_coord(x,y,z));
    }
   return NULL;
}
```

Listing 1-15. The find_coord function, again.

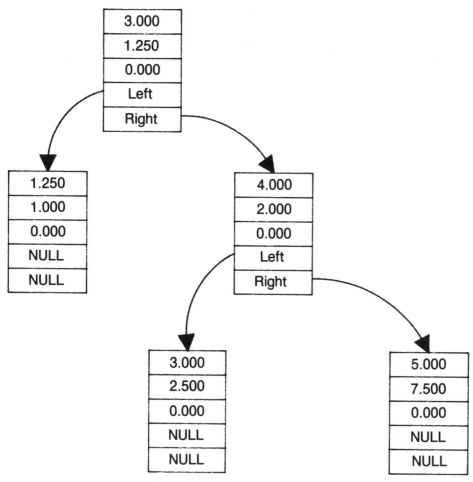

Fig. 1-10. A binary tree of coordinates.

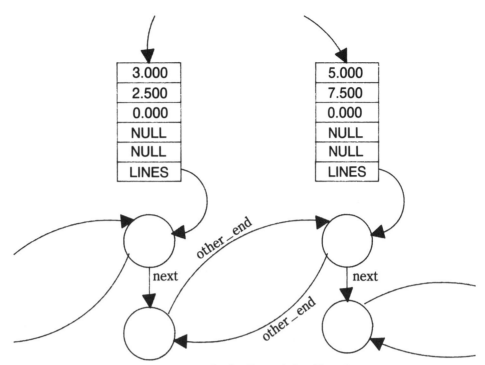

Fig. 1-11. Indicating line ends in a binary tree.

Next we need to redefine the way in which we describe lines. Certainly the line must identify both end points, but a twist in thinking can lead to a new representation. Since there are two end points involved in making a line, what is keeping us from using two separate structures to define the line using those end points? Well, there is no reason; other than how do you relate the two structures? We conveniently packaged our earlier line definitions and made the relation between the end points obvious. The references to both appeared in the single line definition. Now I'm talking about splitting the line definition with its two coordinate pointers.

The solution lies in adding another pointer reference. (Goodness! This guy must love pointers.) We add a reference that says, "Over there is my other end point." Figure 1-11 illustrates the mechanism being suggested.

If we are going out-of-our-way to let the coord structure point at lines, the coord structure must carry those addresses. A reference is built to connect the lines to the coordinate. Listing 1-16 adds the line reference to the coord structure.

```
typedef
  struct a
  {
  double      x;
  double      y;
  double      z;
  struct a    *left;    /* binary tree pointers */
  struct a    *right;
  line        *lines;   /* lines using coordinate */
  }           coord;
```

Listing 1-16. The coord structure with line references.

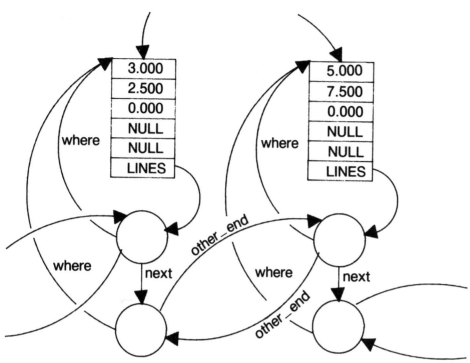

Fig. 1-12. Back referencing lines to their endpoints.

The line structure we've already seen has most of the required variables. However, we may have to take a new look at some of them.

As we move through this network of lines and coordinates, our processing will lead us from line node to line node as we discover connections and relations. If this is true, we will have to look at the associated coordinate node to find out **where** we are. Figure 1-12 expands on this relationship.

So, we've come a full circle. The coordinates identify their lines and once again the lines identify their end points. Therefore we can add a pointer to the line structure that says, "These are my coordinates." As before, this will be a pointer to a coordinate node. Listing 1-17 illustrates the details for this new definition.

What about multiple lines intersecting at a point? The coordinate node references its lines, but there is only one line reference. Will we need several line references (an array of pointers) in the coordinate node? No, one reference is enough if we chain the line definitions together. It would be wasteful to have a bunch of unused line references in a coordinate node because you must always have one more reference than the maximum

```
typedef
  struct b
    {
    struct b    *other_end;
    coord       *where;
    layer       *lyr;
    double       width;
    }            line;
```

Listing 1-17. A split line definition.

```
typedef
  struct b
   {
    struct b    *next;        /* next line node in chain */
    struct b    *other_end;   /* other end of line       */
    coord       *where;       /* where are we?           */
    layer       *lyr;
    double       width;
   }             line;
```

Listing 1-18. A chained line definition.

number of lines ... just to be sure! Not having enough space for line references will cripple the program. Having too many is wasteful. How do we know how many to use? We don't, so we build a chain, a linked list of line nodes. It is slower than having immediately available references as an array provides, but it removes the problem of trying to guess the volume of data. The line node definition with the added chain reference is in Listing 1-18.

The function insert_line now gets a face lift. It has been doing very little in advancing along with the data structures. One of the major changes is to take the line definition nodes out of the array and allocate their memory from heap. These will be nodes that will hang from the binary tree of the coordinates.

The drawing of the decorated tree, Figure 1-13, shows the results of this algorithm over the space of a small number of lines.

So we have a decorated binary tree. The tree gets branches and leaves with coordinates used by the gathered data. We decorate the tree by hanging bits of information about the internal workings of the tree. In this case, we've decorated the tree with the lines that use the coordinates.

Even Christmas comes to an end and the tree has to come down. The same is true for the decorated tree. We've loaded the tree with coordinates and lines. Now is the time to get some benefit from it. The point of this entire exercise is to retrieve line connectivity from a list of unassociated line coordinates.

A later chapter covers the major details for traversing the binary tree and picking up the connected lines. An outline of the algorithm that is used to visit the nodes of the binary tree is shown in Listing 1-20. This is a recursive routine that implements the algorithm description used earlier for finding a node in the tree. Once again, if there is a left side (the lesser side), visit all of the nodes in that sub-tree. When the left side has been processed, perform the designated function on the current node. At the completion of this work, proceed to apply the process to the sub-tree on the right side. Notice that the process is started only when there is a sub-tree on the designated side.

At any given coordinate node in the binary tree, we can find all of the lines attached to that node. In the bit of code in Listing 1-21, we see that the visit to a coordinate node (Listing 1-20) may involve collecting end points for the lines using this coordinate. This is a matter of visiting all of the line values that were attached to a coordinate node. Add a visited flag to the line definition so that you can tell whether a line end point has been used.

STRING STORAGE

When a program needs to use several data types in its processing, it becomes convenient to keep all of the data at the same size. When data is the same size (byte-wise), you can plan the size of the data structures better. Now this seems simple at the outset.

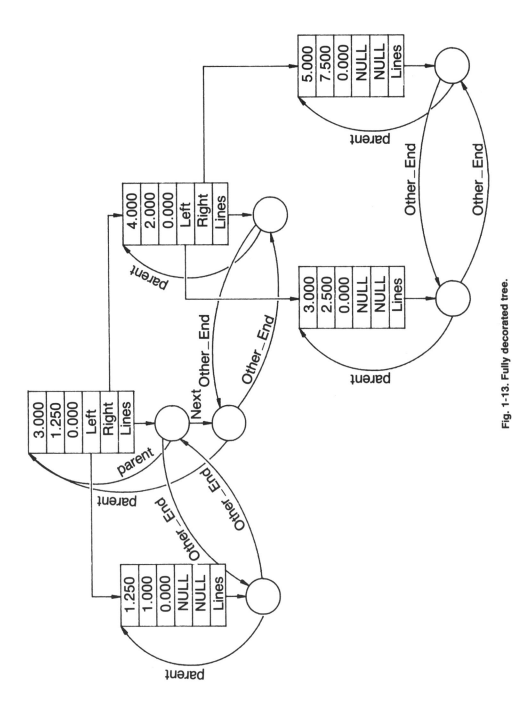

Fig. 1-13. Fully decorated tree.

```
void insert_line(fx,fy,fz,tx,ty,tz)
double          fx;
double          fy;
double          fz;
double          tx;
double          ty;
double          tz;
{
line            *l1;
line            *l2;

/* get two line nodes from heap */
/* see Figure 1-15a              */
  l1 = (line *) malloc(sizeof(line));
  l2 = (line *) malloc(sizeof(line));
/* clear fields that can be added later */
/* see Figure 1-15b                      */
  l1->width = 0.0;
  l1->lyr = NULL;
  l2->width = 0.0;
  l2->lyr = NULL;
/* establish coordinates for lines */
/* see Figure 1-15c                 */
  if (!root) root = new_coord(fx,fy,fz);
  l1->where = find_coord (root,fx,fy,fz);
  l2->where = find_coord (root,tx,ty,tz);
/* connect to each other */
/* see Figure 1-15d       */
  l1->other_end = l2;
  l2->other_end = l1;
/* attach to coordinate node  */
/* see Figure 1-15e           */
  l1->next = l1->where->lines;
  l1->where->lines = l1;
  l2->next = l2->where->lines;
  l2->where->lines = l2;
}
```

Listing 1-19. The decorated binary tree insert_line function.

```
void process_coord(n)
coord        *n
{
   if (n->left) process_coord(n->left);
 /* do whatever you are going to do to the node */
   if (n->right) process_coord(n->right);
}
```

Listing 1-20. Outline for coordinate processing.

```
void visit_node(n)
coord      *n;
{
line       *l;
line       *o;

  l = n->lines;
  while (l)
    {
     if (l->visited == FALSE)
       {
        o = l->other_end;
        /* do things to the line */
        l->visited = TRUE;
       }
      l = l->next;
    }
}
```

Listing 1-21. Visiting the lines attached to a coordinate.

Integers are always 16 bits in a PC (32 bits in some of the more sophisticated machines), floating point numbers are 32 bits (64 bits for double precision). Addresses depend upon the memory model being used, but 16 bits for **NEAR** addresses and 32 bits for **FAR** addresses are the normal sizes. We're looking at this from the view of the 8086 family of processors.

When values are the same size, you know how much memory each data value uses. So, what's the big deal? Strings are the big deal. The old question, "How long is a piece of string?" comes into play here. The revised question is, "How many characters are in a character string?" We will handle all sorts of names when we decipher an AutoCAD **DXF** file. There are layer names, block names, attribute values, text strings, and tag labels.

For internal name fields, names of layers and blocks, for instance, AutoCAD allows up to 32 characters. For text and attribute values, there are no limits. So if it is possible to encounter a string of zero to umpty-ump characters, how are we going to figure out the amount of room to reserve for a character string in our data structures? We certainly aren't blessed with having values of a consistant size.

The AutoCAD approach to internal names (length limit of 32) is to reserve 33 characters to hold the string within the individual structures. 33? Well, the strings can be of any length from zero to 32 characters. There has to be a method for determining how many characters are actually in the string. We can do this in one of two ways.

In Pascal, the first byte of the string is the length byte. Since it is an eight bit field, it could show strings with lengths from zero to 255 characters. In a string with a maximum length of 32 characters, it has a value between zero and 32, indicating the number of valid characters following the length byte. If you reserved 32 bytes for a string, the additional length would raise that count to 33.

However, AutoCAD is not written in Pascal, it is written in C. Well, it's a different ball game in C. In a C string, there is no count to tell how many valid characters are in the string. C uses a terminator character to show the end of the string. The character used to end the string is the one character that is unique in the **ASCII** character set: **NULL** ... nothing, binary zero, zilch.

So, for a 32 character string, there must be room for the terminating **NULL** character; making a total of 33 bytes. Notice there is no logical maximum length to a C string like there is for a Pascal string (255 bytes). There is a physical maximum, the size of a memory segment in an 8086 family machine — 64K.

You must be careful when reserving a fixed space for strings. If you violate you own boundaries with a 40 character string in a 32 byte field, you are liable (very liable) to overrun other data values, rendering your program completely useless or at least unreliable.

On the other hand, I have a question for you. How often have you used a 32 character name for the name of a layer or block? If you are like everyone else, you pick simple and short names. I use names like:

PARTS, SIGNALS, L1, L2, DRILL.

These names become internal AutoCAD names and the amount of reserved memory is static. What happens to the extra spaces in AutoCAD, the 20 or more characters not used with every one of my names? Nothing! They just go to waste. Well, if it's good enough for AutoCAD, then it's good enough for you. Right? If you agree with this, you can skip ahead to the next section.

Still with me? Good. Remember that I mentioned that addresses are all the same size? They are 16 or 32 bits long, depending upon your chosen memory model. I am thinking of a scheme where I save all of the character strings in a nice safe place and then manipulate and move the pointers (addresses) around instead playing with the entire string.

Addresses are always the same size regardless of the length of the string. Therefore it is a simple matter to put these into a complex structure and not worry about unused, good-for-something-else memory.

When you have the address of a string, you simply fetch the character at that location and continue fetching until you find a **NULL** character.

In C, a pointer to a character or character string is declared as:

```
char     *name_of_pointer;
```

The actual memory that holds the character is declared as an array of characters:

```
char     name_of_string[81];
```

A pointer contains the address of a single character. It is not necessarily the first character in a string or array. It can point to the 126th character.

C really helps us out with strings and pointers. When you use an array name and designate a particular element, such as, airplane[4], then C uses the individual element value. However, when you reference the name of the array or string, all by itself, C uses the **ADDRESS** of the array. How convenient. Imagine, getting the address of a memory location automatically by naming it.

The name airplane[4] gets the value of the fifth element (0-1-2-3-4 See? Fifth element.) in the airplane array. airplane produces the address of the airplane array. This only works for arrays, by the way. If you want the address of an integer named bike, for instance, you would use the ampersand (&) form, &bike, to get the address.

Suppose I have an area called words with 1024 bytes reserved for characters. Then I can save the address of words in a pointer called next_word very simply. I assign the value (the address of words) by using the name of the array.

```
char      words[1024];
char      *next_word = words;
```

Notice that the code declares next_words to be a pointer to characters and has been predefined as having the address of the words array. The purpose of the next_word variable is to point to the position of the next available character or string area in the words array. Whenever the program needs to add a new word to the words array, next_word tells it where to put it. At the beginning of the program, there are no words to be put into the array, so next_word points to the beginning of the array.

"That's all well and good," you are probably saying, "but, how do you get words into the words array?" The trite answer is: "You copy the string that you have into the array."

The C function that copies strings is strcpy. When this function receives the addresses of two strings, destination and source, it copies the characters of the source string into the string at the destination address. For a transfer of a string in airplane into the words array, the code would look like this:

strcpy(next_word,airplane);

strcpy requires two addresses. The first address is the destination address. For this value, we used the address of the next available string area in words, next_word holds this value. It is a variable which holds the address value and C passes this address value to the strcpy function. The second address is the address of the source string. Here, the function call uses the name of the string. Since I only used the name of the array, C passes the address of the airplane array for this value.

The strcpy function moves character from the source to the destination, incrementing the addresses as it goes until it finds a **NULL** character.

The official C function returns the address of the destination string. This allows you to nest string copy, string append and string compare functions within each other. All standard C libraries provide the strcpy function, so there is no need to copy this function into any of your programs.

We've just copied a word into the next available word location which means that it is no longer an available position for a word. Where is the next available word going to be put? If I were teaching class, there would a momentary pause here to get responses from the class. And on some days that pause could stretch to several minutes. Since I'm not sure that I can duplicate a pause of that duration in a book (Go read a few pages of *War and Peace,* maybe.), so we'll carry on.

```
char    *strcpy(d,s)
char    *d;
char    *s;
{
char    *t;

  t = d;                    /* save to use as returned address
  */ while d++ = *s++);  /* copy the strings */
  /* last char was the terminating NULL */
  return t;
}
```

Listing 1-22. The strcpy function.

```
char        words[2000];
char        *next_word = words;

char *add_str(s)
char *s;
{
char   *t;

  t = next_word;
  strcpy(next_word,s);
  next_word += strlen(s) + 1;
  return t;
}
```

Listing 1-23. The add_str function.

The next available space immediately follows the word we just copied. We need to bump the address in next_word to the byte following the new string. The new address would be the value of the old address in next_word, plus the length of the added string, plus a byte for the terminating **NULL** character.

Also in the standard C library is the get-string-length function, strlen. Given the address of a string, strlen returns the number of characters in the string, up to but not counting the **NULL.**

If the name of the added string is s, then next_word is updated with:

$$next\_word += strlen(s) + 1;$$

Listing 1-23 shows that all of this is quite painless when organized into separate function, add_str.

The add_str function gives us a way in which to put character strings into a central storage area. In the next chapter, we will look at the retrieval of strings from the string table through the locate function.

THE SYMBOL TABLE

In a complicated program such as AutoCAD, you can expect that there is a wide variety of data types in the input and output files. For instance, in the **DXF** file format, drawing data is presented as: floating point numbers (coordinates, drawing limits, and line width), integers (counts and offsets), text (attribute values, text, and names of tables) and boolean (on/off flags).

If this flow of data is to be handled in a systematic manner, it would be nice to organize a table that contains all of the necessary information for recognizing incoming data and dealing with it properly. This is known as a symbol table. It contains all necessary information for processing symbolic values.

You can create such a table. Each element in the table contains information about one incoming value. The minimum amount of information that you will need is :

> The name of the variable
> The data type of the variable
> The address where the data can be saved to or retrieved from.

Symbol Table Types	C Data Types
INTEGER	int
CHARACTER	char
STRING	char *
REAL	double
COORD	double (x)
	double (y)
	double (z)
ON_OFF	-----

Table 1-1: Symbol Table Data Types.

The first field in the table element is the name of the variable. In the **DXF** file, the name of the AutoCAD header variable, table name, or entity type appears before the value. If we look for these names and search for a match in our table, most of the work is done. To keep the name field in the table consistent throughout the table, we will put the spelling of the name in some safe location (like, the string table or a constant string area) and keep the address of the string in the table. The act of finding the name in the AutoCAD file and this table is another story ... in another chapter.

As previously mentioned, the data that we are expecting is mixed. Some values are integer and others are floating point (real). The second field in this table indicates the type of data being used for the variable. In normal programming we declare variables as being of a certain type (int, double, or char). The words used in the declaration are usually reserved for use by the compiler. We can't use them as programming names. Therefore, to indicate the type of data in our symbol table, we will have to make up some of our own data types. Table 1-1 shows some legal names and a corresponding C name. Notice that some specialized names are in the list. This specialization will aid in later processing. You'll see.

There is no need to save the entire data type name. It is only necessary to save a code number that represents the data type name. By equating a symbolic data type name to a number, you can manipulate the data type name (as a human, you are pretty good at symbolic manipulation) and let the computer handle the numeric value.

I like to keep all of my C definitions in a single file. This file is invariably called defines.h . There is also a types.h file. Using the #include preprocessor command, I can have this definition file in all of my subroutine compilations.

We can neatly encode our data type names with the #define commands in Listing 1-24. Add these definitions to your defines.h file.

Now for handling the values of the variables. If you'll recall, one of my favorite sermons is that all pointer types are the same size. Groan! More pointers. The values that they point to may be of different sizes, but the pointer takes the same amount of space. Therefore, we can build a table with homogeneous elements that refer to inconsistent data sizes.

Listing 1-25 shows the construction of the symbol table entry. Regardless of the fact that some of the values will not be integer, the variable address pointer is declared as a pointer to an integer. We will use "casting" to switch types.

```
#define INTEGER      1
#define REAL         2
#define CHARACTER    3
#define STRING       4
#define ON_OFF       5
#define COORD        6
```

Listing 1-24. Symbol table data type definitions.

```
typedef
struct
 {
  char      *var_name;
  int        type_code;
  int       *var_addr;
 }          sym;
```

Listing 1-25. Symbol table type definition.


```
int     apple;
double orange;
char    pear;
char    tomato[256];
sym     sym_table[] =
                  {{"APPLE", INTEGER, &apple},
                   "ORANGE",REAL,(int *) &orange},
                   "PEAR",CHARACTER,(int *) &pear},
                   "TOMATO",STRING,(int *) tomato},
                   NULL,O,NULL}}:
```

Listing 1-26. Symbol table initialization.

Initializing the table is an interesting piece of work. This table must be initialized before processing starts. We will use the values in the table to control the operation of the program. Listing 1-26 contains a rather fanciful set of initializations. Here the addresses of the variables must be cast to int so that the compiler does not generate warnings. With this table, if a variable with the name tag of **APPLE** appears, we know that it is an integer and the associated value is saved in the apple variable.

REVIEW

This chapter has covered some of the elementary data structures and algorithms that are used in this book. These structures will appear in the next chapter as they are combined with other structures and concepts to form more sophisticated constructs.

2
More Programming Techniques

IT OFTEN AMUSES ME THAT WE BUILD THE MOST COMPLEX PROGRAMS FROM SUCH SIMPLE primitive elements. We have **CAD** packages, spreadsheets, expert systems. Simple instructions such as: **ADD, SUBTRACT, SHIFT, MOVE** and other simple instructions are the building blocks of these programs. Of course, combining these simple instructions in jillions of ways make complex operations. Operations become implemented algorithms; algorithms get written into procedures and functions. Layers and layers of functions become programs.

The purpose of this chapter is to continue our review of the programming techniques regularly used in this book. It is my guess that you might already be familiar with the subjects covered here. If this is the case, skip ahead to the heart of the matter: programming around a **CAD** system.

The subjects covered in this chapter are:

Word Recognition
Translation of Words into an Internal Representation
Sequence Recognition

There will be many hardware dependent code sequences presented here. The code is in Microsoft "C" Version 5.0 for **MS-DOS** 3.1 on an **IBM PC** or **MS-DOS** compatible machine. Microsoft Quick C or Borland's Turbo C are good substitutes. Code for programs on the Sun Workstation, Apollo, or Micro**VAX** computers may require some modifications.

The main motivation for developing a program is:

• to receive some information from some source:
  keyboard,
  communications port or
  file;
• to manipulate the data
• to write the transformed information to some destination.

When developing programs, I have found that reading data and making sense out of it are far more difficult than taking known data values and writing them out. The meaning of data can be so context sensitive that the program must be fully aware of the data surrounding the sample being analyzed.

If we can gather some input and recognize some intelligence in it, we can direct the operations of the program. The actions of the program and its conditions can give us some insight into the context of the data. That is, if the program knows where it is, the there must have been some specific data patterns that put it there. With data and context we can make some wise decisions. This chapter explains a means to this end.

Usually, when an automated means (another program or a piece of hardware) originates data, it is easier to find some intelligence (or recognizable patterns) than when a human enters data. Humans can be so unpredictable. Luckily, we will be dealing with machine generated data. The bad news is that some human probably created the data that produced the output. This means that the patterns of the data will be easy to recognize, but the structures may have meanings that you didn't even know existed.

WORD RECOGNITION

The first key to reading an AutoCAD drawing is to recognize the various words and tags being presented. Getting a single word isn't tough. The "C" function, fscanf, does an excellent job. This routine calls conversion functions to change **ASCII** character sequences to floating point **(REAL),** integer and other data types. Since raw strings (without conversion) are our only interest for the moment, I've chosen to use fgets as the input function. There are no conversion functions called here. Other routines handle the conversions once we have figured out what it is that we have.

So, step one of recognizing words — getting the word — is simple. Use the built-in functions provided by your favorite programming language.

Listing 2-1 is a code sequence which implements fgets. fgets is in most run time libraries so it shouldn't be necessary to use this listing. However, if you want to tune your input to match your needs, it may be handy. fgets reads characters into a string variable until it finds the end-of-line. The end-of-line may be either the carriage return ('\r') or the newline ('\n'), depending upon your local implementation. Now comes the challenge — figuring out what we have. There are a couple of approaches to this problem.

The first approach is to use simplistic brute force. This method calls for getting a word into a variable and carrying that variable wherever you go in the program. By repeatedly comparing this string to several choices, you can figure out what to do. Listing 2-2 illustrates the brute force method of word recognition.

```
int fgets(f,s)
FILE      *f;
char      *s;
{
  while (TRUE)
    {
     c = getc(f);
     if ((c == '\n') ¦¦ (c == '\r')) return;
     *s++ = c;
     *s = '\0';
    }
}
```
Listing 2-1. fgets source code.

```
fgets(s);
if (strcmpi(s,"START") == 0)
  start_process();
else
  if (strcmpi(s,"SEQUENCE") == 0)
    sequence_process();
  else
    printf("Found unknown command : %s\n",s);
```

Listing 2-2. Word recognition through brute force.

This promotes a very long linear search process. These searches devote a lot of time and space to storing and comparing names. This is not to keep you from using linear searches in your programs. Sometimes, brute force is a fair choice in simple situations.

Also, the if-then-else cascading that occurs with brute force methods isn't very easy to maintain or modify. If you are into heavy indentation for your if-then-else blocks, you can run out of page width quickly.

A solution to the cascading if-then-else is to rely on the switch and case statement. In the switch statement a single discrete value (Integers are discrete, individual values. Floating point numbers are continuous values.), selects a block of code for execution as shown in Listing 2-3.

The value in the switch portion of the command must be a discrete single value. A single character will work in the switch, but strings being read may have several characters and are not discrete data types. For instance, the string in a AutoCAD **TEXT** command can be very long. Nevertheless, a process trigger may require just such strings. How do we get past this situation?

In this situation, a standard technique is to associate a discrete value with the string. Since this associated value represents the value of another object (the string), we call the associated value, a token. A bus token represents the money required for a bus ride. A string token is a simple discrete representation of a word or phrase that has value to us.

One major benefit of a token, is that they are all the same size. Well, a bus token isn't the same size as a string token. Subway token gates accept only one type of coin or card. The designers do not expect to recognize various sizes of coins or denominations of bills. You use one size of token to take a subway ride. Similarly, string tokens are all the same size (integer). Even though strings may have one to 32 (or more) characters, a token represents them with homogeneous size. It is easier to pass a two byte integer (faster, too) than to shove an entire string around the program.

Let's get back to the brute force techniques to generate a token. We can start by examining all known or expected words. The program then generates an integer value for

```
switch(value)
  {
  case  0  :  /*  executed when value == 0  */
              break;
  case  1  :  /*  executed when value == 1  */
              break;
    .... etc.....
  }
```

Listing 2-3. Switch-case skeleton.

```
#define FIRSTWORD          1
#define SECONDWORD         2
#define LASTWORD           3

int generate_token(s)
char        *s;
{
   if (strcmpi(s,"FIRSTWORD") == 0) return FIRSTWORD;
   if (strcmpi(s,"SECONDWORD") == 0) return SECONDWORD;
   if (strcmpi(s,"LASTWORD") == 0) return LASTWORD;
   return 0;
}
```

Listing 2-4. Brute force token generation.

a found word. The integer value becomes our token value. This is basically pulling the cascaded if-then-elses of the previous section out of the main stream and putting it off to the side. We will see the conversion of a keyword to a representative integer taking place at several locations in the program. We might as well put it in a subroutine where everyone can get to it. Listing 2-4 shows how this might look.

Like I said, it is simple brute force plagued with inelegance and inefficiencies. On the other hand, if the word list is small and static, at least you know that it will work. You don't worry about it.

Let's take this one step further in efficiency. Eliminate the repetitious strcmpi calls by putting it in a loop. First, put your word list into an array that can be used to find the vocabulary as in Listing 2-5.

```
char        *word_list[12] = {"FIRSTWORD",
                              "SECONDWORD",
                              "LASTWORD"};
```

Listing 2-5. Brute force token generation.

```
#include <stdio.h>
#include <ctype.h>
#include <string.h>

main()
{
int     result_1;
int     result_2;

    result_1 = strcmp("ABCDEFG","ABC_EFG");
    result_2 = strcmpi("ABCDEFG","ABC_EFG");
    printf("strcmp
    results %d\n",result_1);
    printf("strcmpi results
    %d\n",result_2);
}
```

Listing 2-6. Curious little program.

```
int generate_token(s)
char          *s;
{
int           i;

  for(i=0;i<12;i++)
    if (strcmpi(s,word_list[i]) == 0) return i+1;
  return 0;
}
```
Listing 2-7. Better token generation.

Speaking of strcmpi and just as a curiosity, run the following experiment. Write a little program (Listing 2-6) that uses strcmp and strcmpi on the same string. If the string included an underscore character, you can get some startling results. If the results that you get are equal, then you can interchange the two string compares. Beware of mixing them if your results are different (as our tests indicate). Now we can compare the strings within a loop (Listing 2-7).

Once again, the function returns a zero value to show that it made no match. To compensate for the "C" array starting with the index of zero, the function adds one to the index to keep the valid returned value away from the value of zero.

Well, this works well if the word_list is of a known length and is static. However, if you decide to expand your list, you need to change the array range entry — and the upper bound for i in the for loop. This could be done quickly with a #define value for the subscript. Listing 2-8 shows the use of the independent upper bound.

```
#define WORD_LIST_SIZE        12

char                *word_list[WORD_LIST_SIZE] = { ...

for(i=0;i<WORD_LIST_SIZE;i++)
```
Listing 2-8. Using central value for upper bound.

Luckily, there are easier ways to move into an expandable structure without worrying about keeping all of the values correct.

First, we **REMOVE** entirely the subscript range value from the word_list array. By not explicitly stating the size of the array, "C" will automatically size the array to hold the words used to initialize it (Listing 2-9). To be perfectly accurate, the words to be recognized are arrays of characters in their own right and only pointers (addresses) to the strings are saved in the word_list array.

Now we don't explicitly know the size of the array and it really doesn't matter. The important thing is knowing how many words are available for examination for a match. As long as you stop at the last one, the total count is immaterial. Instead of finding a definite number of words to search, why not mark the end of the list with something that catches our attention? Something like: **NOTHING.** Recall that the word_list is actually a list of pointers to the strings (wherever they might be — that's the compiler's problem). Putting a **NULL** pointer in the list certainly separates the valid pointers from other bit patterns

```
char      *word_list[] = {"FIRSTWORD",
                          "SECONDWORD",
                          "LASTWORD"};
```
Listing 2-9. Array with no explicit size.

```
char    *word_list[] = {"FIRSTWORD", "SECONDWORD",
                        "LASTWORD",
                        NULL};

int generate_token(s)
char        *s;
{
char        *p;
int          i;

  i = 0;
  p = word_list;
  while(*(p+i))
    {
      if (strcmpi(s,*(p+i)) == 0) return i+1;
      i++;
    }
  return 0;
}
```

Listing 2-10. The NULL terminated word list and token generator.

that might represent anything. Listing 2-10 shows the token generator with the **NULL** terminated word list.

Assign the address of the first position to the pointer p—a pointer to the string in your word list. Then you can pass the contents of the array element indirectly to the string compare (strcmpi) function for the equality check. Failing to find equality, the program bumps the word pointer to the next word position. Use an integer value, i, as an offset from the pointer to make this easier. An empty array element indicates that it is time to quit the string search as a failure.

Now we can expand our word list without bothering to remember about updating all of the necessary values. Just insert the new word at the end of the list—in front of the terminating **NULL**—and recompile the main program. This treatment is for static lists only. All words must be in place before the program starts.

So far, we have dealt with static lists. Admittedly, this is about all that our **CAD** applications will use. However, there is more to say on the subject. For instance, what if we want to expand the word list as new words are added from the input data. Examples may be **LAYER, BLOCK,** or **STYLE,** names that must be recognized in various applications. We need a method of expanding the word list to accommodate these added names.

There are three considerations when planning this step.

1. Finding a place to save the spelling of the new name.
2. Adding it to the word list.
3. Not saving the same name multiple times.

Listing 2-11 illustrates the strategy we will follow.

The first part of the strategy has been covered: find the word; so we will continue from the point where we would normally "return 0" for an unknown name.

First, we need a place to save the newly found word. For this function we will establish a string table. This is a large array of characters where we can save the names. Only experience can help you decide how much room to reserve for this table. I like 4000 to 8000 characters. This is overkill brought on by time spent designing compilers. We also

```
find the word in the word_list and return the value
if not found
   add word to a string table
   put pointer into the word list
   assign (by position) an integer value
   return the assigned value
```
Listing 2-11. Word recognition strategy.

```
char        str_table[4000];
char        *next_word = str_table;
```
Listing 2-12. The declaration of the name table.

need to keep a pointer into the array that tells us where the **NEXT** word will go. This pointer is the value put into the word list so we can find the spelling of the word later. Listing 2-12 shows the declaration of the name table. This should look familiar. We are finally putting some of the techniques covered in the last chapter into action.

Since the first word is the next word in an empty table, we initialize the **NEXT** pointer value to the beginning of the string table.

To move a string to the string table, copy it to the next available space and update the next word pointer so that it is ready for the next insertion. Listing 2-13 shows how easy this is.

```
strcpy(next_word,new_word);
next_word += strlen(new_word)+1;
```
Listing 2-13. Copying a string to the name table.

The extra one after the strlen function is to accommodate the uncounted trailing **NULL** byte in the string. We still have to remember to save the value of next_word **BEFORE** it is incremented to the next available slot. Now, we move to the word list.

When we last left the word list, we had removed the subscript range values so that it would automatically size itself to the size of the initializing values. This would not leave room for expansion! We return to the point where we may have to either predefine the size of the array or add a number of **NULL** values to the array to allow expansion. If you specify that size of the array, the compiler sets the unused portions of the array to **NULL**. In either case, you need to generate a series of **NULLs** to hold the pointers to the new words.

As long as you don't overrun the last **NULL** in the list when you add a pointer to the end of the valid list, there will be a trailing **NULL** and the search algorithm remains valid. Listing 2-14 puts this altogether to show what I'm talking about.

Even though we are adding words to the string table, it is not necessary to put the original words into the string table. The word_list holds pointers to characters and it is perfectly content to point at a string in the string table or to a string that the compiler has tucked away at its convenience. A pointer to characters is a pointer to characters.

This is all good unless you are handling large lists of names and may be adding an unpredictable number of words. You really learn to hate running off the end of the word_list when you add one more name than you allowed. And you learn to equally detest declaring an unrealistically large array to prevent overflow. This gobbles up memory faster than a runaway spreadsheet.

Let's step away from the static memory management and take a look at dynamic or heap memory. Here is memory that you can request and use as necessary. There is a

```
char            string_table[4000];
char            *next_word = string_table;
char            *word_list[] = {"FIRSTWORD", "SECONDWORD",
                                "LASTWORD",
                                NULL,
                                NULL,
                                NULL,
                                NULL};
char            **next_list;

int generate_token(s)
char            *s;
{
char            *p;
int             i;

  i = 0;
  p = word_list;
  while(*(p+i))
    {
    if (strcmpi(s,*(p+i)) == 0) return i+1;
    i++;
    }
  /* not found -- must be a new word   */
  /* put pointer into open position    */
  *(p+i) = next_word;
  /* save the new word in string table */ strcpy(next_word,s);
  next_word += strlen(s) + 1;
  /* return the new number             */
  return i+1;
}
```

Listing 2-14. Putting the data and the functions together.

penalty for its use, but it allows you to use only the amount needed for a specific purpose without reserving too much or too little. You request it as you need it.

The "C" malloc (memory allocation) and calloc (cleared memory allocation) functions are the prime sources of the memory. You tell these routines how much memory that you want and they return a pointer to the allocated memory. You must save this pointer (the address of the memory) in a reachable place. If you don't, you could accidentally release the memory to float around as long as your program is active. This is analogous to a boat which has slipped its moorings and is adrift in a lake. Without extraordinary means, you aren't going to get that boat back. We need to anchor the dynamic memory to a known location called an anchor.

Just what are we going to ask for in dynamic memory? The obvious thing is enough memory to hold a pointer to a character string. The character string is the name that we have found. The pointer is the address of the string in the name table.

Second, it would not make much sense to anchor each memory module in an array element — although we do need an anchor — because that's what we are trying to get away from! As long as we tie one memory module to a known anchor, all of the other modules can be found. We build a chain of modules. Each module contains a "link" pointer

```
typedef
  struct a
    {
    struct a      *next;      /* link to next */
    char          *spelling; /* address of word */
    }             element;
element           *anchor;
element           *tail;

int generate_token(s)
char         *s;
{
element      *p;
int          i;
  i = 0;
  p = anchor;
  while (p)
    {
    if (!strcmp(s,p->spelling)) return i;
    p=p->next;
    i++;
    }
  p = (element *)calloc(1,sizeof(element));
  if (!anchor) anchor = p;
  if (tail) tail->next = p;
  tail = p;
  p->spelling = next_word;
  strcpy(next_word,s);
  next_word += strlen(s)+1;
  return i;
}
```
Listing 2-15. Linked lists for word pointers.

to the next module. In this way, a chain of memory modules can be built and anchored in a single variable. Listing 2-15 shows a typical data structure containing the link pointer concept and its place in the generation of tokens.

The variable tail keeps a current reference to the end of the chain. This lets you add new modules to the end of the list. Then, as you step through the list with the integer value, i, the numbering of the modules remains consistent.

There is a way to eliminate the need for this tail pointer. This (again!) means more overhead, but easier insertion into the list. If you choose to add the new modules at the beginning of the list, the consistency of numbering is lost with the second insertion. You can overcome this problem by saving the token number in the module with the pointer to the word. Then, no matter how convoluted a list may become, it saves the token identity of the word. Listing 2-16 shows the addition of the token identification to the list element.

You could eliminate all of this saving of names, id numbers, and linked lists if there were a way to directly convert a name into a unique number. The technique is called "hashing"—as in corned beef hash. The original character data is mauled, chopped, sliced, diced and rearranged to form a number. Using the same sequence of manipulation, the same name should always result in the same number. The tricky and elusive quality of

```
typedef
  struct a
    {
     struct a      *next;
     char          *spelling;
     int           id;
    }               element;

int               next_word_value = 1;

int generate_token(s)
char        *s;
{
element     *p;

  p = anchor;
  while(p)
    {
     if(!strcmp(s,p->spelling)) return p->id;
     p=p->next;
    }
  p=(element *)calloc(1,sizeof(element));
  p->next = anchor;
  anchor = p;
  p->id = next_word_value++;
  p->spelling = next_word;
  strcpy(next_word,s);
  next_word += strlen(s)+1;
  return p->id;
}
```

Listing 2-16. Adding the token number.

the process is to get a unique and manageable number for each input. This doesn't seem to be practical. Using practical methods, it is just too easy for two inputs to generate the same number — that is, have a collision.

There is no denying that from a large enough sample of words, we can perform some fast and easy hashing and generate a numeric "class" of words. For instance, in a population of 1000 words, we can hash these words and come up with 128 groups or classes with an average of eight words per group. Or we could generate 64 groups of 16 words or any other grouping that we want. What does this mean to us? If we can hash the words that we encounter, we compare that word to only a few other words in the same class instead of several hundred words to find a match.

I suppose that you've gotten the idea. If you want something to be easier in one way, there is a price to be paid somewhere else. The price of hashing words to form classes of words is:

1. The hashing routine.
2. A separate list and anchor for each hashed class.

However, the more hash classes you use, the fewer comparisons required.

```
element         *hash_table[64];

int generate_token(s)
char            *s;
{
element         *p;
int              h;

  p = hash_table[h=hash(s)];
  while(p)
   {
    if (!strcmp(s,p->spelling)) return p->id;
    p=p->next;
   }
  p=(element *)calloc(1,sizeof(element));
  p->next = hash_table[h];
  hash_table[h] = p;
  p->id = next_word_value++;
  p->spelling = next_word;
  strcpy(next_word,s);
  next_word+= strlen(s)+1;
  return p->id;
}
```
Listing 2-17. Hashing to find word list.

Fundamentally we use the techniques of the earlier method except that we pick the anchor from an array of anchors according to the value of the hashed number. Listing 2-17 illustrates the code for hashing the word to find a word list.

Notice that the index range of the hash_table has been set to 64. I prefer hash tables with a power of 2 number of elements for ease of hash code generation. I recommend numbers such as 32, 64, 128, or 256.

The key to the hash function is to generate a number between 0 and 63 to be valid indexes into the 64 element array. You will need 0 to 127 for 128 elements.

There are two ways to do this that come immediately to mind. First, if you divide any positive number by 64, you can count on a remainder between 0 and 63. The modulo operation ("%" in C) is the simple way to do this. The second method bypasses the need for a divide operation when power-of-2 numbers are used. The binary value of 64 is 0010 0000 and the binary value of 63 is 0001 1111. If we **"AND"** any integer with 63, the

```
int hash(s)
char    *s;
{
int         i;

  i = 0;
  while(*s) i = (i + (*s++)) & 63;
  return i;
}
```
Listing 2-18. Typical hashing function.

```
typedef
struct          token
 {
  struct token          *next;
  char                  *spell;
 }              token;

token          tok[8000];
short          next_token = 0;
token          *hash_table[64];
char           name_table[32000];
char           *next_word = name_table;

int hash(s)
char    *s;
{
int     j;

 j = 0;
 while (*s) j = (j + *s++) & 63;
 return j;
}

char    *locate(s)
char        *s;
{
char        *c;
token       *p;
int         h;

   if (s==NULL ¦¦ *s == '\0') return NULL;

   if (p = hash_table[hash(s)])
     while (p)
       {
        if (p->spell == s) return s;
        if (strcmp (s,p->spell) == 0) return p->spell;
        p = p->next;
       }
   h = hash(s);
   p = &tok[next_token++];
   p->next = hash_table[h];
   hash_table[h] = p;
   p->spell = next_word;
   strcpy(p->spell,s);
   next_word += strlen(s) + 1;
   return p->spell;
}
```

Listing 2-19. Complete listing for locate( ).

result is a number between 0 and 63. Since the lower five bits are all one, the **AND** operation preserves any value in that range and clears away any higher bits. This simple operation is why I choose power-of-2 numbers for hash limits.

How do we get the numbers to hash? All **ASCII** characters are represented by a binary value. I usually add the binary values of the characters in a string and **"AND"** the result so that I always have an in-range number. Listing 2-18 is a typical hashing function. Now we have all of the pieces to a word recognition and encoding system. Listing 2-19 spells it all out.

TRANSLATION TO INTERNAL REPRESENTATION

It is no secret that a **CAD** program uses more than just character strings to represent its internal data. However, from the stand point of reading **ASCII** input files, everything is a character string. A large portion of this book is dedicated to reading AutoCAD **DXF** files which are exclusively **ASCII** characters. This section deals with the systematic conversion of **ASCII** character strings into the proper internal representation of data.

All input information read by programs in this book will come into the program as **ASCII** strings. Since there is such a diverse collection of data types to be considered, it is easier to get the information into the program environment first and then sort out what the data should look like inside the program.

In the last section, the fgets or its equivalent was used to read the strings into the program. the function fscanf has the ability to convert the **ASCII** strings for us to the required data types, when we know what they are. However, at any given point, we may not know what data type to expect.

In following chapters, we will explore the data that is available in the **DXF** file. One of the primary sections of the **DXF** file is the **HEADER** section. This section contains character string, real and integer values. As this file is read, we will want to pick off important pieces of data as we find them in the file. The order in which they come in the file is not necessarily known. Methods to detect specific values in the file are covered later in this chapter and in chapter six. For the moment, we want to look at the methods for storing **ASCII** string information in the proper internal format.

Given these items in the **DXF** file: **$EXTMIN, $EXTMAX, $MENU** and **$ORTHO-MODE. $EXTMIN** is a real number representing the minimum X and Y coordinates of where drawing entities reside in the drawing (the drawing extents). **$EXTMAX** is a real number representing the maximum X and Y coordinates of the drawing extents. **$MENU** is a character string name of the drawing's current menu. **$ORTHOMODE** is an integer representing the current setting of the **ORTHO** value. **$PLINEWID** is a real number indicating the default polyline width. If these values were to appear together in a **DXF** file, they would appear as shown in Listing 2-20. The exact meanings of these numbers is somewhat immaterial for the moment.

What I want to do with these numbers is to save them in variables for later use by my program. For this to happen, I will have to create some variables to hold the values. These variables must have data types that correspond to the data being stored. The numbers between the names and values in the **DXF** listing are tags. They tell us what kind of data follows. There are more details on this point yet to come. The 10 and 20 tags note real numbers. The 2 is for a name. The 70 indicates an integer value. Using this insight, we construct the variables. Listing 2-21 shows the variable definitions.

Next to each variable entry is its size in bytes. Notice (once again) that they are not all of the same size. This is of minor concern when you deal with straight variables. However, our next step is to build a little table that will direct the placement of **DXF** information as it

```
     9
$EXTMIN
    10
1.00
    20
1.00
     9
$EXTMAX
    10
12.00
    20
15.50
     9
$MENU
     2
ACAD
     9
$ORTHOMODE
    70
1
     9
$PLINEWID
    40
0.0125
```

Listing 2-20. Example segment of DXF file.

is found. Each table entry must be the same size, so we will not be putting the exact values into the table.

It is not a great leap of imagination to see that the table will contain pointers to the various variables. Pointers being of one size in memory allow us to keep the structure of our table clean.

Our conversion table will contain the following items:

- Name of **DXF** entry
- Type of **DXF** entry
- Pointer to memory storage

We've previously stated that the data types used here are **REAL, INTEGER,** and **STRING.** However, there is a slight problem here. The extent values have two real numbers to form a coordinate pair. We will note this type to be **COORD** instead of **REAL.**

```
double          extmin_x;    /*  8 bytes  */
double          extmin_y;    /*  8 bytes  */
double          extmax_x;    /*  8 bytes  */
double          extmax_y;    /*  8 bytes  */
char            *menu;       /*  4 bytes  */
int             ortho;       /*  2 bytes  */
double          plinewid;    /*  8 bytes  */
```

Listing 2-21. Example variable declarations.

```
struct
  {
    char        *name;
    int          data_type;
    void        *mem_location;
  }              convert_table;

double              *tmp_real;
double              *tmp_x;
double              *tmp_y;
int                 *tmp_i;
char                *tmp_s;
char                *v;
int                  t;
convert_table       *ctp;

convert_table       *ct = {{"$EXTMIN"  , COORD,&extmin_x},
                           {NULL        , COORD, &extmin_y},
                           {"$EXTMAX"   , COORD, &extmax_x},
                           {NULL        , COORD, &extmax_y},
                           {"$PLINEWID",  REAL , &plinewid},
                           {"$MENU"     , STRING, &menu},
                           {"$ORTHOMODE", INTEGER, &orthomode}
                           {NULL        , 0     , 0}};
```

Listing 2-22. Type conversion table.

This signals the program that uses the table to collect two values instead of the normal one. Listing 2-22 shows a partial table for the conversion.

A tag precedes each value in the **DXF** File. The tag tells us what kind of data follows it. With this advanced information we can direct the **ASCII** character string to the correct software conversion. Once the correct conversion has occurred, we use the pointer in the conversion table to save the value for later use. Listing 2-23 is the overall design for parsing the **DXF** with the conversion table.

Now that we have an idea of where we want to go, take a look at Listing 2-24 for the code that implements these designs. As you can see, the program is easier than the design might indicate.

For this code to compile properly, the pointer assignments in the "9" section will have to be cast (C lingo) so that the types agree. Nothing will be said about the mysterious functions in this passage. These are discussed in later chapters.

The point of this exercise is the establishment of a table that directs the conversion of **ASCII** strings to the proper data type for the information. The structure of the program is wide open, allowing more data types and more recognized names.

SOFTWARE STATE MACHINES

This is a little lecture on states. By the term "state", I mean the condition in which something exists. I understand that California is a state and in some cases a condition in which you find yourself, but that's another matter. I'm talking about the logical state of a program.

```
Loop
  Get value of tag from DXF file
  Get following value for assignment
  If tag is "9"
    Find entry in conversion table using name field
    If conversion table data_type field is INTEGER
      Set integer temporary pointer to mem_location value
    If conversion table data_type field is STRING
      Set string temporary pointer to mem_location value
    If conversion table data_type field is REAL
      Set real temporary pointer to mem_location value
    If conversion table data_type field is COORD Set X coord
      temporary pointer to mem_location value
      Set Y coord temporary pointer to mem_location value in
        the next entry

  If tag is "2"
    Find and store (if required) value in string table
    (Use function locate()) and save string address
      in location referenced by string temporary pointer
    Clear pointer value

  If tag is "10"
    Convert value to real (Use function atof()) and save
      in location referenced by X coord temporary pointer
    Clear pointer value

  If tag is "20"
    Convert value to real (Use function atof()) and save
      in location referenced by Y coord temporary pointer
    Clear pointer value

  If tag is "40"
    Convert value to real (Use function atof()) and save
      in location referenced by real temporary pointer
    Clear pointer value

  If tag is "70"
    Convert value to integer (Use function atoi()) and save
      in location referenced by integer temporary pointer
    Clear pointer value
```

Listing 2-23. Design of simple DXF reader.

Consider an office desk. One in which the drawers work. One state of the desk is when all drawers are closed, another state is when one of the two drawers (Drawer A) is open. Another state is when the other drawer (Drawer B) is open. Still another state is when both drawers are open. It is a small desk. To make the analogy work, please assume that only one thing at a time can happen to the desk. We're going to be opening and closing drawers soon, and I want the situation where two drawers are opened at one time to be illegal. Okay?

```
while (TRUE)
  {
   t = get_tag(dxf_file);
   v = get_value(dxf_file);
   switch(t)
    {
     case    9 : if ((ctp = find_name_in_ct(v)) != NULL)
                    switch (ctp->data_type)
                      {
                       case INTEGER  : tmp_i =
                                           ctp->mem_location;
                                       break;
                       case STRING   : tmp_s =
                                           ctp->mem_location;
                                       break;
                       case REAL     : tmp_r =
                                           ctp->mem_location;
                                       break;
                       case COORD    : tmp_x =
                                           ctp->mem_location;
                                       tmp_y =
                                          (ctp+1)->mem_location;
                                       break;
                      }
                 break;
     case    2 : *tmp_s = locate(v); tmp_s = NULL;
                 break;
     case   10 : *tmp_x = atof(v);
                 tmp_x = NULL;
                 break;
     case   20 : *tmp_y = atof(v);
                 tmp_y = NULL;
                 break;
     case   40 : *tmp_r = atof(v);
                 tmp_r = NULL;
                 break;
     case   70 : *tmp_i = atoi(v);
                 tmp_i = NULL;
                 break;
    }
  }
```

Listing 2-24. Implementing the DXF reader design.

Let's start in state one, drawers closed. Figure 2-1 indicates state one. Now, something happens, an event, that changes the state of the desk. Right! Allied Van Lines moves it to New York. Wrong! You open one of the drawers. Which one? (I don't know ... third base) It doesn't matter; the state has been changed.

Our concern is in mapping the state change. This map is shown with known states and expected events. States are represented by circles. In our examples and program sequences, the states are static. Once a program is in a given state, only certain events can

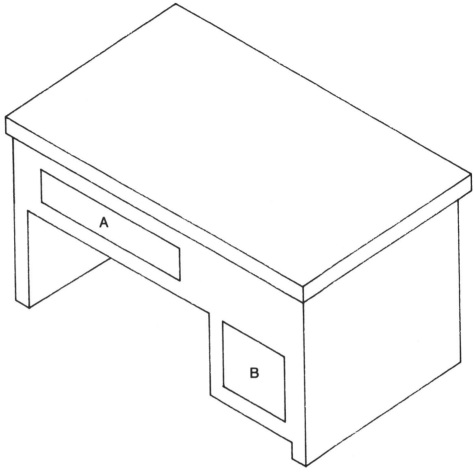

Fig. 2-1. A desk.

change the program state. Arrows show the course of a state change. Arrows represent events.

To map a system, we need to know what alternatives are available and important to our universe. In this example, we are concerned when a drawer is opened or closed. If someone knocks the legs out from under the desk, it doesn't matter to us unless the force of the blow shakes open a drawer or the new tilt of the desk keeps sliding them closed.

Actually, it doesn't even matter then since you no longer have a desk. You have a piece of junk. And this state machine only operates on desks. Figure 2-2 shows the map for the events that can change a desk which is in state one. One event is:

Force is exerted on Drawer A and opens it.

This event leads to state two, Drawer A is open. The other event is to exert force on Drawer B and open it. State three is the result of this event.

Before going for the biggie, both drawers open, consider the event of closing the drawers. Here is another event occurring between states one and two or states one and three. There is no single action that can get us between states two and three.

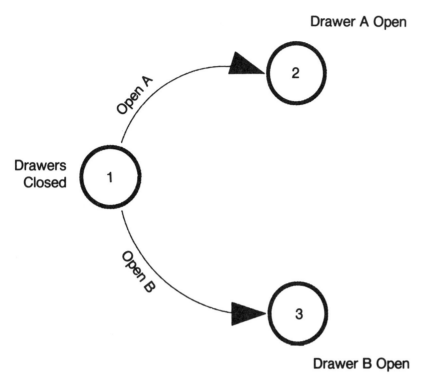

Fig. 2-2. State map of state 1 transitions.

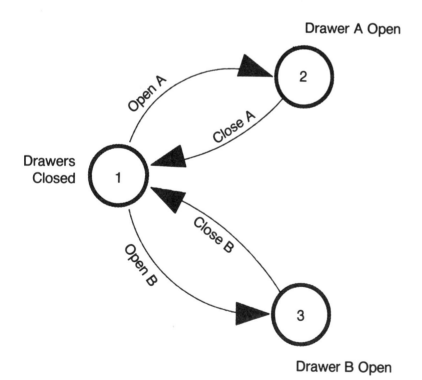

Fig. 2-3. State map with returns to state 1.

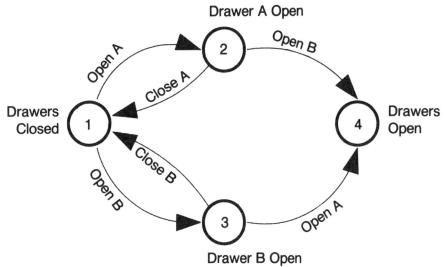

Fig. 2-4. Adding a fourth state.

By closing a drawer, events get added to our map. The states remain constant, only events are added. Figure 2-3 shows the added events for returning to state one.

Suppose we are in state two, Drawer A is open. How do we get to state three. There is no direct connection between the two, so a single event will not do the job. You may not like this answer, but there are an infinite number of ways to get from state two to state three. Only one way is economical and efficient. The one best way (given this state map) is:

1. Close Drawer A — This puts us into state one.
2. Open Drawer B — This puts us into state three.

And, where are the other zillions of ways to get there?

In state one, you have two choices; open Drawer B or reopen Drawer A. If your method of making decisions is somewhat short of being practical (tossing a coin, for

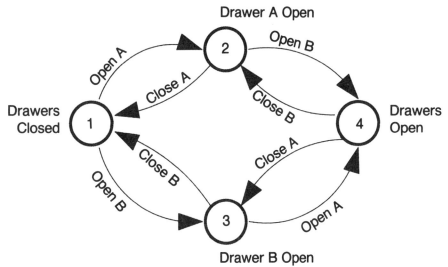

Fig. 2-5. The full state diagram.

instance), you might chose to open Drawer A. This places you back into state two. Now, you have only one choice in your search for state three: Close Drawer A. Once again in state one, you have to decide on an event. You **COULD** choose to reopen Drawer A (Darn! Heads, again.). How many times could you open and close Drawer A before you open Drawer B? Literally an infinite number of times. It's not likely, but it could happen.

There is still a state that has not been mentioned, state four. In state four, both drawers are open. Figure 2-4 shows the new map. The only way that we can get both drawers open is to be in one of the states where one drawer is open and open the other drawer.

```c
/*   state names    */
#define ALL_CLOSED          0
#define DRAWER_A_OPEN       1
#define DRAWER_B_OPEN       2
#define ALL_OPEN            3
/*   event names    */
#define OPEN_A              0
#define CLOSE_A             1
#define OPEN_B              2
#define CLOSE_B             3

int                         desk_transition[4][4] =
    {{DRAWER_A_OPEN, ALL_CLOSED,    DRAWER_B_OPEN, ALL_CLOSED},
     {DRAWER_A_OPEN, ALL_CLOSED,    ALL_OPEN,      DRAWER_A_OPEN},
     {ALL_OPEN,      DRAWER_B_OPEN, DRAWER_B_OPEN, ALL_OPEN},
     {ALL_OPEN,      DRAWER_B_OPEN, ALL_OPEN,      DRAWER_A_OPEN}};


int                         current_state = 0;
operate_desk()
{
  current_state = 0;
  while (TRUE)
    {
    current_state = desk_transition[current_state][get_event()];
    switch(current_state)
      {
      case ALL_CLOSED    : printf("all drawers closed\n");
                           break;
      case DRAWER_A_OPEN : printf("drawer a open\n");
                           break;
      case DRAWER_B_OPEN : printf("drawer b open\n");
                           break;
      case ALL_OPEN      : printf("all drawers open\n");
                           break;
      }
    }
}
```

Listing 2-25. Desk state machine.

Without dragging this out too far, add the events for closing a single drawer., This gives us the transitions from both drawers open to a single drawer open. Figure 2-5 illustrates the full map. All possible and acceptable actions are mapped into this diagram. There is no single state change that will take us from both drawers open to both drawers closed. You must close one drawer first before closing the other.

When you know in which state you are, you know which events are legal and which are illegal. Legal events change the state. Illegal events need to be reported or ignored.

We can transform the state map into a table that can tell us what to do when events occur. When a legal event occurs, the table tells us to which state to transition. The table is called a transition table.

The transition table is a two dimensional table. Its axes represent:

1. the states in the map
2. the possible events.

To use the transition table, you select the row representing the current state of the system. The column is determined by the nature of the event. An event that does not fit into the scheme is ignored or reported as an error. At the intersection of the current state row and the event column is the new state. This is the new state to which the event causes a transition.

When an event cannot effect the state, there is no change made. You can't open drawer A if it is already open. You remain in the original state. If you just have to see it in code, Listing 2-25 shows the desk state machine.

A transition table is not always needed to control the action of the state machine. Oh, yes, the events are still there. However, the machine can be controlled within the program if the transition is (almost) always to the same state. This is practical in a small state machine.

```
while (!quit)
  {
  t = get_tag_token(c = get_tag(f));
  switch (state)
    {
    case 1:   state = 6;
              if (t == NINE) state = 3;
              if (t == ZERO) state = 2;
              if (t == TEN) state = 4;
              if (t == TWENTY) state = 5;
              break;
    case 2:   if (t == ENDSEC) quit = TRUE;
              state = 1;
              break;
         :
         :
         :
    }
  }
```

Listing 2-26. Example implementation of a state machine.

Listing 2-26 is the code for an implemented state machine for reading a **DXF** file. The full details for this code appear in a later chapter. For the moment though, look at the way that the states are changed. There is no transition table to control the state changes. In this case, the majority of the changes take place within state one, caused by events "9", "10", "20" and "0". The change to state four is for the proper detection of tag and value pairs. All other state changes are back to state one.

REVIEW

Armed with a variety of programming techniques, we can move ahead to looking at some real situations where these techniques are used.

Throughout the programming examples, you will see that words form the basis for communication. The translation of words to a managable form (tokens) becomes a necessity for the smooth flow of information in a complex system.

You will also see that the most heavily used technique is the finite state machine. We will be dealing with an input stream — the **DXF** file — that is not always complete nor in any fixed order.

3

The AutoCAD Programming Environment

THIS CHAPTER CONTINUES THE STUDY OF BACKGROUND AND FOUNDATION INFORMATION that will allow you to produce programs that complement the AutoCAD **CAD** program. The last two chapters dealt with the programming techniques that you will encounter throughout the book. This chapter and the next (data and file structures) deal with the aspects of AutoCAD that you will encounter as a programmer.

In particular, this chapter deals with AutoCAD concepts and conventions. We will look at the AutoCAD "instruction set", and the **MS-DOS** environment conventions.

Later sections of this book are divided into the relationships that programs have with AutoCAD. AutoCAD can be used to produce data that drives another program. This section is called "AutoCAD, The Driver". A second section shows how a program can be written to provide AutoCAD with drawing information and this section is called "AutoCAD, The Driven". The last section deals with the Auto**LISP** language for programming within AutoCAD. This section is "AutoCAD, The Host".

I bring this up since the "AutoCAD, The Driven" section is going to deal heavily with script files. The script file is a file of AutoCAD instructions which AutoCAD interprets the same way that it would respond to the same instructions from the keyboard. We are now going to look at the structure of the AutoCAD commands. This detail is necessary to create a successful file for AutoCAD.

I am going to divide the AutoCAD command set into several categories. Actually, there are several ways in which this can be done. They could be divided into operational sets. That is, instructions and command that "go together." In this case, commands for drawing entities, **CIRCLE, LINE, ARC,** and **POINT** would be grouped together. While environment aids such as **SNAP, GRID,** and **ORTHO** would be in another group. I could deal with the commands alphabetically. This would serve as a nice reference for the user. However, the way in which I am going to divide the instruction set is by instruction structure. The structure of a command can be divided into groups of instructions by number and types of parameters. I have chosen this form of division so that similar programming techniques can be adapted to the form of the instruction.

The intent of this summary is to review the instructions so code segments using them in later chapters make more sense. The list includes only the instructions that would typically appear in a script file. The AutoCAD Reference contains further details on all of these instructions.

INSTRUCTIONS WITH NO PARAMETERS

Instructions with no parameters are the easiest to use. Only the name is used. There aren't many of these instructions since there isn't much versatility in them.

In a script file, you separate parameters and terminate all instruction sequences with a space or carriage return. Spaces at the ends of lines are difficult to see, so I would advise you to use spaces only in the middle of lines.

END — Close the current editing session and save the drawing. The **END** command causes AutoCAD to write a **DWG** file representing your drawing. This **DWG** contains all manner of deleted entities, changed entities and unused blocks. To get rid of this extra baggage, you will need to start another editing session. Simply **END**ing this second session reduces the size of the **DWG** file because AutoCAD removes deleted entities when it starts. Use the **PURGE** command to fully clean the **DWG** file.

GRAPHSCR — This instruction changes the visible AutoCAD screen to the graphics screen. If the display is currently a text screen (from a **LIST** or **HELP**), this command forces it back to the normal working graphics screen.

TEXTSCR — This instruction changes the visible AutoCAD screen to the text mode. You normally view the text screen as the two or three lines at the bottom of the graphics screen. This is where you see commands echoed. The **TEXTSCR** command flips the screen so the entire screen shows a list of past commands and information.

REDRAW — This command redraws the graphics screen, cleaning it up after erasures and additions. As the last instruction in a script file, **REDRAW** presents a refreshed screen.

REGEN — This command reevaluates the entities in the database and creates an entirely new drawing representation. It would not be frequently used in script files because it causes a lengthy recalculation and redraw.

RESUME — This command restarts a script file once it has been stopped by an error or human intervention (striking the backspace key). It is unlikely that you would use this command in a script file. However, you will need it to restart one.

DBLIST — This command starts a text dump of all entities in the drawing database. This scrolls on the screen very quickly so it is recommended that the printer be active.

OOPS — This command restores the last erased or blocked item.

RSCRIPT — Placed at the end of a script file, the **RSCRIPT** command restarts a script file for continuous play of slide shows and demonstrations.

INSTRUCTIONS WITH ONE ON/OFF/AUTO TOGGLE PARAMETER

These instructions change the environment of the AutoCAD session. Placed in an initializing script file, they can set up a working environment convenient for your application. Each command has one parameter that follows the keyword. A space or new line separates the parameter from the command. All of these commands accept simple parameters such as **ON** and **OFF** or **YES** and **NO**. As noted, several also accept operating values or the keyword **AUTO**.

BLIPMODE — As you enter AutoCAD coordinates, a small symbol appears on the screen denoting the selected coordinate location. This is a **BLIP.** This command controls the action of the **BLIP.** A **YES** parameter allows the **BLIP**s. A **NO** parameter keeps the screen clear. A **REDRAW** erases the **BLIP**s from the drawing.

GRID — It is handy to have a visual clue of distances on the screen while you are drawing. The **GRID** command toggles the display of a grid of dots on the screen. An **ON**

parameter displays the grid. An **OFF** parameter hides the grid. You may set the grid spacing by offering a scaling coordinate, 0.5, for instance, for a one half unit spacing. A typical script file will set the grid spacing to a comfortable scale. Setting the scale turns on the dots.

SNAP — When **SNAP** is on, it ensures that coordinates fall on predetermined intervals. Pixel resolution can make it appear that a line appears to touch another line, but there is no way to be sure that the coordinates match unless you use some form of **SNAP.** The **SNAP** command toggles the activation of the snapping feature. An **ON** parameter activates the snap. An **OFF** parameter deactivates the snap. You may set the snap spacing by offering a scaling coordinate, 0.5, for instance, for a one half unit spacing. A typical script file will set the snap spacing to a comfortable scale. Setting the scale turns on the snap.

AXIS — The **AXIS** commands provides ruler lines at the edges of the drawing area. The **AXIS** command toggles the display of the ruler lines. An **ON** parameter displays the ruler lines. An **OFF** parameter hides the ruler lines. You may set the spacing of the tick marks along the rulers by offering a scaling coordinate, 0.1, for instance, for a one tenth unit spacing. A typical script file will set the tick spacing to a comfortable scale. Setting the tick spacing turns on the axis.

ORTHO — The activation of the **ORTHO** features restricts the placement of coordinates to locations along the orthogonal (90 degree increments) axes from a given point. With the **ORTHO** feature disabled, you have complete freedom in determining the placement of entities. An **ON** parameter activates the **ORTHO** feature. An **OFF** parameter disables it.

REGENAUTO — Some commands either require or spontaneously initiate a **REGEN** command to properly display their effects. The **REGENAUTO** feature allows this regeneration as required. However, this regeneration may consume a great deal of time. You can control this feature to inhibit the spontaneous regeneration. An **ON** parameter allows the regeneration. An **OFF** parameter stops spontaneous regeneration. When setting **REGENAUTO** to **OFF,** commands that require a regeneration to perform their task send a message informing you that they must regenerate. **ZOOM EXTENTS** is an example. You must okay the request before the operation can continue.

QUIT — This command terminates a drawing session without saving the resulting drawing. It requires a **YES** parameter to proceed with the termination. Script files using **WBLOCK** or **SAVE** commands to save drawing blocks might use this command to terminate a session. AutoCAD does not create a file when you use **QUIT** in a new drawing.

FILL — There is a definite increase in calculations to fill the screen area representing **TRACE, SOLID** or **POLYLINE** entities. The **FILL** command toggles the generation of filled areas. An **ON** parameter allows AutoCAD to fill these entities. An **OFF** parameter renders only the outlines. You must issue a **REGEN** command to regenerate existing entities into the current **FILL** mode.

QTEXT — Text is one of the slowest entities to generate on the screen. Letters can take numerous line strokes to create. The QuickText command **(QTEXT)** allows faster generation of text by showing only the text location and area and not drawing the letters. An **ON** parameter permits the quick text mode. An **OFF** parameter returns AutoCAD to normal text mode.

INSTRUCTIONS WITH FILENAME AS A SINGLE PARAMETER

These instructions require a filename as their parameter. Your application must provide this filename when you generate a script file. You may choose to use the default name (the name of the drawing) in some cases. Select the default name with a space or carriage return.

DXFIN — This command tells AutoCAD to read the contents of a **DXF** file for further drawing information. The name of the file (as found in the disk directory) must have a file extension of **DXF**. AutoCAD assumes the **DXF** file extension. The **DXF** file contains drawing information in **ASCII** format.

DXBIN — This command tells AutoCAD to read the contents of a **DXB** file for further drawing information. The name of the file (as found in the disk directory) must have a file extension of **DXB**. AutoCAD assumes the **DXB** file extension. The **DXB** file contains drawing information in a modified binary format.

DXFOUT — This command tells AutoCAD to create and write the details of the current drawing to a **DXF** file. The name of the resulting file (as found in the disk directory) will have a file extension of **DXF**. AutoCAD assumes the **DXF** file extension. The **DXF** file contains drawing information in **ASCII** format. A second parameter sets the number of significant decimal places. You can use the default by including an extra linefeed in the script file. You can find further information about selecting entities for the **DXF** file in the AutoCAD Reference.

SCRIPT — This command tells AutoCAD to read the contents of a script file for more drawing information. The name of the file (as found in the disk directory) must have a file extension of **SCR**. AutoCAD assumes the **SCR** file extension. The **SCR** file contains drawing information in AutoCAD instruction format. You may start a script file from another script file. This allows you to chain several files together. When a script file starts another script, control does not return to the original file when the second one has been read.

SAVE — This command provides a mid-session write of the drawing to the **DWG** file. The filename may be the current drawing (the default) or another drawing name. The target file will be a **DWG** file. The **SAVE** command does not require the **DWG** extension on the filename.

LOAD — This command instructs AutoCAD to load the drawing instructions in a particular shape file. The filename parameter must have the extension of **SHX**.

MENU — This command loads a menu file into AutoCAD. If you have prepared a special menu for your application, a **MENU** command in an initializing script file gets your menu on the screen without requiring the user to remember to load it. When the user saves the drawing, the drawing file retains the name of the menu. The menu file extension is originally **MNU**. However, AutoCAD compiles the menu into a **MNX** file.

VSLIDE — This command loads an AutoCAD slide file onto the graphics screen. AutoCAD reads the slide data from the file named in the parameter.

MSLIDE — This command creates an AutoCAD slide file from the drawing currently on the viewing screen. AutoCAD writes the slide data into the file named in the parameter. It has the file extension of **SLD.**

·SHELL — The **SHELL** command interrupts the normal drawing activities of AutoCAD to execute an external program. The current activities of AutoCAD may have been to prepare data for an outside program that has calculating abilities beyond those of Auto**LISP** or normal commands. AutoCAD responses to the **SHELL** command with a request for the program name. If the program is available, it is run. AutoCAD will start specific programs if registered in the **PGP** file.

OTHER INSTRUCTIONS WITH A SINGLE PARAMETER

These commands cover a wide variety of uses. However, they share the distinction of accepting a single parameter value. A script file using these commands can present them in one of two ways. First, a single space can separate the command name and the parameter. The second way is to write the command and the parameter on separate lines. There should not be any extra spaces on either line.

APERTURE — This command is an environmental setting. It sets the size of the target box drawn when you use various object snap modes. This target box command does not affect the size of the target box used in selecting items for inclusion in a selection set. The parameter for this command is the size of the target box in pixels. This command may be graphics hardware dependent.

COLOR — Color of an entity is normally controlled by layer. However, it is possible to set the color for individual entities even though they reside on the same layer. The **COLOR** command changes the current entity color. The parameter is a color number (1 to 255) or a specific recognized color name **(BLUE).** You may also specify one of two special color names. The **BYLAYER** color name returns the assignment of entity color to the color of the current layer. The **BYBLOCK** color name assigns color to entities as the color of their parent block.

DELAY — The **DELAY** command offers a method of slowing down the display of slides. I can't think of any other reason to slow down AutoCAD. The parameter to the **DELAY** command is the number of milliseconds (roughly) the process should pause.

LTSCALE — The **LTSCALE** command adjusts the scale of dashed lines in various linetypes to usable proportions. AutoCAD bases linetype specifications to a length of one (on a somewhat arbitrary unit of measure). If your drawing encloses a very large number of these units or a fraction of a unit, the dashes in a linetype can be lost. The parameter in the **LTSCALE** command is a floating point scale factor for adjusting the resolution of the linetype.

INSTRUCTIONS FOR SIMPLE ENTITIES

I am going to make a distinction here between simple and complex drawing entities. Simple entities are drawing constructs with a fixed set of parameters. When a program generates the script file for a simple entity, it is merely a matter of filling in the blanks with known or calculated data. A complex entity does not have a fixed number of entities. As long as you can supply numbers to a complex entity, it will continue drawing. The **LINE** command is an example of this. The **LINE** command does not terminate until you have no more endpoints to give it. Before that point, you will get line segments chaining all points entered.

The following entities meet the requirements for simple entities. Notably the **ARC** and **TEXT** commands have some extensions that make them semi-complex. However, these extensions would not normally be used in a script file.

POINT — The **POINT** command places a point at the coordinates given by its parameter. Its parameter is an **X,Y** coordinate pair. The numbers are separated by a comma and not a space. This entity is the simplest of the drawing entities. Listing 3-1 shows the **POINT** command in script.

CIRCLE — The **CIRCLE** command draws a circle according to the defining coordinates and numbers. There are several ways to determine where and how big to draw a circle. The AutoCAD reference shows five methods. You can easily use four of these in a script file. The **TTR** — tangent, tangent and radius — method is not suited for script work. It deals with selection sets, and requires some extra planning to perform in a script file. Listings 3-2 through 3-5 show these four methods.

```
POINT 5.5,3.12
```
Listing 3-1. The POINT command.

ARC — The **ARC** command forms a partial circle — a circular arc — according to the parameters given. Like the **CIRCLE,** there are several ways to define an arc. The AutoCAD Reference gives eight methods. One method is the continuation of an arc or line. This is the semi-complex nature of this command. Listings 3-6 through 3-13 show the script for the various **ARC** commands.

TEXT — The **TEXT** command is the primary means of placing characters into the drawing. The **ATTDEF** instructions also provide text display, but have additional arguments. Alignment of the text rules the form of the **TEXT** instruction. AutoCAD accepts five different alignment types. Two additional forms allow the setting of a text style (font) and the continuation of text from a previous instruction. Numbers in the instruction show location, height, and rotation of the text. The text string is the last item in the instruction.

```
CIRCLE 1.2,3.4 0.8
```
Listing 3-2. CIRCLE with center and radius.

```
CIRCLE 1.2,3.4 D 1.6
```
Listing 3-3. CIRCLE with center and diameter.

```
CIRCLE 3P 2.4,4.1 5.6,6.8 4.56,5.0
```
Listing 3-4. CIRCLE from three points.

```
CIRCLE 2P 5,5 3,5
```
Listing 3-5. CIRCLE from two points (diameter endpoints).

```
ARC 2.4,4.1 5.6,6.8 4.56,5.0
```
Listing 3-6. ARC from three points.

```
ARC 1,3 C 3,3 5,3
```
Listing 3-7. ARC with start, center and end points.

```
ARC 1,3 C 3,3 A 135
```
Listing 3-8. ARC with start and center points and included angle.

```
ARC 1,3 C 3,3 L 2.134
```
Listing 3-9. ARC with start and center points and chord length.

```
ARC 1,3 E 6,5 R 10.0
```
Listing 3-10. ARC with start and end points and radius.

```
ARC 1,3 E 6,5 A 125
```
Listing 3-11. ARC with start and end points and included angle.

```
ARC 1,3 E 6,5 D 90
```
Listing 3-12. ARC with start and end points and starting direction.

```
ARC

2.3,4.5
```
Listing 3-13. LINE/ARC continuation.

```
TEXT 1.2,2.0 0.08 0.0 How Now Brown Cow
```
Listing 3-14. The left aligned TEXT instruction.

```
TEXT C 5.0,3.6 0.125 90 Slanted Yet Centered Text
```
Listing 3-15. The centered TEXT instruction.

```
TEXT F 1.25,2.5 5.58,2.5 0.10 There is no ROTATION
```
Listing 3-16. The fit TEXT instruction.

```
TEXT M 2.0,4.0 0.125 0.0 Almost Like Centered
```
Listing 3-17. The middle TEXT instruction.

```
TEXT R 3.0,5.25 0.25 0.0 Right Aligned Text
```
Listing 3-18. The right aligned TEXT instruction.

```
TEXT S HELVET C 2.0,3.0 0.30 0.0
Centered Text in Helvetica
```
Listing 3-19. Setting the style in the TEXT instruction.

```
TEXT

You Need a New Line for Continued TEXT
```
Listing 3-20. Continuation of TEXT.

The height argument may be skipped if the text font indicates a fixed height character size. Listings 3-14 through 3-20 show the various forms of the **TEXT** instruction.

SHAPE — The **SHAPE** command inserts instances of shapes into the drawing. Shapes are found in shape files. These are similar to text font files. Shapes don't enjoy the vast number of ways for expression that AutoCAD gives text fonts. The shape file must be loaded before you can use shapes. The **SHAPE** command has arguments for the name of the shape, its location, height and rotation. Listing 3-21 shows a typical **SHAPE** instruction.

INSERT — The **INSERT** command may be the most powerful command in Auto-CAD. This command allows the inclusion of a simple symbol or entire drawing in your drawing. Most other **CAD** systems have this option for the active user, but make it tougher than pulling teeth for an external program to do the same operation. With an **INSERT** command in the script file, you can easily manipulate symbol libraries. The **INSERT** command has a set number of arguments. These include: the name of the inserted block, its location, scale factors and rotation. When an inserted block has attribute values to satisfy, you need to include the values in the script file. There are no

```
SHAPE A_SHAPE 2.25,3.33 1.0
```
Listing 3-21. The SHAPE instruction.

```
INSERT A_BLOCK 4.5,7.65 1.0 1.0 0.0

12-342L

BLUE SPECKS

JONES MANUFACTURING
```
Listing 3-22. The INSERT instruction with attributes.

instructions for inserting attribute values. Listing 3-22 shows the insertion of a block with three attribute values.

INSTRUCTIONS FOR COMPLEX ENTITIES

AutoCAD defines a complex entity as an entity composed of a list of related simple entities. The evidence for this definition is strongest in the **DWG** and **DXF** file formats. The **POLYLINE** and **INSERT** with **ATTRIBUTES** are the only complex entities by that definition. Individual vertex entities form the polyline. The list ends with the **SEQEND** entity. Likewise, an inserted block with attributes is a chain of entities, an **INSERT** entity at the front, **ATTRIB** entities following and a **SEQEND** entity at the end.

However, from the standpoint of the script file, commands that accept an unlimited number of points or values are different and more complex from the previously listed simple entities. So this section deals with complex script commands with multiple arguments.

Since there is no limit to the number of arguments with these complex entities, there must be a means of delimiting and terminating the sequence of arguments. AutoCAD recognizes spaces and new lines as argument delimiters. Placing each argument (usually coordinates) on a separate line makes the script file cleaner and easier to read. Adding a second space or new line where AutoCAD expects an argument terminates the list. Use new lines for terminators. Spaces at the ends of lines are too difficult to see in a text editor. Changing the file with trailing spaces can be a nightmare.

LINE — The **LINE** command is in the complex entities for the reason that it can have an unlimited number of arguments. The arguments themselves are not complex. They are simply coordinates of the next point in a segmented line. Listing 3-23 shows a typical **LINE** command. To emphasize the trailing blank line in the script, I've added a **REDRAW** command.

TRACE — In the early days of AutoCAD, before the advent of the polyline, the **TRACE** command was the premier form of drawing a line with width. Especially suited to printed circuit board work, the **TRACE** became a fixture in the AutoCAD stable. Easy to

```
LINE 1.0,2.0

1.0,5.5

1.34,6.78


REDRAW
```
Listing 3-23. The LINE instruction.

```
TRACE 0.015

2.5,3.321

4.0,4.0

4.0,5.5

6.3,5.5



REDRAW
```

Listing 3-24. The TRACE command.

draw, but difficult to edit, the **TRACE** has lost its popularity and necessity to the polyline. The form of the **TRACE** command is similar to the **LINE.** The only difference is the inclusion of a width value as the first argument. Listing 3-24 shows a typical **TRACE** command.

   SOLID — For filling large areas of the drawing with color — or ink, the **SOLID** command comes to the rescue. Limited to triangles and rectangular areas, it took a patchwork of solids to fill a complex area. By hand, this could entail a great deal of work. With a program calculating the bounds of the solid area, it can be done efficiently and accurately. However, as in using the command in the manual mode, you must be careful about the order of the arguments, lest you create the dreaded **BOW- TIE.** If you haven't made one of these, you are really missing out on one of AutoCAD's more mysterious features. Since the **SOLID** command will allow multiple arguments, building solid area upon solid area, I include it in the complex entity list. Listing 3-25 shows a typical **SOLID** command sequence. This is not a **BOW-TIE.**

   POLYLINE — Here is the papa of the complex entities. With so many variations, I am hesitant to even list them for fear of missing some of them. Accepting the basic list of coordinates defining continuous line segments, you can change the appearance of the polyline with the introduction of modifiers. AutoCAD recognizes these modifiers because it identifies them by name (or at least, a letter) instead of a number. Modifiers in a script

```
SOLID

1.0,1.0

1.0,3.0

4.0,1.0

4.0,3.0



REDRAW
```

Listing 3-25. Using SOLID for a simple rectangle.

```
PLINE 3.0,2.5

W 0.010 0.010

3.25,2.5

3.25,5.0

4.0,5.0



REDRAW
```

Listing 3-26. The POLYLINE command.

format are best for making a change in line width or defining a polyarc. You can change polylines even further through the **PEDIT** command. This command is too complex for script file work since it involves selection sets and human judgement. Listing 3-26 shows a script sequence for a polyline with the assignment of width at the beginning. Setting a width involves values for a starting and an ending width. Therefore, there are two values following the "W" in the example.

INSTRUCTIONS FOR LAYER COMMANDS

The **LAYER** command meets the criteria for being a complex AutoCAD command, but it has enough differences to warrant a section to itself. In the earlier complex commands, the coordinates were related to each other. They were all a part of the same entity.

Drawing entities do not play a part in the **LAYER** command. Yet, there is a hint of a similarity. Both command types terminate with an extra linefeed. Both command types allow multiple arguments. As the drawing commands build entities, the **LAYER** command builds table entries. The other commands build one entity or group of related entities — although they are not necessarily stored as one entity within the framework of AutoCAD. On the other hand, the **LAYER** command can build or modify several table entries with one invocation. This is the major reason for splitting the discussion.

Open the layer command processor with the **LAYER** command. You continue using the layer command until you add the terminating extra linefeed. Most layer operations involve the name of the operation and the name of the effected layer. Exceptions to this rule are **COLOR** and Line**TYPE** which require an extra entry — a color for the **COLOR** command and a linetype name for the **LTYPE** command.

You may specify several layer names where a single layer name is used. Separate the names with commas. AutoCAD accepts wildcard characters where several layer names are permitted. Since there can only be one active layer at a time, the **MAKE** and **SET** commands demand a single layer name.

The following operations are available in the layer command:

NEW — This operation creates a new layer with the given layer name. You may use several layer names with this operation.

SET — This operation sets the current active layer. All following drawing entities will appear on this active layer. You may only specify a single layer name for this operation.

MAKE — This operation combines the action of **NEW** and **SET** into a single entry.

OFF — This operation removes (does not delete) a layer from the display screen.

```
LAYER

NEW LYR_1,FLOOR,WING,SURFACE

COLOR RED LYR_1

COLOR BLUE FLOOR

COLOR 14 WING

COLOR 4 SURFACE

LTYPE DASHED SURFACE

ON *

SET WING



REDRAW
```
Listing 3-27. The LAYER command.

You may specify several layers. This operation helps to clear a cluttered screen of extraneous drawing information.

    ON — This operation undoes the work of the **OFF** operation. Listed layers are once again displayed. You may specify several layers.

    COLOR — This operation establishes the default color of entities drawn to a particular layer. This operation has two arguments. The first argument is the color. This color may be a color number between 1 and 255; or it may be one of the recognized AutoCAD colors: **RED, YELLOW, GREEN, BLUE, CYAN, MAGENTA** or **WHITE.** The second argument is the names of the colored layers. **WHITE** is the default color.

    LTYPE — This operation establishes the default linetype of entities drawn to a particular layer. This operation has two arguments. The first argument is the name of the linetype. The second argument is the names of the layers to which the linetype is assigned. **CONTINUOUS** is the default linetype. Listing 3-27 shows several of the layer operations in a script file format. It creates and colors several layers.

MS-DOS CONVENTIONS

To lend some flexibility to the operation of a program, the software designers will often allow several operating parameters to be set by the user.

    In some cases, a configuration file is used. AutoCAD uses such a configuration file to establish the types of hardware drivers being used, initial drawing parameters and general, not-changed-often values.

    However, there are operating parameters which can affect the operation of the program from one usage to the next. These are values which must be quickly and easily changed to reflect the needs of the program in special ways. For instance, symbol libraries may be saved in several directories according to their purpose. AutoCAD would need to be notified of which library is being used.

Normally, **MS-DOS** will provide a program with files from the current directory without the extra overhead of a pathname construction and it will also provide the path to the directory containing the original **.EXE** file being executed. In case you are interested, the path of the executing program is in the argc and argv arguments of the main function. argv[1] is usually a pointer to the first parameter on the activating command line. It is the first one that a program usually looks at. However, if your compiler supplies it (Microsoft "C" does.), a pointer to the path to the program is in argv[0]. This argument includes the name of the program. This must be removed to find the pathname. Place a **NULL** character behind the last backslash to remove the program name.

The **MS-DOS PATH** command will not provide path information to data directories and files. The **PATH** command is used for finding executable files and batch files.

The path to any other library directory must be provided from another source. AutoCAD accomplishes this task of finding a library directory through the **MS-DOS SET** command.

One of the features of **MS-DOS** is an inter-program communications area known as the environment. This is a chunk of memory reserved for short messages between the user, **MS-DOS,** and an application program. The **SET** command is the user level entry into this area. Programs also can gain access to the environment to see if something has been left for them.

The normal mode of operation of the **SET** command is for setting a parameter. The form of the command is:

SET name_of_parameter=value_of_parameter

The name of the parameter as well as its value is quite arbitrary. Various software companies will pick parameter names which are descriptive of their function; yet unique so that they don't collide with other parameters.

Once in the environment, the parameters become public. Knowing the name of the parameter, the program can request an environment access to that parameter.

Using Microsoft "C" (and presumably other C compilers as well) function getenv, a program can request a particular parameter from the environment space. The getenv accepts a single argument. This argument is a string (or more correctly, the address of a string) containing the "name_of_parameter". The getenv returns the address of a string containing the associated "value_of_parameter". For instance, if the user had entered the following **MS-DOS** command:

SET ABCD=C:\LIBRARY

Listing 3-28 shows a program segment that checks the environment space for a specific value. The results of this code would be:

C:\LIBRARY

```
char        s[64];

s = getenv("ABCD");
printf("The value for ABCD is %s\n",s);
```
Listing 3-28. Using the getenv function.

AutoCAD uses several of these environment messages to let the user make operational changes between editing sessions. The big problem is that the environment area must be changed from outside of AutoCAD. Once AutoCAD starts, it checks its environment messages, sets them in concrete and doesn't look back. Using the **DOS SHELL** to modify the environment won't change things.

AutoCAD recognizes the following environment messages.

ACAD — The acad environment message should be set to a **MS-DOS** pathname. This path leads to a secondary library of drawings (blocks). AutoCAD will search the directory associated with the path in an attempt to satisfy an insertion request when the request is not known internally. For example, if you have a directory of piping symbols, they may be in a directory called **PIPES.** You do not have to use the **PIPES** directory as your main drawing directory to use these symbols. You should **NEVER** use the **ACAD** (or whatever you named it) directory. If you had entered: **SET ACAD=\PIPES** at a **MS-DOS** prompt, AutoCAD will search the directory **\PIPES** for a requested block. The backslash ("\") indicates that the directory is attached to the root directory of the current disk drive. Removing the backslash will make AutoCAD search a directory named **PIPES** which is attached to the current working directory. This is probably not what you are after, so remember the leading backslash in the **SET** command.

The path is assumed to belong to the current drive unless specifically named otherwise. If you have a partitioned disk, several physical drives or a **RAM** disk to hold libraries, the drive identifier should be included:

SET ACAD=D:\PIPES

ACADCFG — This environment message tells AutoCAD where to find a current configuration file. When you set the operating constraints for AutoCAD, it asks if it should save the changes in the current configuration. The configuration information is saved to the file. This file is read whenever AutoCAD is started to help configure its operation. The first check is in the current directory; followed by a check in the **ACAD** (or whatever) directory; and finally in the directory referred to in the **ACADCFG** environment message. Each configuration would be saved in a separate directory. By setting this message before entering AutoCAD, a distinctly different AutoCAD configuration can be seen. This would make a lot of sense if you want your pen plotter configured in several ways, depending upon the type of drawing on which you are working. Although the screen and digitizer may stay constant, different pen assignments, linesytle, etc. could be saved for various occasions.

ACADFREERAM — This environment setting notifies AutoCAD to reserve a certain amount of memory for ????. Since most drawings of any decent size have problems without this setting, I haven't the faintest idea why it has to be a user setting. Set **ACADFREERAM** to 24 (i.e., 24000).

LISPSTACK — This value tells AutoCAD to reserve a certain amount of memory for the operational stack for Auto**LISP.** If your Lisp programs exhibit a high rate of recursion or if you pass massive structures, this value should be large. A value of 8000 works well for everyday situations. The **LISPSTACK** and the **LISPHEAP** total should not exceed 45000.

LISPHEAP — This value tells AutoCAD to reserve a certain amount of memory for the dynamic memory area for Auto**LISP.** This is the area for global data structures. For most applications, this value is the larger of the two (**LISPSTACK** and **LISPHEAP**). A value of 37000 works well here. The **LISPSTACK** and the **LISPHEAP** total should not exceed 45000. That sounds familiar.

4

AutoCAD File Structures

NOW THAT WE'VE LOOKED AT THE INTERNAL REPRESENTATIONS OF AUTOCAD data, it is time to investigate the external representations. The thrust of this book is to provide information about writing applications for AutoCAD. Therefore, it is with the external structures that we must become intimately involved.

The purpose of this chapter is to introduce the numerous file structures that Auto-CAD either accepts or creates. I'll discuss the details of these file structures in later chapters. I've divided these chapters to show the origins and destinations of the files. Chapters five and six deal with the files that AutoCAD creates and applications read. Chapters seven and eight cover the input files for AutoCAD. Finally, Chapters nine and ten deal with the files that modify AutoCAD to the user's needs.

AutoCAD designates its files through the filename extension or filetype. This extension to the filename is the short (up to 3 characters) name that follows the normal filename. A period separates the filename from the extension.

The files that we will discover are:

DXF — The Drawing Exchange File. This structure is the **ASCII** equivalent of the binary drawing file **(DWG).** Since the **DWG** format is proprietary in nature, I will not discuss its structure. (footnote: Just so that you won't think that I am avoiding the issue: I have developed commercial software that decodes and uses the **DWG** file. To maintain my strong relationship with Autodesk, I have chosen not to publish the **DWG** structure.) Chapters 5 and 8 deal with the reading and writing of the **DXF** file.

DXB — The Drawing Exchange File (Binary Format). This structure is a simple binary encoded file without the rigors of **DXF** or **DWG.** Translation of **ASCII** values to their true internal format can take a relatively long time to perform. The **DXB** allows binary encoded data to be entered quickly without the need for character to numeric conversion. Refer to Chapter 8 for more details about generating the **DXB** file.

TXT — The Attribute Template. The Attribute Template File is a user generated file that indicates the identity and format of attribute and attribute definition values to be written when the Attribute Extraction Instruction **(ATTEXT)** is used.

TXT — The Attribute Output. Just to confuse the issue, there are two **TXT** file types. The second **TXT** is the extension name for the output of the **ATTEXT** file. The difference is in the filename. The template file is usually named independently of the drawing. The output file takes the name of the drawing for its filename. The user can override this filename at the time that the **ATTEXT** instruction is used.

You can structure the Attribute Output File in one of three ways. If your application uses the attribute output file, you should pick the structure that best suits your needs. The three forms are:

1. **Comma Delimited (CDF)** — The Comma Delimited format separates all attribute values with commas. This is the normal file structure used by some database programs. Character strings — which could conceivably contain commas — are enclosed by double quotes. AutoCAD will generate a single line of attribute information for each entity containing at least one user-defined attribute value listed in the attribute template. If the entity does not contain all of the attributes listed in the attribute template, AutoCAD writes a **NULL** field. A **NULL** field appears as two adjacent commas.

2. **Space Delimited (SDF)** — Space delimited format is not a format where the fields are separated by spaces. Instead it is a specification of how much space each field takes. This is quite similar to format of a **FORTRAN** program.

3. **DXF Format (DXF)** — The **DXF** format generates a **DXF**-like file. With this format, it writes only entities containing selected attributes (one user defined attribute present) and those selected attribute entities in **DXF** style. AutoCAD reveals attribute values associated with internal AutoCAD data as normal **DXF** fields (e.g., block coordinates, scale factors, rotation angle, et.al.). See Chapter 6 for more details about reading **DXF** files.

SCR — The **SCRIPT** File. The Script file is the easiest method of directing the actions of AutoCAD from an outside source. The Script File contains AutoCAD commands and data you would use if you were typing the commands and data from the command line. AutoCAD temporarily diverts its attention away from the tablet and keyboard and accepts the file input as if someone were typing very quickly. All of the commands are available. However, the means for identifying individual entities is a bit different. With no pointing facilities, all entity selections must be made through windows, exact coordinate selections or use of **LAST** and **PREVIOUS** selection sets. Since a program probably generated the script, it should know the location of the entities that it has added. This means that it can identify their locations for later selection set selection. Further details follow in Chapter 7.

PGP — The Program Parameters File. Programs external to AutoCAD may be executed as if they were AutoCAD commands if they appear in the Program Parameters File. The values in a **PGP** record inform AutoCAD about the name of the program, its memory requirements, and the internal command name that invokes it. The **PGP** program can be tied to the **DXB** input form, allowing for automatic inclusion of drawing entities. Further details follow in Chapter 8.

LSP — The Auto**LISP** Source File. Auto**LISP,** AutoCAD's own version of Lisp allows programmers and users to add custom commands to AutoCAD repertoire. The **LSP** file is the file extension for the Lisp source code.

MNU — The Menu Source File. The ability to customize AutoCAD to the specific application of the application writer adds greatly to the flexiblity of the product. Adding a menu to the system that allows easy access to the special combination of commands needed to accomplish a task makes the job easier for the user and support easier for the author. The **MNU** file is the file extension of the source code of a custom menu.

MNX — The Compiled Menu File. AutoCAD compiles menus for faster response to menu picks. AutoCAD saves the compiled menu in an **MNX** file. AutoCAD generates the **MNX** file when the file does not exist for the corresponding **MNU** or when the **MNU** is newer than the **MNX** file (suggesting that a change has been made).

SHP — Shape and Font Source File. AutoCAD allows the creation of new lettering fonts and frequently used shapes in a special shape format. This format is an abbreviated drawing language for fast reproduction on the screen. The **SHP** is the file extension for the source code of the shape file.

SHX — Shape and Font File. AutoCAD saves the compiled **SHP** shape or font file in the corresponding **SHX** file. This file is a binary equivalent to the source **SHP** file.

5

The DXF Format

BEFORE DIGGING INTO THE DETAILS OF PARSING THE **DXF** FILE FORMAT, A BRIEF OVER-view of what we will encounter is warranted. The **DXF** file contains nearly all of the information required to reconstruct a drawing. It is our main source of documented drawing information. The **DWG** file is the primary source of information. However, its structure is not public knowledge.

The one necessary element that is missing from the **DXF** file is the drawing details for shapes and fonts. These are found in the shape and font **(SHX)** files.

The **DXF** file is divided into four separate sections. If you were producing a **DXF** file, only the sections important to your constructed drawing would be included. However, when AutoCAD produces the **DXF** file, it includes all sections and you must handle them.

The four sections of the **DXF** file are:

> The **HEADER** Section
> The **TABLE** Section
> The **BLOCKS** Section
> The **ENTITIES** Section

HEADER SECTION OVERVIEW

The **HEADER** Section contains the operational and environmental values of the drawing. A more extensive list of the values in the header section follows in Appendix B. To give you an idea of the values in the header, you will find:

- The originating AutoCAD version.
- The coordinates of the drawing limits.
- The coordinates of the drawing extents.
- Dimension parameters.
- Current Menu name.

The usefulness of this information depends upon your application. I usually pick out the drawing limits and extents and ignore the rest. These values prove useful in gauging scale factors when converting the AutoCAD drawing to a photoplotter language.

Another important value in the **DXF** file is the version record. This record is a key to which other values exist in the **DXF** file. A program that converts a newer version of **DXF** file to an earlier version (so that drawing can be backward compatible) needs to locate the AutoCAD version record and then disregard any **DXF** values which are not appropriate to the older version.

TABLE SECTION OVERVIEW

Whereas the header section dealt with simple operating values, the table section contains groups of information about the more complex operating values of the AutoCAD drawing. The table section is divided into four subsections. Each subsection may have several entries. The four subsections are:

LINETYPE
LAYER
STYLE
VIEW

Each subsection contains enough entries to maintain all applicable drawing information. If you use ten layers in your drawing (including layer 0), the layer table will have ten entries.

The **LINETYPE** table defines the active linetypes used in your drawing. These linetypes are added through the **LINETYPE** command. Common linetypes are **DOT, DASHED, PHANTOM,** and **DOTDASH.** The default linetype, **CONTINUOUS,** is always included in the **DXF. A LINETYPE** entry includes an **ASCII** based example of how the linetype appears when drawn.

The **LAYER** table contains the definition of each layer in the drawing. This structure is the information center for retrieving color, linetype, and visibility data. Layers are created and named through the **LAYER/NEW** command. AutoCAD always includes the default layer 0. The name of this layer, 0, should be handled as a character string and not as an integer value. This makes comparisons and mixing with alphabetic names easier. In the olden days of AutoCAD 1.4, layer names were numeric. This changed with AutoCAD 2.0.

The **STYLE** table contains implementation information about text fonts and shapes. Default characteristics are maintained in each table entry. The name of the font or shape file appears in each entry. The name of the style may be the same as the font file name. Since it is possible to derive several styles from a single font, the **STYLE** table entry saves the style name separately. AutoCAD includes the default text style, txt, in the **DXF** file.

The **VIEW** table contains the list of named views and view points added during the drawing session.

BLOCKS SECTION OVERVIEW

The blocks section of the **DXF** file contains the entity details for all blocks defined in the drawing. These blocks may be the result of dimensions, hatching, inserted drawings of library symbols or blocks designed during a drawing session. Even blocks that have been visually erased from the AutoCAD screen still exist in the blocks section.

In the blocks section, the file structure introduces each block with its name and registered insertion point. Following the introduction is the list of entities composing the block.

The blocks section defines each block individually. Although it is possible for a block insertion to be a part of another blocks definition, no blocks are defined within each other. There is no nesting of block definitions in the **DXF** file.

ENTITIES SECTION OVERVIEW

The entities section lists all active entities of the drawing. All details to construct the drawing reside in this section. Since there are constant references to the blocks section and the tables, these items are already defined and ready to be used by the individual drawing entities. Each entity has its own **DXF** format. These are covered in great detail in later sections.

PARSING THE DXF FILE

Now that we know what we are up against, let's get into the particulars involved in reading and parsing the **DXF** file.

The entire **DXF** file is built with a tag-value structure. A tag is an integer value indicating the type (integer, real, or character string) and general use (name, coordinates, or on/off flag) of the value portion of the structure. Knowing the data type of the trailing data value, you can switch to the proper conversion routine. All values are read as **ASCII** values. Their conversion to their proper internal representation is up to you. The tag and the value are on separate lines in the **DXF** file.

The tag is in **FORTRAN** format I3. This means that the tag is an integer value occupying a three character, right-justified field. A tag of a single digit, for instance, would have two leading spaces. AutoCAD and several applications use this standard. Most application programs don't enforce this standard because the Pascal and C languages will skip the leading spaces anyway. AutoCAD does not enforce this standard when reading **DXF** files created by application programs. However, some other applications insist upon this format.

AutoCAD follows a very rigid system of data type tags. This makes it quite simple to extract exactly the pieces of data that you want. It also means that your program must be accurate when reading and writing **DXF** files.

For example, let's look at a simplified **DXF**-like tag-value file and the program code that parses it. Listing 5-1 shows our simple example **DXF** file.

The file contains two pieces of interesting data, the name **APPLE** and the real number, 5.216. Preceding each value is a tag. In our example, 2 denotes that a character string name follows. 10 is the tag for a real number.

The program segment which recognizes this file structure is a fairly simple loop. Control remains in the **WHILE** loop until the **END-OF-FILE** is encountered. At the top of the loop, the code segment reads the input file to extract the tag value. We are in **BIG** trouble if there isn't a tag (or **EOF**) available when the top fscanf reads a line from the input. Listing 5-2 shows the code for reading our simple example.

In the case of missing a tag, we would lose control and the results would become unpredictable. You can add detection code to make sure that the tag is always a valid value. Luckily, if AutoCAD or some other properly operating program generates the file, the structure should be valid. It's when people start hand coding the data that inconsistencies creep in. And, for our little example, I'm not expecting problems.

Here is how this little program works. Having read the tag value and converted it to its integer form (in the **WHILE** statement), we let the tag select the type of input method

```
  2
APPLE
 10
5.216
```
Listing 5-1. Simple DXF file.

```
read_dxf(dxf)
FILE      *dxf;
{
int       tag;
char      name[256];
char      garbage[256];
double    real;

  while(fscanf(dxf,"%d",&tag) != EOF)
    switch (tag)
      {
        case  2 : fgets(dxf,name,256);
                  break;
        case 10 : fscanf(dxf,"%f",&real);
                  break;
        default : fgets(dxf,garbage,256);
                  break;
      }
}
```

Listing 5-2. Simple DXF file reader.

and required conversion for the value. This occurs in the switch statement. I chose to use fgets for the string input. This places the entire line into the local buffer variable. fscanf, on the other hand, it would stop reading the input stream at the first space it encountered. fscanf is the proper function for a single name **(APPLE)** in the input string. It spells disaster for a more complex string **(AN APPLE A DAY).** fscanf reads only the first word **(AN)** in the string. This leaves the second word **(APPLE)** as the input for the next tag, placing the input stream out of sequence. Disaster ensues. AutoCAD lets us know through the tag whether to expect a single name or a complex string.

Tables 5-1 and 5-2 show the tags used by AutoCAD. Tags have specific uses and must appear in the correct context to be valid. Not having a valid tag causes AutoCAD to issue an error message. AutoCAD stops reading your **DXF** file at that point and quits.

We've looked at the idea of tag-value pairs for directing the program in deciding how to interpret the data. The entire **DXF** file is constructed from these primitive pairs. At the next layer of complexity, AutoCAD combines a **GROUP NAME** and attendant values together. Each **GROUP NAME** and associated value is a tag-value pair. For instance, a **LINE** entity has at least five tag-value pairs with a **LINE GROUP.** Listing 5-3 shows a simple **LINE** group.

I say, "simple line group" because a typical line group may contain layer, color, thickness, and elevation information. In the example, the tag of 0 announces the start of an entity. A 0 also indicates the start of blocks, sections, and tables, but that is not a concern here. The value following the 0 tag tells us the kind of entity described in the remainder of the group. Detecting the **LINE** value, the program calls the line processor to handle it. The example line stretches from location 1.0,1.5 to 6.32,7.233. The trailing tag-value pairs

```
 0 -  9   Strings (Names, Attributes, Text)
10 - 59   Real Numbers (coordinates, angles, distances)
60 - 79   Integer (toggle switches, counts, selections)
```

Table 5-1. DXF Tags By Range.

0	Identifies the beginning of a division in the DX file. Used to start SECTIONS, each of the TABLES, and ENTITIES. The value is a string without spaces.
1	Primary Text. For a TEXT, ATTDEF or ATTRIB, the main text is found following this tag. The value is a string which may contain spaces.
2	A name. The name of a block or attribute tag follows this tag. INSERT uses this tag to name the inserted block. The value is a string which may contains spaces when used with ATTRIBUTE. There are no spaces in a BLOCK name.
3-5	Other text values. Default attribute values and prompting text is found here. "3" is also the font name in the style entry. The value is a string which may contain spaces.
6	Linetype Name. The value is a string without spaces.
7	Text Style Name. The value is a string without spaces.
8	Layer Name. One of the most common tags in the DXF. The value is a string without spaces.
9	Used in HEADER to introduce the variable name. The value is a string without spaces.
10	Primary X Coordinate. The value is the ASCII representation of a floating point number.
11-18	Other X Coordinates. Used to identify the other end of a line, corners on a trace or solid and the vertexes on a 3DFACE. The value is the ASCII representation of a floating point number.
20	Primary Y Coordinate. The value is the ASCII representation of a floating point number.
21-28	Other Y Coordinates to match other X coordinates. The value is the ASCII representation of a floating point number.
30	Primary Z Coordinates. Not very common yet. The value is the ASCII representation of a floating point number.
31-36	Other Z Coordinates corresponding to other X and Y coordinates. The value is the ASCII representation of a floating point number.

Table 5-2. Specific DXF Tags.

38	The Elevation of an Entity (When not 0.0). The value is the ASCII representation of a floating point number.
39	The Thickness of an Entity (When not 0.0). The value is the ASCII representation of a floating point number.
40-48	Other real numbers. The value is the ASCII representation of a floating point number.
49	Multiple Values - Used the Linetype definitions to define the individual visible and invisible line lengths for dashed and dotted lines. The value is the ASCII representation of a floating point number.
50-58	Angles (degrees). The value is the ASCII representation of a floating point number.
62	Color number (Found in LAYER definition and with individual entities when color is different than layer color.) The value is a string representation of a color number. It may also carry the values of BYLAYER or BYBLOCK.
66	Additional information follows. This is usually to indicate that attributes follow an entity. However, this flag also appears in polyline to indicate that vertices follow.
70-78	Integer values. The value is the ASCII representation of a integer number.

Table 5-2. (cont'd)

indicate these coordinates. Further details are forthcoming. I'm just setting the stage of what you will see in the **DXF** file.

```
  0
LINE
 10
1.0
 20
1.5
 11
6.32
 21
7.223
```

Listing 5-3. LINE group in DXF file.

READING THE DXF FILE

Before getting into the details of each of the **DXF** sections, let's look at the overall structure of the file. This structure study will lead us into the details of the various sections.

So far we have looked at the strategy of the **DXF** structure. Next, we will look at the tactics and details.

Autodesk designed the **DXF** file so that one central routine controls the activation of the section parsers. A parser is a routine that "tears apart" or separates the pieces of a structure so that information can be retrieved.

When you diagram a sentence (Remember high school English diagramming?), you are parsing a sentence into its subject-predicate-phrase pieces. Parsing the **DXF** file is easier than parsing an English sentence. I know. In the **DXF** file, all sections lead off with a **SECTION** tag and label pair. Listing 5-4 shows what this looks like in the file.

When your program sees one of these pairs, it should start looking for the type of section. This information immediately follows. It has a tag of 2. Listing 5-5 shows the header used to introduce the **HEADER** section.

```
    0
SECTION
```
Listing 5-4. The SECTION header.

```
    2
HEADER
```
Listing 5-5. The HEADER header.

When the program recognizes the particular section that follows the 2 tag, it calls the correct section parser. In this example, the program calls the **HEADER** parser. The information following the section name displays a certain pattern, meaningful to specific parsing routines.

The **DXF** format also indicates the end of the section. This is your signal that your program should return control to the central parsing routine. This prepares the central parser to recognize the next section and call the proper section parser (**HEADER, TABLE, BLOCK,** or **ENTITIES** parser).

The end of the section appears as a tag and label pair. It is a tag of 0. Listing 5-6 illustrates the end of section sequence.

```
    0
ENDSEC
```
Listing 5-6. The END OF SECTION.

I want to introduce a couple of routines that appear all of the time in programs dealing with **DXF** files. These routines provide the low level support for producing the tags and values represented in the **DXF** files.

BASIC DXF ROUTINES AND STRUCTURES

The code segments in the rest of the chapter (or the book, for that matter) will use, time and again, a couple of routines for reading the **DXF** file. The numerous program segments that follow merely use the information gathered and somewhat converted by two routines, get_tag and get_tag_token.

The routine get_tag (Listing 5-7) is the direct interface to the **DXF** file. It has a fairly simple job, read some **ASCII** characters from the file and remove extraneous spaces, tabs and linefeeds. When it is finished, it returns a pointer to the text read. This routine is

```
char *get_tag(dxf)
FILE      *dxf;
{
int       i;

/*                                                              */
/* read a line of text from DXF file                           */
/* limit to 255 characters                                     */
/* remove the newline character at the end of the string */
/* find first character following spaces or tabs              */
/* return pointer to text found in dxf file                   */
/*                                                              */

  fgets(tag_str,255,dxf);
  if (tag_str[strlen(tag_str)-1] == '\n')
    tag_str[strlen(tag_str)-1] = '\0';
  i = strspn(tag_str," \t");
  return &tag_str[i];
}
```
Listing 5-7. The get_tag routine.

rather simplistic and does not even recognize an end-of-file when it encounters one. In this case, the program has faith that the **DXF** file is complete and includes the **EOF** entry at the end of the file. You can be more restrictive by generating the tag and value for **EOF** if it is found prematurely.

On the other hand, the get_tag_token function is the direct interface of tag recognition and token translation to the rest of the program. Given a tag name (generated by

```
int get_tag_token (s)
char      *s;
{
tok_tab   *t;

/* hash word -- s -- to get class of word    */
/* get anchor -- t -- to list of words       */
/* look at each word in list                 */
/* (use NExT link to get next word)          */
/*   if spelling is the same (strcmp == 0)   */
/*     return with internal value            */
/* return with 0 for not found               */

  t = tok_hash[hash(s)];
  while (t)
   {
    if (!strcmp(t->tok_name,s)) return t->tok_value;
    t = t->next;
   }
  return 0;
}
```
Listing 5-8. The get_tag_token routine.

```
init_tok_table()
{
tok_tab      *t;
int           j;

/*   initial values for token table have          */
/*   spelling and internal value                  */
/*   the NULL value is for the NEXT field for linking */
/*   words with same HASH values                  */
/*                                                 */
/*   for each value in token name list            */
/*   (while name is not NULL)                      */
/*     hash name to get class                      */
/*     link name through NEXT field to hash table  */
/*            entry for class                      */
/*                                                 */
     t = tok_table;
     while (t->tok_name)
       {
        j = hash (t->tok_name);
        t->next = tok_hash[j];
        tok_hash[j] = t;
        t++;
       }
}
```

Listing 5-9. Initializing the token table.

get_tag), it uses a hash code to reduce the number of token names it must search to find the token in question. Finding a name that matches the **DXF** tag name, it returns the associated token number. Not finding a match (and this is quite often for non-token names and values found in the **DXF**), it returns a zero. Listing 5-8 features get_tag_token.

There is an initialization routine for the token table, init_token_table. Execute this routine at the beginning of your program. It makes the names of the **DXF** field values available during **DXF** parsing. Listing 5-9 shows the source code for the init_tok_table function. The code includes a reference to tok_table. Another listing (Listing 5-12) defines this table.

Since the definition list for the integer token values is rather large, this is the only place in the book where the tag names and values are shown. The internal values used in the definitions are arbitrary except **NONE** which is set to zero. I took all of the words and names (I gave names to the numbers.) normally encountered, alphabetized them and assigned token values.

The programs in this book consistently use the definition names. If I care to change an internal value, the only thing I change is the definition file (defines.h) and then I recompile the program, the whole program.

Listing 5-10 is the token value definition source code, Listing 5-11 is the type declaration source code, and Listing 5-12 is the variable declaration source code.

Here's how it all works. Suppose that I am looking for a line, the geometric entity that defines the shortest distance between two points. In the **DXF** file, this would be identified by the word, **LINE.** The first thing that I need to do is to get the next tag. Listing 5-13 is the code line used to fetch the tag from the **DXF** file.

```
#define FALSE       0       #define  POLYLINE   33
#define TRUE        1       #define  SECTION    34
                           #define  SEVEN      35
#define  NONE       0       #define  SEVENTY    36
#define  ARC        1       #define  SEVENTY1   37
#define  ATTDEF     2       #define  SEVENTY2   38
#define  ATTRIB     3       #define  SEVENTY3   39
#define  BLOCK      4       #define  SHAPE      40
#define  BLOCKS     5       #define  SIX        41
#define  CIRCLE     6       #define  SIXTY2     42
#define  EIGHT      7       #define  SIXTY6     43
#define  ELEVEN     8       #define  SOLID      44
#define  ENDBLK     9       #define  STYLE      45
#define  ENDSEC     10      #define  TABLE      46
#define  SEQEND     11      #define  TABLES     47
#define  ENDTAB     12      #define  TEN        48
#define  ENTITIES   13      #define  TEXT       49
#define  EOFILE     14      #define  THIRTEEN   50
#define  FIFTY      15      #define  THIRTY1    51
#define  FIFTY1     16      #define  THREE      52
#define  FORTY      17      #define  TRACE      53
#define  FORTY1     18      #define  TWELVE     54
#define  FORTY2     19      #define  TWENTY     55
#define  FORTY3     20      #define  TWENTY1    56
#define  FORTY4     21      #define  TWENTY2    57
#define  FORTY5     22      #define  TWENTY3    58
#define  FORTY9     23      #define  TWO        59
#define  FOUR       24      #define  VERTEX     60
#define  HEADER     25      #define  VIEW       61
#define  INSERT     26      #define  ZERO       62
#define  LAYER      27      #define  LIMMIN     63
#define  LINE       28      #define  EXTMIN     64
#define  LTYPE      29      #define  DIMENSION  65
#define  NINE       30      #define  LIMMAX     66
#define  ONE        31      #define  EXTMAX     67
#define  POINT      32
```

Listing 5-10. Token values (#define).

```
typedef
struct   z
  {
  struct z    *next;
  char        *tok_name;
  int          tok_value;
  }            tok_tab;
```

Listing 5-11. Type declaration for token structure.

```
tok_tab        tok_table[] = {{NULL,"0",ZERO},
                               {NULL,"1",ONE},
                               {NULL,"10",TEN},
                               {NULL,"11",ELEVEN},
                               {NULL,"12",TWELVE},
                               {NULL,"13",THIRTEEN},
                               {NULL,"2",TWO},
                               {NULL,"20",TWENTY},
                               {NULL,"21",TWENTY1},
                               {NULL,"22",TWENTY2},
                               {NULL,"23",TWENTY3},
                               {NULL,"3",THREE},
                               {NULL,"31",THIRTY1},
                               {NULL,"4",FOUR},
                               {NULL,"40",FORTY},
                               {NULL,"41",FORTY1},
                               {NULL,"42",FORTY2},
                               {NULL,"43",FORTY3},
                               {NULL,"44",FORTY4},
                               {NULL,"45",FORTY5},
                               {NULL,"49",FORTY9},
                               {NULL,"50",FIFTY},
                               {NULL,"51",FIFTY1},
                               {NULL,"6",SIX},
                               {NULL,"62",SIXTY2},
                               {NULL,"66",SIXTY6},
                               {NULL,"7",SEVEN},
                               {NULL,"70",SEVENTY},
                               {NULL,"71",SEVENTY1},
                               {NULL,"72",SEVENTY2},
                               {NULL,"73",SEVENTY3},
                               {NULL,"8",EIGHT},
                               {NULL,"9",NINE},
                               {NULL,"ARC",ARC},
                               {NULL,"ATTDEF",ATTDEF},
                               {NULL,"ATTRIB",ATTRIB},
                               {NULL,"BLOCK",BLOCK},
                               {NULL,"BLOCKS",BLOCKS},
                               {NULL,"CIRCLE",CIRCLE},
                               {NULL,"DIMENSION",DIMENSION},
                               {NULL,"ENDBLK",ENDBLK},
                               {NULL,"ENDSEC",ENDSEC},
                               {NULL,"$EXTMIN",EXTMIN},
                               {NULL,"$EXTMAX",EXTMAX},
                               {NULL,"SEQEND",SEQEND},
                               {NULL,"ENDTAB",ENDTAB},
                               {NULL,"ENTITIES",ENTITIES},
                               {NULL,"EOF",EOFILE},
                               {NULL,"HEADER",HEADER},
                               {NULL,"INSERT",INSERT},
                               {NULL,"LAYER",LAYER},
                               {NULL,"LINE",LINE},
                               {NULL,"$LIMMIN",LIMMIN},
```

```
                                    {NULL,"$LIMMAX",LIMMAX},
                                    {NULL,"LTYPE",LTYPE},
                                    {NULL,"ONE",ONE},
                                    {NULL,"POINT",POINT},
                                    {NULL,"POLYLINE",POLYLINE},
                                    {NULL,"SECTION",SECTION},
                                    {NULL,"SHAPE",SHAPE},
                                    {NULL,"SOLID",SOLID},
                                    {NULL,"STYLE",STYLE},
                                    {NULL,"TABLE",TABLE},
                                    {NULL,"TABLES",TABLES},
                                    {NULL,"TEXT",TEXT},
                                    {NULL,"TRACE",TRACE},
                                    {NULL,"VERTEX",VERTEX},
                                    {NULL,"VIEW",VIEW},
                                    {NULL,NULL,0}};

double              limit_x = 0.0;
double              limit_y = 0.0;
double              extent_x = 0.0;
double              extent_y = 0.0;
double              limit_mx = 0.0;
double              limit_my = 0.0;
double              extent_mx = 0.0;
double              extent_my = 0.0;
char                tag_str[40];
```
Listing 5-12. Token and variable declarations.

Having the tag (pointer to character string), we want the integer token value for the tag. This is the job of get_tag_token. It compares this tag's string value against all of the expected tag names. It performs a hash function to narrow the number of words to be checked. When it finds a match, it returns the internal value as the token (Listing 5-14).

Since the name **"LINE"** is associated with the defined integer value **LINE** in the token table, get_tag_token should return the integer value **LINE** when the word **"LINE"** is found in the **DXF.** In the extreme case where you are looking for only **LINE**s in the **DXF,** the following line of code found in Listing 5-15 will do the trick.

There is a tag of 0 which precedes the **LINE** value. A program should recognize this 0 before checking for the word, **LINE.** This check eliminates the embarrassment of finding a **LAYER** named **LINE** or a text entity with the word **LINE** in it. Both are legal and quite common.

```
tag = get_tag(dxf);
```
Listing 5-13. Calling get_tag.

```
token = get_tag_token(tag);
```
Listing 5-14. Calling get_tag_ token.

```
if (get_tag_token(get_tag(dxf)) == LINE)
```
Listing 5-15. Using token routines to find a LINE.

```
switch(get_tag_token(get_tag(dxf))
 {
  case LINE    : line_processor(dxf);
                 break;
  case CIRCLE  : circle_processor(dxf);
                 break;
  case ARC     : arc_processor(dxf);
                 break;
  case POINT   : point_processor(dxf);
                 break;
  default      : break;
 }
```
Listing 5-16. Simple parsing of entities.

A more logical action is to change the flow of the program control as determined by the token's value. Then the program may pick out and process several entity types. An example of this is in Listing 5-16.

The Central Parser Control

The central control procedure is a little piece of code that starts the various detail parsers as they arrive in the **DXF** file. Of course, the detail parsers have to cooperate so that the control gets returned to the central control in an orderly fashion. Figure 5-1 is the finite state diagram for the parser. Since the **DXF** file is not complicated at this stage of the game, the processor doesn't have much to do. Listing 5-17 is the central control module. Once the program opens the **DXF** file, it starts the ball rolling by calling the central control procedure with the **DXF** file reference (Listing 5-18). Control is eventually returned to the main program when the **DXF** file has been completely read. In the example code, detecting the **EOF** value causes the program control to leave the finite state loop.

Reading the HEADER Section

The **HEADER** section contains specific operational values for the drawing. Some of the information is relevant to your needs, some isn't. There are conditions where the **HEADER** section can be ignored. This being the easiest and most used condition in my programs. This is what we cover first. For ignoring the **HEADER** section, look at all of the tags in the **HEADER** section until the **ENDSEC** value appears. Exit when **ENDSEC** is found. First, Listing 5-19 illustrates the strategy in narrative form.

It is necessary to **ALWAYS** get the value that follows the tag. Reading every field as if it were the tag field can lead to trouble. In this instance, we are looking for a **ZERO** tag. If we read every field, then it is possible to find a **ZERO** value (indicating a switch setting or layer 0) and accidentally treat it as a tag. Then, trying to find out whether the value for the misread **ZERO** is **ENDSEC**, a tag is read. This isn't catastrophic unless the tag that is mistaken for a value is the **ZERO** tag for the **ENDSEC.** Then you are out of sync and nothing will work correctly.

Listing 5-20 is the program code for reading and ignoring the **HEADER** section. The central control procedure calls this procedure with the **DXF** file reference as an argument. The procedure reads the **DXF** file until the first **ENDSEC** record. This **ENDSEC** marks the end of the header section.

There are a number of cases where you want to know specific values in the **DXF** file. If this is the case, you want to detect and read specific values. We will set up a finite state

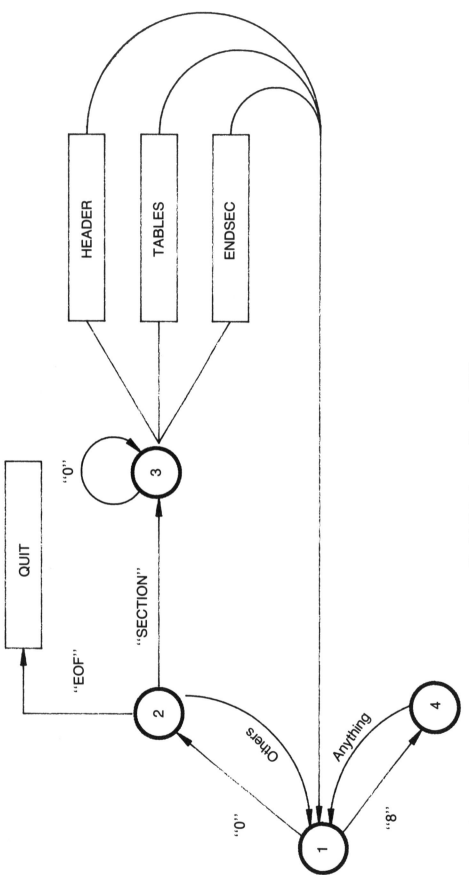

Fig. 5-1. State diagram of the central DXF parser.

```
dxf_in(f)
FILE          *f;
{
char          buf[132];
int           state;
int           quit;
int           t;
matrix        m1;
matrix        m2;

  quit = FALSE;
  state = 1;
  while (!quit)
    {
    t = get_tag_token(get_tag(f));
    switch (state)
      {
      case 0:   quit = TRUE;
                break;
      case 1:   if (t == ZERO) state = 2;
                if (t == EIGHT) state = 4;
                break;
      case 2:   state = 1;
                if (t == SECTION) state = 3;
                if (t == EOFILE) quit = TRUE;
                break;
      case 3:
                switch(t)
                  {
                  case HEADER   : header(f); state = 1;
                                  break;
                  case TABLES   : tables(f); state = 1;
                                  break;
                  case ENDSEC   : state = 1;
                                  break;
                  }
                break;
      case 4:   state = 1;
                break;
      }
    }
}
```

Listing 5-17. Central control module.

machine to recognize the fields in the **DXF** file. Since we cannot be sure of which values will actually be in the **DXF;** the order in which they will appear; or the form (data type) the data will be presented, the finite state mechanism is our surest method of being ready for all contingencies. Figure 5-2 is the finite state diagram for the Header Section parser. Actually, we know the form that data will appear in the **DXF** file—it will be **ASCII.** However, the working value of the data may be in some other internal form, integer,

```
strcpy (fn_dxf,path);
strcat (fn_dxf,".dxf");
init_tok_table();
if (fd = fopen (fn_dxf,"r"))
 {
  dxf_in (fd);
  fclose(fd);
 }
else
 {
  printf (" DXF File <%s> not found\n",fn_dxf);
  printf (" Press a key to continue\n");
  c = getch();
 }
```

Listing 5-18. Starting DXF input from the main program.

```
Repeat
   Get a tag from the DXF file
   Get a value from the DXF file
   If the tag is ZERO and the value is ENDSEC -- Done!
Until Done
```

Listing 5-19. Strategy for reading the DXF header.

```
header (f)
FILE     *f;
{
int          quit;
int          state;
int          t;
char         *c;

  quit = FALSE;
  state = 1;
  while (!quit)
   {
     t = get_tag_token(c = get_tag(f));
     switch (state)
      {
        case 1:  state = 3;
                 if (t == ZERO) state = 2;
                 break;
        case 2:  if (t == ENDSEC) quit = TRUE; state = 1;
                 break;
        case 3:  state = 1;
                 break;
      }
   }
}
```

Listing 5-20. Skeleton code for reading the DXF HEADER.

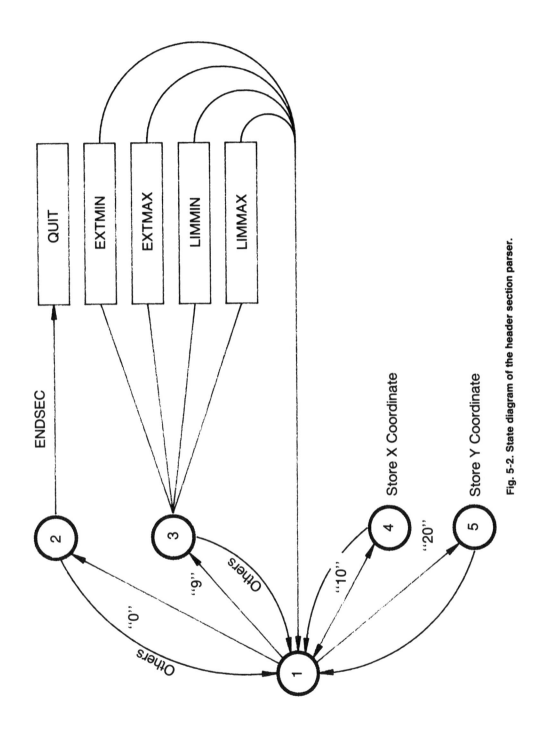

Fig. 5-2. State diagram of the header section parser.

string, character or floating point. Listing 5-21 shows a narrative strategy for finding values in the **DXF HEADER.** Listing 5-22 amplifies upon this strategy with actual code.

Appendix B contains descriptions of each of the values found in the **DXF HEADER** section. Appendix B also has the tag number for the data associated with each field in the **HEADER** section.

READING THE TABLES SECTION

The **TABLES** Section contains the working environment of the AutoCAD drawings. The entries in later sections of the **DXF** file continuously reference these tables to determine the form in which to display the drawing entities. In these tables the entities find color, font, linetype and viewing angle information. The **TABLES** section has four parts. Each part determines a specific piece of information about the appearance of a drawing.

The **DXF** file introduces the **TABLES** section with its own heading. The signal for this heading is a 0 tag and a value of **TABLES.** Notice that this word is plural. The introduction of the individual tables is through the word **TABLE.** This word is singular. Listing 5-23 shows the **DXF** lines that signal the beginning and the end of the **TABLES** section. The central parser control program should recognize the **TABLES** token and start the tables parser.

It becomes the task of the **TABLES** parser to determine the time and order of calling the individual parsers for each table. The **DXF** file introduces each table with a special sequence. Without showing the inside details of the **DXF** file, Listing 5-24 shows the structure of the **DXF** file for the **TABLES** Section. This listing includes the introduction tags for the individual tables. You will find details of the tables in the following sections.

The parser at the **TABLES** section level must anticipate and recognize all of the tags and values shown in the listing. Since there is no requirement that any of the tables exist in the **DXF** file, a finite state machine based algorithm will allow us to detect and parse whatever the **DXF** presents. Figure 5-3 shows the finite state diagram for this processor. Listing 5-25 implements the diagram. Each table in this section has its own structure and usefulness. The following discussions cover each of the tables.

The LINETYPE Table

The **LINETYPE** table entry defines the physical appearance of various line types on the drawing. Linetypes contain the first drawing information of the **DXF** file. Being associated with layers, the **DXF** file defines the linetype before the layers. This provides an existing reference for the layer definition.

```
Get tag from DXF file
Get value from DXF file
If tag is NINE and value is a wanted field
   assign proper pointers to receiving values
Else
   If tag is one of the following:
      10 - save X coordinate (floating point)
      20 - save Y coordinate (floating point)
      30 - save Z coordinate (floating point)
      50 - save angle (floating point)
```

Listing 5-21. Strategy for finding values in the DXF HEADER.

```
header (f)
FILE    *f;
{
int         quit;
int         state;
int         t;
char        *c;
double      p2;

  p1 = NULL;
  p2 = NULL;
  quit = FALSE;
  state = 1;
  while (!quit)
    {
      t = get_tag_token(c = get_tag(f));
      switch (state)
        {
        case 1:
                state = 6;
                if (t == NINE) state = 3;
                if (t == ZERO) state = 2;
                if (t == TEN) state = 4;
                if (t == TWENTY) state = 5;
                break;
        case 2:  if (t == ENDSEC) quit = TRUE;
                state = 1;
                break;
        case 3:  state = 1;
                switch(t)
                  {
                    case EXTMIN : p1 = &extent_x;
                                  p2 = &extent_y;
                                  break;
                    case EXTMAX : p1 = &extent_mx;
                                  p2 = &extent_my;
                                  break;
                    case LIMMIN : p1 = &limit_x;
                                  p2 = &limit_y;
                                  break;
                    case LIMMAX : p1 = &limit_mx;
                                  p2 = &limit_my;
                                  break;
                  }
                break;
        case 4:  if (p1) p2 = atof(c);
                p2 = NULL;
                state = 1;
                break;
        case 6:  state = 1;
                break;
        }
    }
}
```

Listing 5-22. Finding values in the DXF HEADER.

```
     0
  SECTION
     2
  TABLES
     :
     :
     :
     0
  ENDSEC
```

Listing 5-23. DXF file for TABLES section bounds.

```
     0
  SECTION
     2
  TABLES
     0
  LTYPE
     :
     :
     0
  ENDTAB
     0
  TABLE
     2
  LAYER
     :
     :
     0
  ENDTAB
     0
  TABLE
     2
  STYLE
     :
     :
     0
  ENDTAB
     0
  TABLE
     2
  VIEW
     :
     :
     0
  ENDTAB
     0
  ENDSEC
```

Listing 5-24. Structure of DXF TABLES section.

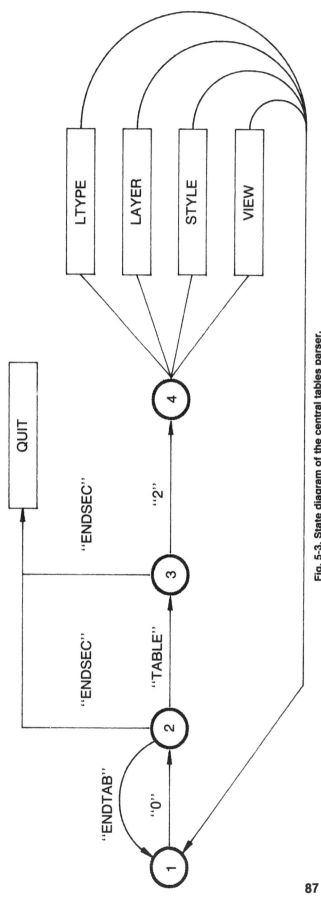

Fig. 5-3. State diagram of the central tables parser.

87

```
tables (f)
FILE    *f;
{
char            quit;
int             state;
int             t;

  quit = FALSE;
  state = 1;
  while (!quit)
    {
    t = get_tag_token(get_tag(f));
    switch (state)
      {
      case 1:  if (t == ZERO) state = 2;
               break;
      case 2:  state = 1;
               if (t == ENDSEC) quit = TRUE;
               if (t == ENDTAB) state = 1;
               if (t == TABLE) state = 3;
               break;
      case 3:  state = 1;
               if (t == ENDSEC) quit = TRUE;
               if (t == TWO) state = 4;
               break;
      case 4:  state = 1;
               switch(t)
                 {
                 case LTYPE : ltype(f);
                              break;
                 case LAYER : layer(f);
                              break;
                 case STYLE : style(f);
                              break;
                 case VIEW  : view(f);
                              break;
                 }
               break;
      }
    }
}
```

Listing 5-25. Controlling the input of the TABLES section.

There isn't a huge amount of information tied to a linetype. Its prime importance is to direct AutoCAD in the correct presentation of lines. Not all lines are solid, continuous lines. Some are dotted, some are dashed and some are a combination of the two.

If you really care about linetypes, you will want to pick up this information. Most likely, you don't care and will want to bypass this table as quickly as possible. Since your most probable goal is to ignore linetypes, the read-it-and-skip-it code comes first.

```
ltype(dxf)
FILE      *dxf;
{
char          quit;
int           state;
char      *s;
int           t;

  quit = FALSE;
  state = 1;
  while (!quit)
   {
    t = get_tag_token(s = get_tag(dxf));
    switch (state)
     {
      case 1:   state = 3;
                if (t == ZERO) state = 2;
                break;
      case 2:   state = 1;
                if (t == ENDTAB) quit = TRUE;
                break;
      case 3:   state = 1;
                break;
     }
   }
}
```

Listing 5-26. Getting through LINETYPE quickly.

The key to getting through the linetype quickly is to look for the **ENDTAB** value. Listing 5-26 gets you through the linetype table with a minimum of problems. The finite state diagram for this routine is simple. Figure 5-4 illustrates the state diagram. The linetype definition has two parts. Look at the **DXF** example in Listing 5-27 to see these parts.

The main part of the definition contains the name, description and scaling data. The second part contains the mathematical definition of the drawn line.

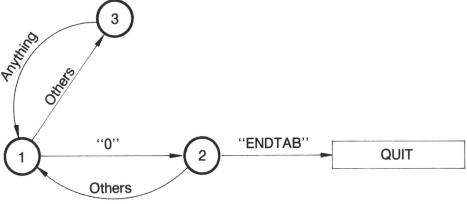

Fig. 5-4. State diagram of the linetype quick parser.

```
    0
LTYPE
    2
CENTER
   70
   64
    3
```

```
   72
   65
   73
    4
   40
2.000000
   49
1.250000
   49
-0.250000
   49
0.250000
   49
-0.250000
```

Listing 5-27. Example LINETYPE table entry in the DXF.

Lines consist of visible line segments, invisible line segments and dots. The standard linetype **"CONTINUOUS"** is the regular solid line with no dots or dashes. Each linetype contains a list of these elements to direct the drawing of lines. These directive elements follow the main portion of the linetype definition. The elements are floating point numbers defining the lengths of the line segments. Positive values represent visible line segments. Negative values represent invisible line segments. Values of 0.0 represent dots. The sum of the absolute values of the line segments should equal the length parameter found in the main portion of the linetype definition.

Since the number of segment definitions can vary from linetype to linetype, there is no efficient fixed record for keeping the segment definitions. My choice is to use a linked list of values for the segments. Listing 5-28 shows the type definition for this linked record. I called it the dash_type because no linetypes would be using this data type unless they included dashes. Figure 5-5 shows the linked structure of the dash definition and its relation to the rest of the linetype structure.

The main portion of the linetype definition also has a type definition. This type includes all of the gathered information about a linetype. It includes an anchor pointer to the list of dash definitions as discussed above.

```
typedef
  struct c
    {
    struct   c    *next;
    double        length;
    }             dash_type;
```

Listing 5-28. Th dash_type definition.

90

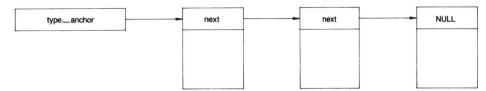

Fig. 5-5. Linking linetype definition to linetype node.

Once the information about a line type has been transferred from the **DXF** file to the internal representation, the program attaches the linetype definition to a linked list of other linetype definitions found in the **DXF.** The linetype definitions are anchored by the variable, lt_anchor. Listing 5-29 shows the type definition for the linetype (ltype_type). Figure 5-6 shows the linked list of linetype definitions.

Since this is **DXF** information, the file represents each value in a tag-value pair. Each field has a unique tag with the linetype structure. Table 5-3 shows the tags found in the linetype definition. These values will aid in understanding the parsing code.

The full linetype parser reads a **DXF** tag and depending upon the tag's value, the

```
typedef
  struct d
  {
    struct   d    *next;
    char          *name;
    char          *descript;
    int            flags;
    int            alignment;
    int            dashes;
    double         length;
    dash_type     *dash_length;
  }              ltype_type;
```

Listing 5-29. The linetype type definition.

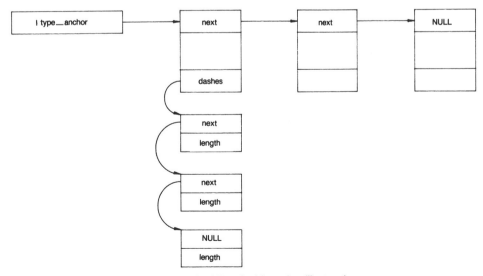

Fig. 5-6. Linked list of table nodes (linetype).

2	String	Name of Linetype
3	String	ASCII depiction of linetype
72	Integer	Alignment
73	Integer	Number of Dash Elements
40	Real	Total Length of Pattern
49	Real	Dash Length Value
70	Integer	Flags

Table 5-3. LINETYPE DXF Tags.

```
ltype(dxf)
FILE      *dxf;
{
char          quit;
int           state;
char          *s;
ltype_type    *l;
dash_type     *dl;
int           t;
int           used_flag;

  /* get a ltype node and add to chain  */
  /* set defaults */
  l = NULL;
  quit = FALSE;
  state = 1;
  while (!quit)
    {
    t = get_tag_token(s = get_tag(dxf));
    switch (state)
      {
      case 1:  state = 1;
               switch(t)
                 {
                   case ZERO     : state = 2;
                                   break;
                   case TWO      : state = 3;
                                   break;
                   case THREE    : state = 4;
                                   break;
                   case SEVENTY2 : state = 5;
                                   break;
                   case SEVENTY3 : state = 6;
                                   break;
                   case FORTY    : state = 7;
                                   break;
                   case FORTY9   : state = 8;
                                   break;
                   case SEVENTY  : state = 9;
                                   break;
                 }
```

```
                break;
        case 2:  state = 1;
                 l= NULL;
                 if (t == ENDTAB) quit = TRUE;
                 break;
        case 3:  state = 1;
                 if (l = (ltype_type *) calloc(1,sizeof(ltype_type)))
                   {
                    l->next = lt_anchor;
                    lt_anchor = l;
                    l->name = locate(s);
                   }
                 else
                   printf("Out of Memory -- LINETYPE\n");
                 break;
        case 4:  state = 1;
                 if (l) l->descript = locate(s);
                 break;
        case 5:  state = 1;
                 if (l) l->alignment = atoi(s);
                 break;
        case 6:  state = 1;
                 if (l) l->dashes = atoi(s);
                 break;
        case 7:  state = 1;
                 if (l) l->length = atof(s);
                 break;
        case 8:  state = 1;
                 if (!l) break;
                 d1 = l->dash_length;
                 if (!d1)
                   {
                    l->dash_length = (dash_type *)
                                      calloc(1,sizeof(dash_type));
                    l->dash_length->length = atof(s);
                   }
                 else
                   {
                    while (d1->next) d1 = d1->next;
                    d1->next = (dash_type *) calloc(1,sizeof(dash_type));
                    d1->next->length = atof(s);
                   }
                 break;
        case 9:  state = 1;
                 used_flag = atoi(s);
                 if (l) l->flags = used_flag;
                 break;
      }
   }
}
```

Listing 5-30. Completely parsing the linetype.

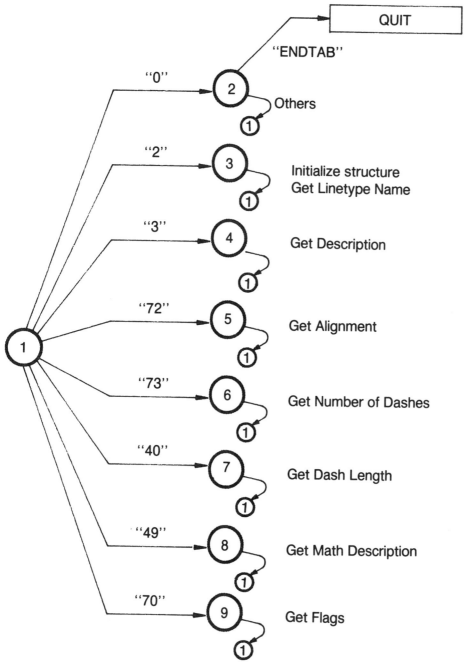

Fig. 5-7. State diagram of the LINETYPE parser.

proper state captures the value and saves it in the internal structure. Listing 5-30 shows the full linetype parser. Figure 5-7 illustrates the finite state diagram for this parser.

The next discussion is not about parsing linetypes. It involves finding information about a linetype after the **DXF** has been read. The earlier code segments gathered information about the linetypes and stored it in a linked list of linetype packets. Sometime in your program, you will want to access this information. If you don't want to use the linetype data, use the routine that bypasses this table. The routine in Listing 5-31 shows how to retrieve a linetype packet by using the name of the linetype as an argument.

```
ltype_type  *find_ltype(s)
char    *s;
{
ltype_type     *l;
l = lt_anchor;
while (l)
  {
   if (!strcmpi(s,l->name)) return l;
   l = l->next;
  }
printf("line type not found\n");
return NULL;
}
```
Listing 5-31. Finding a linetype packet.

The routine searches the linked list (anchored at lt_anchor) by comparing the name of the desired linetype with the names saved in the packets. When two names match, the routine returns a pointer to the correct packet. If no linetype packet can be found with the given name, the routine reports the error and returns a **NULL** pointer.

The LAYER Table

The **LAYER** table entry defines the characteristics of each layer in the AutoCAD drawing. A single layer entry contains information regarding color, linetype, and visibility. This information is easily extracted from the **DXF** file.

Unlike the **LINETYPE** table entry which you may have chosen to ignore in the **DXF** file, the **LAYER** table entry is often referenced through the file. Every drawing entity in the **ENTITIES** section contains a layer reference. Listing 5-32 shows a typical **LAYER** entry in the **DXF** file.

This layer entry describes a layer named **A_LAYER**. The default color is **RED** (1). Lines drawn on **A_LAYER** are the **CONTINUOUS** linetype.

Since the layer table contains the least information of all of the tables, it should be the

```
1
  6
CONTINUOUS
 70
64
  0
ENDTAB
```
Listing 5-32. Typical DXF LAYER entry.

2	String	Name of Layer
62	Integer	Color Number
		Negative = Layer is OFF
6	String	Linetype Name
70	Integer	Flags
		1 = Frozen

Table 5-4. Tags of the LAYER Table Entry.

```
typedef
  struct e
    {
    struct e    *next;
    char        *name;
    int          flags;
    int          color;
    char        *lt;
    }            layer_type;
```

Listing 5-33. Data structure for saving layer information.

easiest to construct. It is. It also has the distinction of being the most highly used table. Table 5-4 shows that tags found in the layer definition.

Listing 5-33 shows the data structure for storing layer information. Like the linetype entry, I've designed the layer entry structure to reside on a linked list of layers. This allows access to each entry as necessary. Each field in the structure corresponds to one of the tag and value pairs found in the layer table.

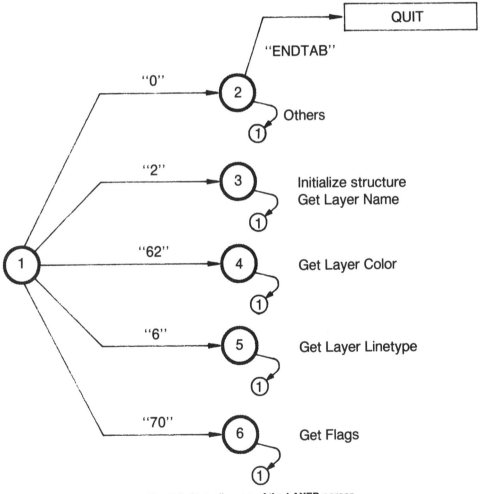

Fig. 5-8. State diagram of the LAYER parser.

```
layer(dxf)
FILE        *dxf;
{
char            quit;
int             state;
char        *s;
layer_type  *l;
int             t;
char        *c;
int             used_flag;

 l = NULL;
 quit = FALSE;
 state = 1;
 while (!quit)
   {
    t = get_tag_token(s = get_tag(dxf));
    switch (state)
      {
       case 1:  state = 1;
                switch(t)
                  {
                    case ZERO     : state = 2;
                                    break;
                    case TWO      : state = 3;
                                    break;
                    case SIXTY2   : state = 4;
                                    break;
                    case SIX      : state = 5;
                                    break;
                    case SEVENTY  : state = 6;
                                    break;
                  }
                break;
       case 2:  state = 1;
                l = NULL;
                if (t == ENDTAB) quit = TRUE;
                break;
       case 3:  state = 1;
                if (l = (layer_type *)
                            calloc(1,sizeof(layer_type)))
                  {
                    l->next = ly_anchor;
                    ly_anchor = l;
                    l->name = locate(s);
                  }
                else
                  printf("Out of Memory -- LAYER\n");
                break;
       case 4:  state = 1;
                if (l) l->color = atoi(s);
                break;
       case 5:  state = 1;
                if (l) l->lt = locate(s);
                break;
       case 6:  state = 1;
                used_flag = atoi(s);
                if (l) l->flags = used_flag;
                break;

      }
    }
  }
```

Listing 5-34. Parser for the LAYER entry.

```
layer_type  *find_layer(s)
char        *s;
{
layer_type        *l;
l = ly_anchor;
while (1)
  {
   if (!strcmpi(s,l->name)) return l;
   l = l->next;
  }
printf("layer not found\n");
return NULL;
}
```

Listing 5-35. Finding a layer.

The listing for ignoring linetype declarations could be modified for ignoring layers. There isn't much need to repeat a skeleton piece of code like that. This is especially true when you consider that most applications don't want to ignore layers. They need the information. Figure 5-8 illustrates the diagram for this parser. Listing 5-34 is the implementation of the diagram.

There is an important note about the color value in the layer table. The value of the color will usually be a number between 1 and 255. The number of colors that you can display depends upon your hardware. If the number is negative, the layer is **OFF.** The color is the absolute value of the negative number.

Speaking of layers being turned off, there is a layer flag entry in the **DXF** file. This is the 70 tag in the file. These are generally flags to indicate some condition. A value of one in the flag value indicates that the layer is frozen. This is a device for AutoCAD to skip over certain entities when it performs a **REGEN** operation. To you and me, it is another way to say that the layer is off.

Since we are placing the layer table entries into a linked list for later reference, it is necessary to have a method of finding a required layer. The code in Listing 5-35 is similar to the code used in the linetype search. In this case, the linked list has ly_anchor as its anchor variable. The algorithm moves from layer reference to layer reference, comparing the layer names against the requested name. When a match is made, the routine returns the address of the layer block as a pointer. When there are no matches, the routine returns a **NULL** pointer, indicating no match. You may want to modify this code so that it returns a pointer to layer 0. Then, even with a problem **DXF** file, a valid layer is still available.

The STYLE Table

The **STYLE** Table records the form in which AutoCAD is to display specific type faces or fonts. Since shapes are virtually identical to lettering fonts in their internal structure, this table also maintains shape file information.

A particular typeface may be twisted, mirrored and scaled in any number of ways to create different styles. Each style has an entry in the Style Table. There may be several styles based upon a single typeface.

The style table entry is the second most complicated of the tables. No doubt about it, linetypes are the most complicated. Listing 5-36 shows a typical **DXF** file sequence for a style table.

```
       0
   STYLE
       2
   SIMPLEX
      70
  64
      40
   0.000000
      41
   1.000000
      50
   0.000000
      71
   0
      42
   0.160000
       3
   simplex
       4
```

Listing 5-36. STYLE table entry in the DXF file.

Table 5-5 lists the tags found in the style entry. Shapes do not require all of the fields of the style entry. Only the file name is necessary. Although the other fields may be in the **DXF** file, your program may ignore them. The **DXF** file indicates a shape file by setting the value of the 70 tag **(FLAGS)** to one.

A style may actually use two font definition files. The 3 tag indicates the primary font file. AutoCAD uses the drawing instructions in this font for "normal" **ASCII** characters. Extended characters (as required for Japanese Kanji) use the Big Font file for drawing instructions. The codes for Big Font match the established 16 bit codes used by Japanese personal computers. If you were to display a **DXF** file with Big Font characters (using the **MS-DOS TYPE** command, for instance), you would see the Kanji characters and not some weird numeric values. There is always at least one style in the **DXF** file. This style is called **"STANDARD."** It's font is usually "txt."

2	String	Name of the Style
70	Integer	Flags
		1 = SHAPE File
		4 = Vertical Font
40	Real	Fixed Text Height
		0 = Not Fixed
41	Real	Width
50	Real	Oblique (Slant) Angle
71	Integer	Text Generation Flags
42	Real	Last Text Height Used
3	String	Primary Font File
4	String	"Big" Font File
		Blank = No Big Font

Table 5-5. Tags of the STYLE Table Entry.

```
typedef
  struct f
    {
    struct f          *next;
    char              *name;
    int                flags;
    int                gen_flags;
    double             txt_scale;
    double             height;
    double             oblique;
    double             last_height;
    char              *font;
    char              *big_font;
    }                  style_type;
```

Listing 5-37. Data structure for STYLE table entry.

```
style(dxf)
FILE        *dxf;
{
char            quit;
int             state;
char           *s;
style_type     *l;
int             t;
char           *c;
int             used_flag;

  l = NULL;
  quit = FALSE;
  state = 1;
  while (!quit)
    {
    t = get_tag_token(s = get_tag(dxf));
    switch (state)
      {
      case 1:   state = 1;
                switch(t)
                  {
                  case ZERO     : state = 2;
                                  break;
                  case TWO      : state = 3;
                                  break;
                  case FORTY    : state = 4;
                                  break;
                  case FORTY1   : state = 11;
                                  break;
                  case FIFTY    : state = 5;
                                  break;
                  case SEVENTY1 : state = 6;
                                  break;
```

```
                case FORTY2    : state = 7;
                                 break;
                case THREE     : state = 8;
                                 break;
                case FOUR      : state = 9;
                                 break;
                case SEVENTY   : state = 10;
                                 break;
            }
          break;
    case 2:  state = 1;
             l = NULL;
             if (t == ENDTAB) quit = TRUE;
             break;
    case 3:  state = 1;
             if (l = (style_type *)calloc(1,sizeof(style_type)))
              {
                l->next = s_anchor;
                s_anchor = l;
                l->name = locate(s);
              }
             else
               printf("Out of Memory -- Text Style\n");
             break;
    case 4:  state = 1;
             if (l) l->height = atof(s);
             break;
    case 5:  state = 1;
             if (l) l->oblique = atof(s);
             break;
    case 6:  state = 1;
             if (l) l->gen_flags = atoi(s);
             break;
    case 7:  state = 1;
             if (l) l->last_height = atof(s);
             break;
    case 8:  state = 1;
             if (l) l->font = locate(s);
             break;
    case 9:  state = 1;
             if (l) l->big_font = locate(s);
             break;
    case 10: state = 1;
             used_flag = atoi(s);
             if (l) l->flags = used_flag;
             break;
    case 11:  state = 1;
             if (l) l->txt_scale = atof(s);
             break;
    }
  }
}
```

Listing 5-38. The STYLE table parser.

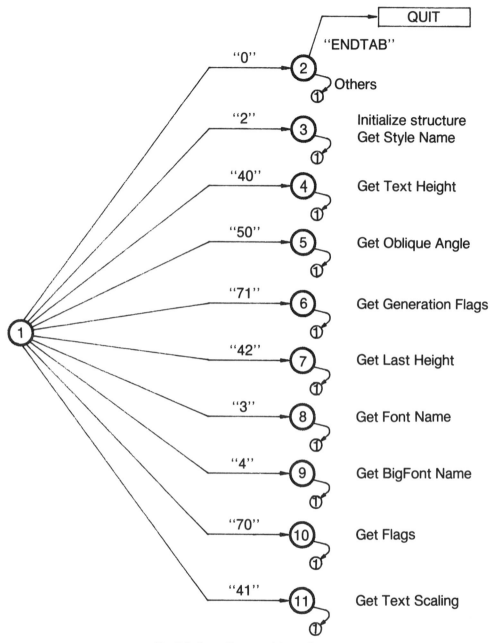

Fig. 5-9. State diagram of the style parser.

Well, there are a lot of fields in a style entry. Listing 5-37 shows the data structure for receiving this information. Each entry corresponds to a tag and value pair in the **DXF** file.

Following what must now seem like a tradition, Figure 5-9 is the design diagram of the style table parser. Listing 5-38 is the implementation of this design.

Since we are placing the style table entries into a linked list for later reference, it is necessary to have a method of finding a required style. The code in Listing 5-39 is quite similar to the code used in the linetype and layer searches. In this case, the linked list has s_anchor as its anchor variable. The algorithm moves from style to style reference,

```
style_type *find_style(s)
char      *s;
{
style_type    *t;
    t = s_anchor;
    while (t)
      {
       if (!strcmpi(s,t->name)) return t;
       t = t->next;
      }
    return NULL;
}
```

Listing 5-39. Finding a style.

comparing the style names against the requested name. When a match is made, the routine returns the address of the style block as a pointer. When there are no matches, the routine returns a **NULL** pointer, indicating no match. You may want to modify this code so that it returns a pointer to the **"STANDARD"** style. Then, even with a problem **DXF** file, a valid style is still available.

The VIEW Table

Probably the least used of the tables is the View Table. This table records the names and coordinates of viewpoints established for the drawing. Until a good three dimensional package comes forth, this will continue to be an unused table. Listing 5-40 shows a typical **DXF** representation of a view table entry. Table 5-6 lists the tags found in the view table entry.

There are several fields in a view entry, but they are all fairly normal. There are no surprises. Listing 5-41 shows the data structure for receiving this information. Each entry

```
   0
VIEW
   2
ONE
  70
0
  40
3.994192
  10
4.372212
  20
7.490436
  41
5.480400
  11
0.000000
  21
0.000000
  31
1.000000
```

Listing 5-40. Example DXF VIEW table entry.

```
2       String              Name of the View
40      Real                View Height
41      Real                View WIdth
10      Real                X Coordinate of View Center
20      Real                Y Coordinate of View Center
11      Real                X Coordinate of View Origin
21      Real                Y Coordinate of View Origin
31      Real                Z Coordinate of View Origin
```

Table 5-6. Tags of the VIEW Table Entry.

```
typedef
  struct g
      {
        struct g      *next;
        char          *name;
        int            flags;
        double         v_height;
        double         v_width;
        double         v_ctr_x;
        double         v_ctr_y;
        double         v_dir_x;
        double         v_dir_y;
        double         v_dir_z;
      }                view_type;
```

Listing 5-41. Data structure for VIEW table entry.

```
view(dxf)
FILE       *dxf;
{
char           quit;
int            state;
char        *s;
view_type   *l;
int          t;
char        *c;
int           used_flag;

  l = NULL;
  quit = FALSE;
  state = 1;
  while (!quit)
    {
     t = get_tag_token(s = get_tag(dxf));
     switch (state)
       {
       case 1:  state = 1;
                switch(t)
                  {
```

```
                        case ZERO      : state = 2;
                                          break;
                        case TWO       : state = 3:
                                          break;
                        case FORTY     : state = 4;
                                          break;
                        case FORTY1    : state = 5;
                                          break;
                        case TEN       : state = 6;
                                          break;
                        case TWENTY    : state = 7;
                                          break;
                        case ELEVEN    : state = 8;
                                          break;
                        case TWENTY1   : state = 9;
                                          break;
                        case THIRTY1   : state = 10;
                                          break;
                        case SEVENTY   : state = 11;
                                          break;
                     }
                  break;
        case 2:   state = 1;
                  l = NULL;
                  if (t == ENDTAB) quit = TRUE;
                  break;
        case 3:   state = 1;
                  if (l = (view_type *)calloc(1,sizeof(view_type)))
                   {
                    l->next = v_anchor;
                    v_anchor = l;
                    l->name = locate(s);
                   }
                  else
                          printf("Out of Memory -- VIEW\n");
                     break;
            case 4:  state = 1;
                     if (l) l->v_height = atof(s);
                     break;
            case 5:  state = 1;
                     if (l) l->v_width = atof(s);
                     break;
            case 6:  state = 1;
                     if (l) l->v_ctr_x = atof(s);
                     break;
            case 7:  state = 1;
                     if (l) l->v_ctr_y = atof(s);
                     break;
            case 8:  state = 1;
                     if (l) l->v_dir_x = atof(s);
                     break;
```

```
    case 9:   state = 1;
              if (1) l->v_dir_y = atof(s);
              break;
    case 10:  state = 1;
              if (1) l->v_dir_z = atof(s);
              break;
    case 11:  state = 1;
              used_flag = atoi(s);
              if (1) l->flags = used_flag;
              break;
    }
  }
}
```
Listing 5-42. VIEW table parser.

```
view_type *find_view(s)
char       *s;
{
view_type      *v;

  v = v_anchor;
  while (v)
    {
     if (!strcmpi(s,v->name)) return v;
     v = v->next;
    }
  return NULL;
}
```
Listing 5-43. Finding the view.

corresponds to a tag and value pair in the **DXF** file. There are no default views. This table may be empty or missing. Figure 5-10 is the design diagram of the view table parser. Listing 5-42 is the implementation of this design.

Since we are placing the view table entries into a linked list for later reference, it is necessary to have a method of finding a required view. The code in Listing 5-43 is quite similar to the code used in the linetype, layer, and style searches. I usually keep all of these parsers in one source file to make it easy to transport from one application to the next. In this case, the linked list has v_anchor as its anchor variable. The algorithm moves from view to view, comparing the view names against the requested name. When a match is made, the routine returns the address of the view block as a pointer. When there are no matches, the routine returns a **NULL** pointer, indicating no match.

READING THE ENTITIES SECTION

The **ENTITIES** section of the **DXF** file is the portion of the file that describes the pieces of the actual drawing. Here are the definitions of what actually appears on the screen or gets plotted to paper.

Normally the discussion of the **BLOCKS** section would appear here since it appears next in the **DXF** file. However, the **BLOCKS** section is very similar to the construction of the **ENTITIES** Section. Therefore, to keep everything in a logical and progressive order

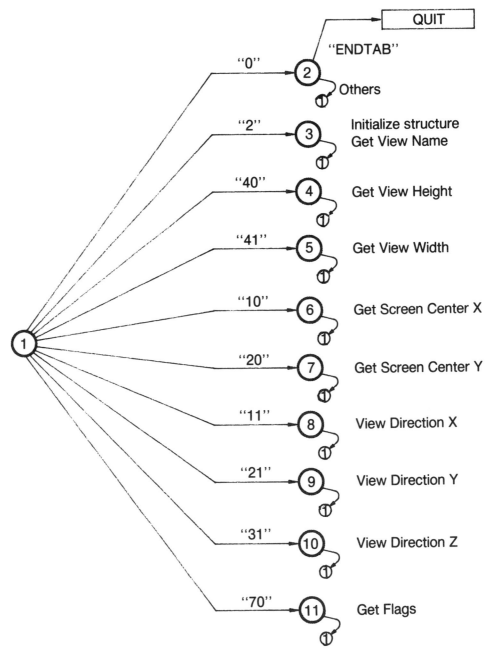

Fig. 5-10. State diagram of the view parser.

—in a programming sense—the **BLOCKS** section (or what's left to say about it) is covered in the next section.

The heart of any program that reads a **DXF** file revolves around the information about the individual entities. To this point in the discussion, we've only parsed and defined the environment of the drawing. We know how big the drawing area is through the **LIMITS** and **EXTENTS** values in the header. We know what colors are used and with which layers they are associated from the layer tables. We know how lines will appear when they are drawn from the linetype tables. What we don't know is what the drawing looks like. We are going to change that situation.

As in all previous sections, we see the section being introduced by a special tag-value sequence. In the entities section leader, we see the same thing. Listing 5-44 shows the section tags that precede and follow the entities.

Since the first lines of the **ENTITIES** section is exactly the same as all of the other sections, we can fold the recognition of these lines back into the already existing recognition procedure, the central control module. The only difference is that we need to add the recognition of the **ENTITIES** sequence. Once it is found, the program invokes the entities parser. Figure 5-11 shows the finite state diagram with the entities being recognized. The updated central parser control sequence is in Listing 5-45. This takes us into the entity parser.

Each entity is identified by a leading tag value pair. We use this pair to activate special handling for the entity type. The data following the entity identifier is unique for the entity.

Here is the strategy the you can use in parsing entities.

1. Upon recognizing an entity type, activate a function to handle the upcoming sequence.
2. While in the special handler, pick up all of the information about the entity, filling in the fields of a data structure. This data structure can be saved for later use — when more information has been found and organized — or passed as a whole to some processor.
3. The results of the special function is a pointer to the data structure containing the entity characteristics.

The **DXF** file introduces each entity through an identifying tag-value pair. The tag is always **ZERO**. The identifying value is a character string with the name of the entity. A list of entity names is in Table 5-7.

The details for each particular entity parser may vary. However, the strategy of each is very similar. Therefore, I will discuss and illustrate the strategy in great detail. This discussion will be further illustrated by designing a specific handler. This will give you a very detailed model for building other parsers. Following the discussion of strategy, you will find a series of tables. Each table shows the structure of an entity. The table contains:

- Name of field
- TAG used to identity field
- Data type of field
- Default value of field

By closely following the structure and logic of the model and using the information in an entities table, you will be able to gather all of the available information about an entity. What you do with the information is up to you. Once a particular entity is encountered, there are things that must be done to prepare the parser for the drawing details.

I am quite partial to collecting all available information in a data structure. You could gather and process data on a piecemeal basis, but you could lose some of the context of the entity in that way. Having all of the information in a central organized location, I can pass the information as a blocked parameter for further processing — using a pointer argument instead of several numeric arguments. You can also save the information for later use with this method.

Regarding the "later use" tactic, I skipped the **BLOCKS** section in favor of the **ENTITIES** section. We will get back to the **BLOCKS** section. However — and this is the

```
    0
SECTION
    2
ENTITIES
    :
    :
    :
    0
ENDSEC
```

Listing 5-44. Header tags and values for ENTITIES section.

reason for doing this — the **BLOCKS** section is 90% identical to the **ENTITIES** section. The only difference is that you find **BLOCK, ENDBLK** and **ATTDEF** entities in the **BLOCKS** section. These don't appear in the **ENTITIES** section. Since blocks are not entities — they are definitions of commonly used entity groups — the entities used to define a block must be saved so that the details of the block are available when the **INSERT** entities introduce an instance of the block into the drawing. Aha! You'll get more details about this later.

Now that I've alluded to the possibility of saving drawing information in a data structure, our first step in planning a drawing parser is to design the data structure. All entity data structures will tend to be different. Use the detailing tables to identify the fields that you will need. All structures will require two identical fields. The first common field is the link pointer allowing for the chaining of several entities.

The second common field is the entity identifier. You certainly know which entity you have when the parser is active. However, when the entity gets chained to other entities (as is the case for a block definition), you quickly lose that identity. You've got to have a method for remembering what kind of entity you have. These two fields should appear in every entity structure, assuming that you plan to save entities.

Several different entity types may have to be chained together in a complicated block. In this case it may be handy to have a generic data type to which all references to the next pointer and the ident fields can be cast (That's C language talk for overriding the data type checking of the compiler). This is pulling the wool over the eyes of the compiler, but it works very well. Listing 5-46 is the type definition of this generic structure.

Listing 5-47 shows a possible use of the generic type in action. In this sequence, the procedure runs through a linked list of entities, activating procedures based upon the entities identity. The casting in this example satisfies the type checking imposed by any function prototypes that you might have.

Regardless of the true specific data type, this scheme works if the data structures are constructed consistently. The operative word here is "consistently." All structures must have the link pointer and the identity field in the same absolute locations.

Getting to specifics, I've chosen the **TEXT** entity as my specific example. It offers a rich assortment of data types and situations. Listing 5-48 shows the type definition of the **TEXT** entity. Compare this structure with the **DXF** Definition tables.

Returning to the discussion about entity parsing, the next thing to consider is the function declaration. Since the circumstances may require that the data be saved, it is quite reasonable to return a pointer to the parsed data and its structure.

Also consider the input arguments to the parser. First and foremost is the handle or file reference for the source of the **DXF**. It is a matter of personal preference as to which you use. My examples use the **FILE** reference.

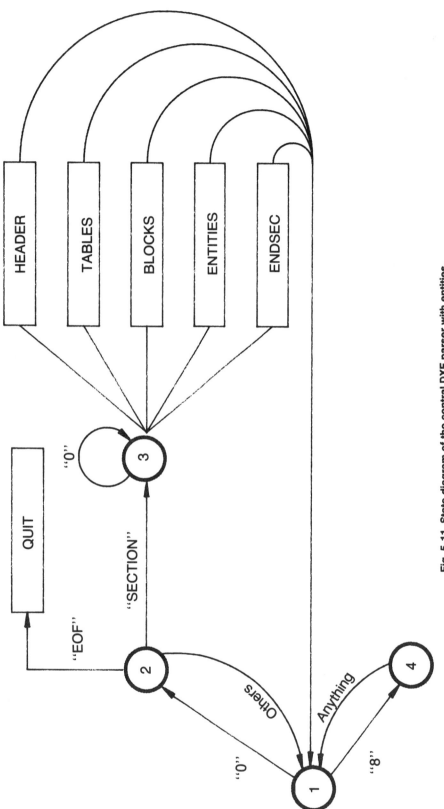

Fig. 5-11. State diagram of the central DXF parser with entities.

```
  switch(state)
{
 case  1  : state = 2;
            if (t == ZERO) state = 3;
            break;
 case  2  : state = 1;
            break;
 case  3  : state = 1;
            if (t == SECTION) state = 4;
            break;
 case  4  : state = 2;
            if (t == TWO) state = 5;
            break;
 case  5  : state = 1;
            switch(t)
              {
                case HEADER   : header_parser(f); state = 3;
                                break;
                case TABLES   : tables_parser(f); state = 3;
                                break;
                case BLOCKS   : blocks_parser(f); state = 3;
                                break;
                case ENTITIES : entity_parser(f,NULL); state = 3;
                                break;
              }
            break;
}
```

Listing 5-45. Central parser control — updated.

LINE	ENDBLK
POINT	INSERT
CIRCLE	ATTDEF
ARC	ATTRIB
TRACE	POLYLINE
SOLID	VERTEX
TEXT	SEQEND
SHAPE	DIMENSION
BLOCK	3DLINE
	3DFACE

Table 5-7. The DXF Entities.

```
typedef
  struct a
    {
    struct a      *next;
     int          ident;
    }             generic;
```

Listing 5-46. The generic data type.

```
generic      *e;
  /* pointer is originally a reference to a generic */
  /* data type                                      */
  e = first_entity;
  while(e)
    {
    /* here is where the entity identity comes in handy * /
    switch (e->ident)
      {
            /* cast the pointer to fit the situation */
      case LINE  : line_processor((line_entity *)e);
                   break;
      case ARC   : arc_processor((arc_entity *)e);
                   break;
      }
    e = e->next;
    }
```
Listing 5-47. Using the generic datatype.

```
typedef
  struct tex
    {
    generic        *next;
    int             ident;
    double          x;
    double          y;
    double          angle;
    double          oblique;
    double          height;
    double          x_scale;
    short           generation_flag;
    short           justification;
    layer_node     *layer;
    char           *words;
    style_node     *font;
    }               text_entity;
```
Listing 5-48. The TEXT entity data type.

```
text_entity  *text_parser(f,lyr)
FILE *f;
char *lyr;
```
Listing 5-49. The text entity parser prototype.

```
text_entity  *text_parser(FILE *f,char  *lyr);
```
Listing 5-50. The text entity parser ANSI prototype.

112

Another possible argument is the layer on which the entity exists. Looking at a real **DXF** file, you see that the layer declaration (**TAG** = 8) precedes the entity. So here is a situation where we know what layer an entity occupies, but nothing about the entity. The operation is obvious. Save the layer information and pass it to the entity processor where it can be used. Listing 5-49 shows our text parser declaration. Listing 5-50 shows the **ANSI** prototype.

The next thing to consider is generating the memory block for holding the drawing data. This is just a matter of requesting a block of heap memory using malloc.

Further consideration must be given to the initialization of the memory. It is not enough to take the block from malloc and assume that all fields will be set at some time.

```
text_entity        *te;

if ((te = (text_entity *)malloc(sizeof(text_entity))) == NULL)
    return NULL;
te->next = NULL;
te->ident = TEXT;
te->x = 0.0;
te->y = 0.0;
te->angle = 0.0;
te->oblique = 0.0;
te->height = 1.0;
te->x_scale = 1.0;
te->generation_flag = 0;
te->justification = 0;
te->layer = find_layer((lyr)?lyr:"0");
te->words = NULL;
te->font = find_style("STANDARD");
```
Listing 5-51. Initializing the text entity structure.

Malloc delivers uninitialized blocks — garbage filled. The **DXF** file does not necessarily contain data for all parameters of an entity. It contains only the fields that have been set in the drawing. Default values do not normally appear in the **DXF** file.

Neither is it correct to set all fields to **ZERO.** Although this is safer than leaving garbage in the fields (as delivered by malloc), it may not fit the requirements of tracking with AutoCAD expectations.

Not wanting to have the wrong values in the structure — a scale factor of zero can prove disastrous — we are careful and initialize all structure fields for ourselves. First, we need to make sure that the "next" pointer is **NULL.** This software is complex enough without having to chase uninitialized pointers.

Second, the entity identifier needs to be set. Values for the identities of the entities are defined for the token generator. Use the same values. It makes life easier.

Next, several of the fields in an entity have a default value other than **ZERO.** This is the value that a field would normally have unless it is explicitly set by a tag-value pair in the **DXF.** Default values are not always **ZERO.** For instance, scaling values have a default value of 1.0. A scale factor of **ZERO** would leave us with no visible element at all. So, let's try this for the text entity. Listing 5-51 shows the initialization of the text entity structure. You'll see this code again when the parser is finally put together. So you see how the find_layer and find_style procedures come into play.

Now the tough part comes. As the program detects each tag of the text entity, it must arrange for the following **ASCII** value to be read, converted to the proper data type and

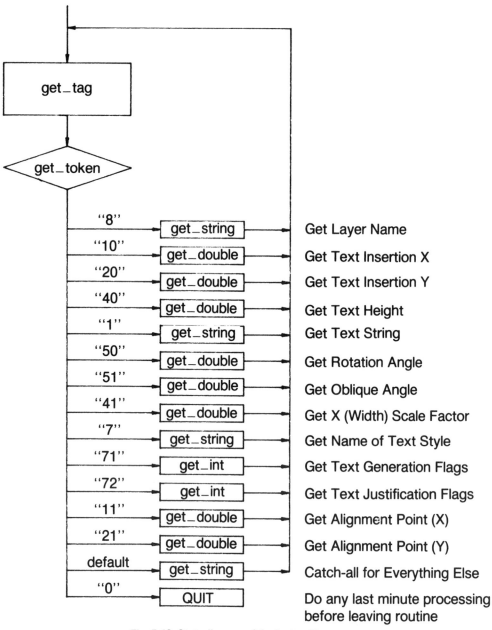

"8"	get_string	Get Layer Name
"10"	get_double	Get Text Insertion X
"20"	get_double	Get Text Insertion Y
"40"	get_double	Get Text Height
"1"	get_string	Get Text String
"50"	get_double	Get Rotation Angle
"51"	get_double	Get Oblique Angle
"41"	get_double	Get X (Width) Scale Factor
"7"	get_string	Get Name of Text Style
"71"	get_int	Get Text Generation Flags
"72"	get_int	Get Text Justification Flags
"11"	get_double	Get Alignment Point (X)
"21"	get_double	Get Alignment Point (Y)
default	get_string	Catch-all for Everything Else
"0"	QUIT	Do any last minute processing before leaving routine

Fig. 5-12. State diagram of the text entity parser.

saved in the correct field of the structure. Since there are no requirements that the entity fields arrive in the **DXF** file in any particular order (They are in a set order in an AutoCAD **DXF** file, but there is no requirement for this.), we can plan for the unexpected with another finite state machine. Figure 5-12 shows the text entity finite state machine. This same engine can easily be adapted to the other entities.

You need to be aware of one feature of this machine. I stressed earlier that the **DXF** file introduces each entity with a zero tag. This is the only instance of the zero tag in the **ENTITIES** section. Therefore, it is the start of a new entity when your program finds a

```
quit = FALSE;
while(!quit)
  {
   t = get_tag_token(c = get_tag(f));
   switch(t)
     {
      case ZERO     : if (te->lyr == NULL) te->lyr = lyr;
                      if (te->text && *(te->text)) te->lt = NULL;
                      quit = TRUE;
                      break;
      case EIGHT    : te->lyr = get_string(f);
                      break;
      case TEN      : te->ix = get_double(f);
                      break;
      case TWENTY   : te->iy = get_double(f);
                      break;
      case FORTY    : te->height = get_double(f);
                      break;
      case ONE      : te->text = get_string(f);
                      break;
      case FIFTY    : te->angle = get_double(f);
                      break;
      case FORTY1   : te->x_scale = get_double(f);
                      break;
      case FIFTY1   : te->oblique = get_double(f);
                      break;
      case SEVEN    : t_font = find_style(ts = get_string(f));
                      if (t_font)
                         te->font = t_font;
                      else
                         printf ("STANDARD used for %s Text Font\n",ts);
                      break;
      case SEVENTY  : te->att_flags = get_int(f);
                      break;
      case SEVENTY1 : te->gen_flags = get_int(f);
                      break;
      case SEVENTY2 : te->justify = get_int(f);
                      break;
      case ELEVEN   : te->ax = get_double(f);
                      break;
      case TWENTY1  : te->ay = get_double(f);
                      break;
      default       : get_string(f);
                      break;
     }
```

Listing 5-52. The text entity parser.

```
double get_double(f)
FILE      *f;
{
   return atof(get_tag(f));
}
```
Listing 5-53. get_double( ).

```
char *get_string(f)
FILE      *f;
{
char       s[256];

   fgets(s,255,f);
   if (s[strlen(s)-1] == '\n') s[strlen(s)-1] = '\0';
   return locate(s);
}
```
Listing 5-54. get_string( ).

```
int get_int(f)
FILE      *f;
{
   return atoi(get_tag(f));
}
```
Listing 5-55. get_int( ).

zero tag. It is also the end of the current entity and it is time to process the accumulated data. Since the very next item in the **DXF** file is the identity of the next entity, the parser control for entities must be left in the state of detecting the identity of the entity.

Listing 5-52 implements the finite state machine for the text parser. By substituting values and structure fields for those found in the tables to follow, you can construct a parser for any entity.

In this listing, there are references to type conversion functions (get_double( ), get_string( ) and get_int( )). Before the parser calls these functions, the parser has already decoded the tag from the **DXF** file. These functions read the next line from the **DXF** file, this being the value. These functions supervise the conversion of the **ASCII** characters to the designated type and return this value. String values return with a pointer to the string table where to locate the string. Listings 5-53 through 5-55 show these functions.

Arriving at the state for the zero tag, it is time to do something with the parsed text. One possible suggestion would be to process the text in a meaningful way. To do this, simply pass the filled structure to a special procedure. When the procedure has finished, the program no longer needs the text entity and you can return the block of memory to the heap manager. The transaction for the entity is complete.

I've conducted this part of the discussion in a "bottom-up" fashion. We've seen the fine details of the parsers and data structures already, but haven't seen the controlling factors. Since the emphasis of the chapter is the parsing of the **DXF** file, I feel that these details warrant this kind of attention.

116

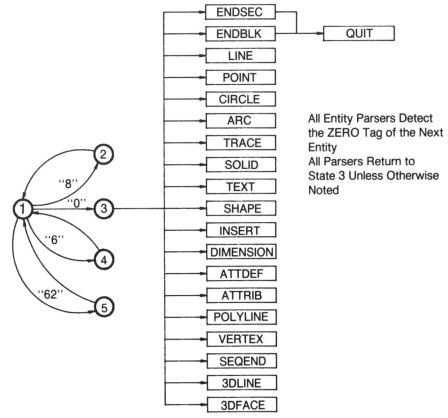

Fig. 5-13. State diagram of the central entity parser.

Surrounding the entity parsers is a central entity parser control module. Every other main section of the program has had one and now is the time to get into the entity control. Similar to other control modules that I've talked about in this chapter, I've designed the entity parser control procedure around a finite state machine. I've made the point that a **DXF** file reading program cannot depend upon the elements of any section to appear in the same order as the AutoCAD Reference shows. This is clearly stated in the reference. Well, we're going to see the same thing in the **ENTITIES** section — only to a greater extent. Can you imagine a **DXF** file where all of the **LINE** entities appear before the **POINT** entities or any other entities (and so forth)? Truly, we can not expect entities in any order or for any given entity to appear at all!

Using the list of entities in Table 5-7 as transition events in the finite state machine, Figure 5-13 shows the design of the central entity parser. Listing 5-56 implements this design. This listing gets modified in the next section to handle block definitions. In this listing (Listing 5-56), the routine called in each of the states handles all parsing and processing.

READING THE BLOCKS SECTION

Remember how there were two things that you could do with an entity. Immediately processing it was one thing, saving the entity was the other thing that you can do with it. This occurs during the **BLOCKS** section parsing.

```
entities(f,blk)
FILE            *f;
block_type      *blk;
{
int             t;
int             quit;
char            *c;
int             state;
char            *lyr;
generic         *en;
line_type       *vl;
int             closed_pline;    /* make global */

pl = NULL;
state = 1;
quit = FALSE;
lyr = NULL;
while(!quit)
  {
   t = get_tag_token(c = get_tag(f));
   switch (state)
     {
     case  1 : if (t == ZERO) state = 3;
               if (t == SIX) state = 4;
               if (t == EIGHT) state = 2;
               break;
     case  2 : state = 1;
               lyr = locate(c);
               break;
     case  3 : state = 1;
               en = NULL;
               switch(t)
                 {
                   case ENDSEC :
                   case ENDBLK : quit = TRUE;
                                 break;
                   case LINE   : state = 3;
                                 en = (generic *)line_parser(dxf,lyr);
                                 break;
                   case POINT  : state = 3;
                                 en = (generic *)point_parser(dxf,lyr);
                                 break;
                   case CIRCLE : state = 3;
                                 en = (generic *)circle_parser(dxf,lyr);
                                 break;
                   case ARC    : state = 3;
                                 en = (generic *)arc_parser(dxf,lyr);
                                 break;
                   case TRACE  : state = 3;
                                 en = (generic *)trace_parser(dxf,lyr);
                                 break;
                   case SOLID  : state = 3;
                                 en = (generic *)solid_parser(dxf,lyr);
                                 break;
```

```
        case TEXT    : state = 3;
                       en = (generic *)text_parser(dxf,lyr);
                       break;
        case SHAPE   : state = 3;
                       en = (generic *)shape_parser(dxf,lyr);
                       break;
        case INSERT  : state = 3;
                       en = (generic *)insert_parser(dxf,lyr);
                       break;
        case DIMENSION  : state = 3;
                       en = (generic *)dimen_parser(dxf,lyr);
                       break;
        case ATTDEF  : state = 3;
                       en = (generic *)attdef_parser(dxf,lyr);
                       break;
        case ATTRIB  : state = 3;
                       en = (generic *)attrib_parser(dxf,lyr);
                       break;
        case POLYLINE : state = 3;
                       pl = pline_parser(dxf,lyr);
                       break;
        case VERTEX   : state = 3;
                       vertex_parser(dxf,pl,lyr);
                       break;
        case SEQEND   : state = 1;
                       if (pl) en = pl;
                       break;
        }
    }
  }
}
```

Listing 5-56. Central entity parser control.

```
       0
     BLOCK
       8
       0
       2
     A_BLOCK
      70
     64
      10
    0.000000
      20
    0.000000
```

Listing 5-57. Block entry in DXF file.

A block is a named group of drawing entities which may appear together any number of times in a drawing. Each time that a block appears in a drawing is an instance of the

```
2        STRING      BLOCK NAME
70       INTEGER     BLOCK FLAGS
                     1 = Anonymous (Hatch or Dimension)
10       REAL        BASE X COORDINATE
20       REAL        BASE Y COORDINATE
```

Table 5-8. Tags of the BLOCK Entity.

block. The **INSERT** command creates an instance. The entities associated with a block form a template which AutoCAD duplicates for each instance.

The **BLOCKS** section parser takes some programming elements from the **TABLE** section parsers and wholly shares the entity parser to organize its defining entities.

This half-table and half-entity situation illustrates part of the nature of the block. Block definitions reside in a table structure. In this structure we find a block name, a block layer and a set of base coordinates. These are the types of information that might be found in the other tables. However, the block contains something that is completely different. It contains drawing entities — any number and type of drawing entity. This is where the entity parser comes to our aid. We have to figure out what the block looks like and then save the entities for later instantiation (the act of creating an instance). Listing 5-57 shows a typical **BLOCK** entry in the **DXF** file.

This block entry describes a block named **A_BLOCK**. The layer of creation is "0". Blocks created on layer "0" have a great deal of flexiblity when inserted into drawings. Table 5-8 shows the tags found in the **BLOCK** entity.

Listing 5-58 shows the data structure for storing block information. Like the table entries, I've designed the block structure to reside on a linked list of blocks. This allows access to each entry as necessary. Each field in the structure corresponds to one of the tag and value pairs found in the block definition. Figure 5-14 illustrates the diagram for this parser. Listing 5-59 is the implementation of the diagram.

Following the block defintion in the **DXF** are the entities defining the template of the block. These are regular entities. The end of the entities is the **ENDBLK** entity. In the code you will see that the **ENDBLK** has the same effect as the **ENDSEC**. Both show the end of a collection of entities. The **ENDBLK** shows the end of a block's definition. The **ENDSEC** shows the end of the drawing definition. The **BLOCKS** section has an **ENDSEC** also, but the **ENTITIES** parser should not be active when it is encountered.

As stated time and time again, the major difference between the entities for a block and those for a drawing is that the block entities must be saved for later instantiation (Imagine that, Christian entities!). We trigger that difference by providing a place to save the block entities. In the example code, it is the "ent" field in the data structure. When the

```
struct k
{
  struct k          *next;
  int                what;
  char              *name;
  int                flags;
  struct e          *lyr;
  struct d          *ltype;
  double             base_x;
  double             base_y;
  int               *ent;
}                    block_type;
```

Listing 5-58. Data structure for block entry.

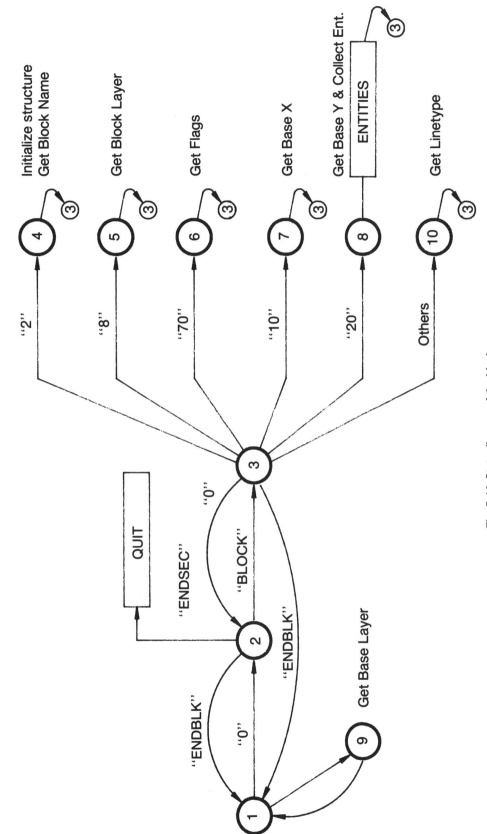

Fig. 5-14. State diagram of the block parser.

```
blocks (f)
FILE        *f;
{
int             t;
int             quit;
char            *c;
int             state;
block_type      *b;
layer_type      *ly;
int             used_flag;

    b = NULL;
    ly = NULL;
    state = 1;
    quit = FALSE;
    while(!quit)
      {
       t = get_tag_token(c = get_tag(f));
       switch (state)
         {
         case  1 :if (t == ZERO) state = 2;
                   if (t == EIGHT) state = 9;
                   b = NULL;
                   break;
         case  2 : state = 1;
                   if (t == BLOCK) state = 3;
                   if (t == ENDBLK) state = 1;
                   if (t == ENDSEC) quit = TRUE;
                   break;
         case  3 : state = 1;
                   switch(t)
                     {
                       case ZERO     : state = 2;
                                       break;
                       case TWO      : state = 4;
                                       break;
                       case EIGHT    : state = 5;
                                       break;
                       case SEVENTY  : state = 6;
                                       break;
                       case TEN      : state = 7;
                                       break;
                       case TWENTY   : state = 8;
                                       break;
                       case ENDBLK   : state = 1;
                                       break;
                       default       : state = 10;
                                       break;
                     }
                   break;
         case  4 : state = 3;
                   if (b = (block_type *)calloc(1,sizeof(block_type)))
                     {
```

```
                b->next = b_anchor;
                b_anchor = b;
                b->name = locate(c);
                b->flash = NULL;
                b->ent = NULL;
                if (ly)
                  {
                    b->lyr = ly;
                    ly = NULL;
                  }
              }
            else
              printf("Out of Memory -- BLOCKS\n");
            break;
  case   5 : state = 3;
             if (b && !b->lyr)
               b->lyr = find_layer(c);
             else
               ly = find_layer(c);
             break;
  case   6 : state = 3;
             used_flag = atoi(c);
             if (b) b->flags = used_flag;
             break;
  case   7 : state = 3;
             if (b) b->base_x = atof(c);
             break;
  case   8 : state = 3;
             if (b)
               {
                 b->base_y = atof(c);
                 entities(f,b);
               }
             else
               printf ("No entities attached to block\n");
             break;
  case   9 : state = 1;
             break;
  case 10 : state = 3;
            if (b && !b->ltype) b->ltype = find_ltype(c);
            break;
  }
}
```

Listing 5-59. The block parser.

program calls the entity parser from the **BLOCKS** section parser, it passes a pointer to ent. When it is time to parse the **ENTITIES** section, the program does not pass a pointer.

The logic is simple. If there is a pointer to the block, then you save the entity on the chain anchored at ent. If there isn't a pointer, then this is just a vanilla entity and it should be processed.

```
case TEXT      : state = 3;
                 en = (generic * )text_parser(dxf,lyr);
                 if (blk)
                 {
                   (generic *)en->next = (generic *)blk->ent;
                   (generic * )blk->ent = (generic *)en;
                 }
                 else
                 {
                   text_processor(en);
                   free(en);
                 }
                 break;
```

Listing 5-60. Linking to the block after parsing.

There are several ways in which you can do this. You can implement the check for the block pointer and the subsequent call to the processor for every entity. Listing 5-60 shows this for the text entity. This passage of code represents an excerpt from the main entity parser control module (Listing 5-56). All other entity processors would be virtually identical.

Another way to implement this feature is to postpone the block check and call to the processor until the flow of control merges after the parsers. This occurs at the close of the switch statement. Now you need only one code sequence to link the entity to the block. Casting all data structures to the generic type facilitates the ease in making the link. However, you will need another switch statement to break out the various entity processors. Of note here is the fact that some processors may be identical for several entities. For instance, **SOLID** and **TRACE** are identical at this point and could use the same processor. Listing 5-61 shows the block pointer linkage and second switch statement. The linking of the entity to the parent block concludes the formation of the block.

With the block entities saved in the block structure, you might be wondering what to do with them. The details for the blocks becomes needed when your entity parser encountered an **INSERT** command in the **ENTITIES** section. All **INSERT** commands found in the **BLOCKS** section get saved like all other entities. The processor (not the parser) for the **INSERT** command is somewhat special. Given a block to be inserted, the insert command processor must:

- Find the block
- Get the chain of parsed entities
- Invoke the processor for each entity found

Since we placed the block entries into a linked list for later reference, we need to find a required block from that list. The code in Listing 5-62 is similar to the code used in the table searches. In this case, the linked list has bl_anchor as its anchor variable. The algorithm moves from block to block, comparing the layer names against the requested name. When a match is made, the routine returns the address of the block as a pointer. When there are no matches, the routine returns a **NULL** pointer, indicating no match.

Listing 5-63 shows the code for getting the start of the entity list and invoking the processor for each entity. If your application requires geometric and trigonometric manipulations, you will want to include the insertion point from the **INSERT** command and the base point of the block in your positioning calculations.

124

```
if (blk)
 {
  (generic *)en->next = (generic *)blk->ent;
  (generic *)blk->ent = (generic *) en;
 }
else
 {
  switch(t)
   {
    case LINE      : line_processor(en);
                     break;
    case POINT     : point_processor(en);
                     break;
    case CIRCLE    : circle_processor(en);
                     break;
    case ARC       : arc_processor(en);
                     break;
    case TRACE     :
    case SOLID     : solid_processor(en);
                     break;
    case ATTDEF    :
    case ATTRIB    :
    case TEXT      : text_processor(en);
                     break;
    case SHAPE     : shape_processor(en);
                     break;
    case INSERT    : insert_processor(en);
                     break;
    case DIMENSION : dimen_processor(en);
                      break;
    case SEQEND    : if (en) pline_processor(en);
                     break;
   }
  if (en->ident == POLYLINE) pline_free(en);
  free(en);
 }
```

Listing 5-61. Linking to the block at a common point.

DXF ENTITY DEFINITION TABLES

The following tables contain the promised outlines for all **DXF** entities. Creating code for any entity should be a matter of including the tag number in the finite state machine, making the proper data conversion and saving the result in the data structure.

There's always an exception to anything. Polylines are the exception in this case. Polylines are a complex entity. They have three components: **POLYLINE, VERTEX** and **SEQEND.** The **POLYLINE** entity is the base piece for the entity. To processors it is the entity. Chained to it are the **VERTEX** entities. This is where the complexity shows up. As **VERTEX** entities are found, they must be parsed (as the tables here indicate) and attached to the **POLYLINE** entity. This explains the extra parameter being passed to the vertex

```
block_type *find_block(s)
char     *s;
{
block_type    *b;

   b = b_anchor;
   while (b)
     {
      if (!strcmpi(s,b->name)) return b;
      b = b->next;
     }
   return NULL;
}
```

Listing 5-62. Finding a block.

parser. It is the pointer to the **POLYLINE** entity so that the **VERTEX** may be attached to it. On this chain of vertices, the latest one is added to the end of the chain. The **SEQEND** entity signals the end of the **POLYLINE.** This is the place for introducing the processor for the polyline.

The first table (Table 5-9) includes tags and values which might be found in any entity. These are optional values and overrides. They do not occur in every entity, but must be expected and processed.

The remaining tables (Tables 5-10 through 5-27) describe the entities.

```
block_type    *b;
generic        *this;
  b = find_block(inserted->block_name);
  this = (generic *)b->ent;
  while (this)
    {
     switch (this->what)
       {
        case LINE      : line_processor(this);
                         break;
        case POINT     : point_processor(this);
                         break;
        case CIRCLE    : circle_processor(this);
                         break;
        case ARC       : arc_processor(this);
                         break;
        case TRACE     :
        case SOLID     : trace_processor(this);
                         break;
        case TEXT      : text_processor(this);
                         break;
        case SHAPE     : shape_processor(this);
                         break;
        case INSERT    : insert_processor(this);
                         break;
        case ATTRIB    : attrib_processor(this);
                         break;
        case ATTDEF    : attdef_processor(this);
                         break;
        case POLYLINE  : pline_processor(this);
                         break;
        case DIMENSION : dimen_processor(this);
                          break;
        default        : printf
                            ("unknown entity found in inserted block\n");
                         break;
       }
     this = (generic *)this->next;
    }
```

Listing 5-63. Processing an INSERT command.

6	STRING	LINETYPE NAME (default = BYLAYER)
38	REAL	ELEVATION (default = 0)
39	REAL	THICKNESS (default = 0)
62	INTEGER	COLOR (default = BYLAYER)
8	STRING	LAYER NAME

Table 5-9. Non-Entity Specific Tags.

10	REAL	START X COORDINATE
20	REAL	START Y COORDINATE
11	REAL	END X COORDINATE
21	REAL	END Y COORDINATE

Table 5-10. Tags for LINE Entity.

10	REAL	X COORDINATE
20	REAL	Y COORDINATE

Table 5-11. Tags for POINT Entity.

10	REAL	CENTER X COORDINATE
20	REAL	CENTER Y COORDINATE
40	REAL	RADIUS

Table 5-12. Tags for CIRCLE Entity.

10	REAL	CENTER X COORDINATE
20	REAL	CENTER Y COORDINATE
40	REAL	RADIUS
50	REAL	START ANGLE
51	REAL	END ANGLE

Table 5-13. Tags for ARC Entity.

10	REAL	FIRST CORNER X COORDINATE
20	REAL	FIRST CORNER Y COORDINATE
11	REAL	SECOND CORNER X COORDINATE
21	REAL	SECOND CORNER Y COORDINATE
12	REAL	THIRD CORNER X COORDINATE
22	REAL	THIRD CORNER Y COORDINATE
13	REAL	FOURTH CORNER X COORDINATE
23	REAL	FOURTH CORNER Y COORDINATE

Table 5-14. Tags for TRACE Entity.

10	REAL	FIRST CORNER X COORDINATE
20	REAL	FIRST CORNER Y COORDINATE
11	REAL	SECOND CORNER X COORDINATE
21	REAL	SECOND CORNER Y COORDINATE
12	REAL	THIRD CORNER X COORDINATE
22	REAL	THIRD CORNER Y COORDINATE
13	REAL	FOURTH CORNER X COORDINATE
23	REAL	FOURTH CORNER Y COORDINATE

Table 5-15. Tags for SOLID Entity.

10	REAL	INSERTION X COORDINATE
20	REAL	INSERTION Y COORDINATE
40	REAL	HEIGHT
1	STRING	TEXT VALUE
50	REAL	ROTATION ANGLE (default = 0)
41	REAL	X SCALE FACTOR (default = 1)
51	REAL	OBLIQUE ANGLE (default = 0)
7	STRING	STYLE NAME (default = STANDARD)
71	INTEGER	GENERATION FLAGS (default = 0)
		2 = Mirrored in X
		4 = Upside down
72	INTEGER	JUSTIFICATION FLAGS (default = 0)
		0 = Left Justified
		1 = Centered
		2 = Right Justified
		3 = Aligned
		4 = Middle
		5 = Fit
11	REAL	ALIGNMENT X COORDINATE
21	REAL	ALIGNMENT Y COORDINATE

Table 5-16. Tags for TEXT Entity.

10	REAL	INSERTION X COORDINATE
20	REAL	INSERTION Y COORDINATE
40	REAL	SIZE
2	STRING	SHAPE NAME
50	REAL	ROTATION ANGLE (default = 0)
41	REAL	X SCALE FACTOR (default = 1)
51	REAL	OBLIQUE ANGLE (default = 0)

Table 5-17. Tags for SHAPE Entity.

NO TAGS

Table 5-18. Tags for ENDBLK Entity.

66	INTEGER	ATTRIBUTES FOLLOW
2	STRING	BLOCK NAME
10	REAL	INSERTION X COORDINATE
20	REAL	INSERTION Y COORDINATE
41	REAL	X SCALE FACTOR (default = 1)
42	REAL	Y SCALE FACTOR (default = 1)
43	REAL	Z SCALE FACTOR (default = 1)
50	REAL	ROTATION ANGLE (default = 0)
70	INTEGER	COLUMN COUNT (default = 1)
71	INTEGER	ROW COUNT (default = 1)
44	REAL	COLUMN SPACING (default = 0)
45	REAL	ROW SPACING (default = 0)

Table 5-19. Tags for INSERT Entity.

10	REAL	TEXT START X COORDINATE
20	REAL	TEXT START Y COORDINATE
40	REAL	TEXT HEIGHT
1	STRING	DEFAULT VALUE
3	STRING	PROMPT
2	STRING	ATTRIBUTE NAME
70	INTEGER	ATTIBUTE FLAGS
		1 = Invisible
		2 = Constant
		3 = Invisible & Constant
73	INTEGER	FIELD LENGTH (default = 0)
50	REAL	TEXT ROTATION ANGLE (default = 0)
41	REAL	X SCALE FACTOR (default = 1)
51	REAL	OBLIQUE ANGLE (default = 0)
7	STRING	STYLE NAME (default = STANDARD)
71	INTEGER	GENERATION FLAGS (default = 0)
		2 = Mirrored in X
		4 = Upside down
72	INTEGER	JUSTIFICATION FLAGS (default = 0)
		0 = Left Justified
		1 = Centered
		2 = Right Justified
		3 = Aligned
		4 = Middle
		5 = Fit
11	REAL	ALIGNMENT X COORDINATE
21	REAL	ALIGNMENT Y COORDINATE

Table 5-20. Tags for ATTDEF Entity.

10	REAL	TEXT START X COORDINATE
20	REAL	TEXT START Y COORDINATE
40	REAL	TEXT HEIGHT
1	STRING	VALUE
2	STRING	ATTRIBUTE NAME
70	INTEGER	ATTIBUTE FLAGS
		1 = Invisible
		2 = Constant
		3 = Invisible & Constant
73	INTEGER	FIELD LENGTH (default = 0)
50	REAL	TEXT ROTATION ANGLE (default = 0)
41	REAL	X SCALE FACTOR (default = 1)
51	REAL	OBLIQUE ANGLE (default = 0)
7	STRING	STYLE NAME (default = STANDARD)
71	INTEGER	GENERATION FLAGS (default = 0)
		2 = Mirrored in X
		4 = Upside down
72	INTEGER	JUSTIFICATION FLAGS (default = 0)
		0 = Left Justified
		1 = Centered
		2 = Right Justified
		3 = Aligned
		4 = Middle
		5 = Fit
11	REAL	ALIGNMENT X COORDINATE
21	REAL	ALIGNMENT Y COORDINATE

Table 5-21. Tags for ATTRIB Entity.

70	INTEGER	POLYLINE FLAGS
		1 = Closed Polyline
		2 = Curve Fit Vertices
66	INTEGER	COMPLEX ENTITY FOLLOWS
40	REAL	STARTING WIDTH
41	REAL	ENDING WIDTH

Table 5-22. Tags for POLYLINE Entity.

10	REAL	X COORDINATE
20	REAL	Y COORDINATE
40	REAL	STARTING WIDTH (default = 0)
41	REAL	ENDING WIDTH (default = 0)
42	REAL	BULGE
70	INTEGER	VERTEX FLAGS
		1 = Curve Fit Vertex
50	REAL	CURVE FIT TANGENT

Table 5-23. Tags for VERTEX Entity.

```
          NO TAGS
```
Table 5-24. Tags for SEQEND Entity.

```
 2          STRING       Block Name of Dimension Image
10          REAL         Base Definition Point X
20          REAL         Base Definition Point Y
11          REAL         Middle of Dimension Text X
21          REAL         Middle of Dimension Text Y
12          REAL         Clone Insertion Point X
22          REAL         Clone Insertion Point Y
70          INTEGER      Dimension Type
                            0 = Rotated, Horizontal or Vertical
                            1 = Aligned
                            2 = Angular
                            3 = Diameter
                            4 = Radius
 1          STRING       User Defined Text
13          REAL         First Definition Point X
23          REAL         First Definition Point Y
14          REAL         Second Definition Point X
24          REAL         Second Definition Point Y
15          REAL         Diameter Definition Point X
25          REAL         Diameter Definition Point Y
16          REAL         Arc Definition Point X
26          REAL         Arc Definition Point Y
40          REAL         Leader Length for Diameter
50          REAL         Angle of Rotation
```
Table 5-25. Tags for DIMENSION Entity.

```
10          REAL         Start X Coordinate
20          REAL         Start Y Coordinate
30          REAL         Start Z Coordinate
11          REAL         End X Coordinate
21          REAL         End Y Coordinate
31          REAL         End Z Coordinate
```
Table 5-26. Tags for 3DLINE Entity.

10	REAL	First Corner X Coordinate
20	REAL	First Corner Y Coordinate
30	REAL	First Corner Z Coordinate
11	REAL	Second Corner X Coordinate
21	REAL	Second Corner Y Coordinate
31	REAL	Second Corner Z Coordinate
12	REAL	Third Corner X Coordinate
22	REAL	Third Corner Y Coordinate
32	REAL	Third Corner Z Coordinate
13	REAL	Fourth Corner X Coordinate
23	REAL	Fourth Corner Y Coordinate
33	REAL	Fourth Corner Z Coordinate
70	INTEGER	Edge Visibility Flags

Bit Set	Meaning
0	First edge is invisible
1	Second edge is invisible
2	Third edge is invisible
3	Fourth edge is invisible

Table 5-27. Tags for 3DFACE.

6

Attributes

THE MOST IMPORTANT DEVELOPMENT IN AUTOCAD TO THE THIRD PARTY APPLICATION developer was the introduction of attributes in AutoCAD 2.0. Well, I should hedge a little on that remark since Auto**LISP** allowed specific AutoCAD functionality to be described by anyone. Let's say that for external programs, attributes allow a dimension of flexibility not found in other drawing packages. My own experience leads me to state that the uses of attributes can be so far reaching as to limit the movement of some AutoCAD applications to other **CAD** systems.

What are attributes? Attributes are specific pieces of data, defined by the user, which become attached to block references in a drawing.

So, why the fuss about attributes? There isn't much argument that AutoCAD introduced attributes to provide a hook into the drawing database for the production of bill of materials listings. This is the basis for the examples in the user guide. The data attached to various blocks of furniture describe various bill of material entities. There may be several attributes in a block. Each attribute contains one piece of information. Several attributes describe the non-graphic properties of the furniture. These non-graphic properties might include:

> Name of Article
> Name of Manufacturer
> Stock Number
> Available Colors
> Delivery Time
> Price
> Discount Rates

These values don't necessarily have to be displayed on the screen for everyone to see. It may very well be advantageous to keep some of the information hidden. Besides, the screen would get cluttered with all of this information spread all over the place. A chair may simply be labeled, by means of a visible attribute, **"EXECUTIVE CHAIR"** or **"DIN-ING CHAIR."** Other information would still be available; it would simply be hidden from view.

When the designer completes the drawing containing the attribute information, the designer has AutoCAD prepare the attribute information for transfer to an outside program. The **ATTEXT** command affects this transfer. **ATTEXT** means **ATTRIBUTE EXTRACTION.** Following a user defined output template, AutoCAD scans its active database, looking for instances of blocks containing one or more of the fields set forth in the template. AutoCAD then writes a formatted record to the output file.

This certainly raises some questions. One of these must be: what is in the template file? Another question would be: What is the format of the output file?

The template file describes the names of the attributes collected during the **ATTEXT** operation and the kind of data which the individual attributes represent. These data representations are either **NUMERIC** or **CHARACTER** in nature. Specifically, the template file is a list of records. Each record contains the name of the attribute and its data representation. The attribute name is the generic title of the attribute. This is not the value assigned to the attribute (which is what you want to extract). The name of an attribute might be something like:

ITEM_NAME
MANUFACTURER
STOCK_NUMBER
PATTERN_NAME

The other field of the attribute template record is the format of the representation. The format field has three sub-fields.

DATA TYPE
WHOLE NUMBER COUNT
FRACTIONAL NUMBER COUNT

Figure 6-1 shows the structure.

The data type field is pretty easy. The position contains the letter **C** for character or the letter **N** for numeric. Any attribute that will always carry numeric information can use the **N** format. However, when the attribute can change from time to time, it may be wiser to choose the character form. For example, it is possible to expect only a number in an attribute known as price; but it doesn't take long for somebody to enter **"NO CHARGE"** or **"NC"** in the otherwise numeric attribute to mess things up. Mixed data makes AutoCAD issue warning messages. Warning messages terrify users. Terrified users call for technical support. Technical support takes time and money. Leaning on this truth, I would suggest that the following attributes be numeric: those that are constant (generated when the block is formed), those that are generated automatically by another program and those that are internal to AutoCAD (most notably, coordinates). All other

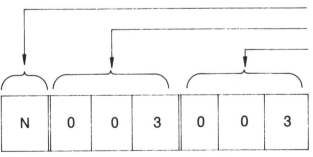

Fig. 6-1. The characters of the attribute template.

```
C008000 -- Character string of 8 characters (max)

C060000 -- Character string of 60 characters (max)

N003000 -- Integer number from -99 to 999
```
Table 6-1. Character and Integer Template Fields.

```
N003003--Floating point number with the form xxx.fff

N004001--Floating point number with the form xxxx.f
```
Table 6-2. Floating Point Template Fields.

attributes extractions should be in character mode. A user-introduced space in the front of a legitimate number can be enough to cause AutoCAD to have problems.

The next three character positions in the second template field indicate the number of digits or characters to the left of the decimal point. Since character strings and integers are entirely to the left, this is only significant count positions in the field. There must be three digits in this sub-field. Fill the unused positions with zeroes. Table 6-1 shows character and integer template fields.

The last three digits indicate the number of significant digits that follow the decimal point. This field is used for floating point numbers. Internal attributes such as coordinates, scale factors, and angles of rotation are floating point numbers.

The form of the third sub-field is the same as the first count field. It must be there, and it must be three digits in length. Table 6-2 shows two floating point template fields.

With that out of the way, we can construct a template file. A template file is a list of attribute names and formats. Sample attribute template records appear in Listing 6-1. The list may be a bit ragged looking since I have not tabbed to make a "pretty" list. I tried using a pretty list once. AutoCAD didn't like it. I haven't used one since. In fact, I don't know if modern AutoCAD allows multiple spaces and tabs. You find something that works and you stick with it. This doesn't mean that you stop looking for new and better ways, but I don't test the waters for old mistakes.

The order of the records in the template file is of critical importance. The order in the output records follows exactly the order in the template file. Since there is no point in going through all of this without using it, it is safe to assume that your program expects the fields in the very same order. I have put stern warnings in my user's guides against

```
BL:NAME C016000
BL:X N008004
BL:Y N008004
BL:LAYER C016000
BL:ORIENT N008004
BL:XSCALE N008004
BL:YSCALE N008004
STOCK_NUMBER C012000
FABRIC C020000
COLOR C012000
```
Listing 6-1. Attribute template records.

BL:LEVEL	Nwww000
BL:NAME	Cwww000
BL:X	Nwwwfff
BL:Y	Nwwwfff
BL:LAYER	Cwww000
BL:ORIENT	Nwwwfff
BL:XSCALE	Nwwwfff
BL:YSCALE	Nwwwfff

Table 6-3. Internal Attributes and Templates.

tampering with the order of attributes. You cannot guarantee the proper operation of your program if the input gets scrambled.

There are several attributes which are internal to AutoCAD. You may access these through the attribute extraction when you include them in the template file. Internal attributes carry a **"BL:"** prefix. These attributes refer directly to values associated with the inserted block. Table 6-3 shows these predefined attributes.

Let's look at the pieces that we have so far and figure out what we want to do. We have constructed a template for attribute extraction. The complete template is in a file. The file extension for this file must be **TXT.** So let's say that the templates file name is **SAMPLE.TXT.** We also, presumably, have a drawing active in AutoCAD. What we want to do is to extract attribute information from the blocks in the drawing and put that information into an output file for further processing. This processing may update a database or generate a report.

The programming examples in the following discussion expect a comma delimited format for the output attribute file. You may modify the algorithms to fit the space delimited format if you wish.

To extract the attribute information from the drawing, start the **ATTEXT** command. Enter **ATTEXT** on the AutoCAD command line. The first prompt that you will see is:

CDF, SDF or **DXF** Attribute extract (or **E**ntities)? **<C>**

Now is that a cryptic command or what? Respond to this command with a **"C"** for command, delimited format. The default value in the brackets is comma delimited format.

Respond to this command with an **"S"** for space delimited format. The fields are fixed in size which may not allow any space characters between the fields. If you are familiar with **FORTRAN,** this format matches the rigid input format of a **FORTRAN** program.

Respond to this command with a **"D"** for **DXF** format. This option writes a modified **DXF** file for the block references with attributes. The next major discussion deals with the extraction of attribute information from a **DXF** file. If you follow the techniques in that discussion, you will not have to use the attribute extraction method.

Respond to this command with **"E"** for a chance to select the blocks for attribute extraction before actually generating the output file. **ATTEXT** gives you a chance to use selection set methods to narrow the range of the extraction. When the selection is complete, you will see the **CDF, SDF** and **DXF** prompt line again. For **CDF** and **SDF** options, AutoCAD requires the template file for directing the extraction. The next prompt from AutoCAD is:

Template file <default>:

The default template file is the last one used. Enter the name of the template file. It is not necessary to include the **TXT** file extension name. Next, AutoCAD wants the name of an output file. It prompts you with:

Extract file name <drawing name>:

The default name for the extraction file is the name of the drawing. The file extension name is **TXT.** You may pick any name that you would like for the extraction file name. However, since the file will get an extension of **TXT** whether you want it to get this name or not, do not pick the same name as the template file for the extraction file. You **WILL** lose the template file when AutoCAD writes extraction information over it. Stick with the default name and don't name your drawings with the same name as the template file.

Once AutoCAD writes the extraction file, it really doesn't matter what you do next. You can continue with your editing session, you may quit the session or you may end (with a drawing save) the session. The extraction file does not cease to exist if you **QUIT** the session. Listing 6-2 illustrates a typical attribute file after the **ATTEXT** experience.

```
"CHAIR",12.5,24.0,"FLOOR",0.0,1.0,1.0,"BR-549","M15-6","RED"
"COUCH",23.5,17.9,"FLOOR",90.0,1.0,1.0,"ML-123"," 1-23","AQUA"
```
Listing 6-2. Extracted attribute records.

The remainder of this discussion deals with producing a program that parses the attribute extraction records. Let me outline some things about the records in the attribute extraction file.

1. Each record has the same number of fields.
2. These fields exactly match the template records in the template file.
3. There are empty fields for attributes not found in a block
4. The fields are in the same order as the template fields in the template file.
5. All of the field values are represented as ASCII characters.
6. For comma delimited fields, all fields are separated with commas.
7. Character strings are surrounded by quotes. Commas within the quotes are not delimiters.

Figure 6-2 illustrates a portion of the attribute extraction record. This is a byte by byte illustration to show the construction of the input record. The program reads the

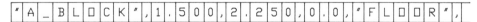
Fig. 6-2. Detail of attribute record.

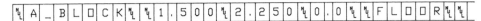

Fig. 6-3. NULs added to attribute record.

entire record into the input buffer at one time. We will not be reading a field at a time, it's too much work.

Since each field is a string of **ASCII** characters and there are all of these extra bytes containing commas which are outside of the information strings, it is not too difficult to see that by replacing the commas with **NUL** characters, you get a number of smaller, perfectly formed **C** strings. Figure 6-3 shows the transformation.

Our task is complete when we generate a pointer variable to each field. And to make life even nicer, we will keep the pointers in an array of pointers with indexes that match the position of the string. Let's get started.

Following the lead of the template file, Listing 6-3 shows the defined constants that we will use to reference the table of pointers. I've borrowed the names from the template attribute names.

Listing 6-4 shows the array of pointers for referencing the fields in the input buffer. The variable for the input buffer is also in this listing. Since this data will be required throughout the program, it is best that these variables be global. Figure 6-4 shows what all of this fuss is about. Listing 6-5 describes the strategy that the program flow will follow to get the attribute information into the program.

The top layer of program code isn't much more complex. Listing 6-6 shows the code for this top layer. I am leaving the algorithm for separating the fields to the next listing so that I can cover it in detail.

The separation process is a matter of finding the commas and newline characters and changing them into **NUL** characters. When you find a comma, the **NEXT** character is the start of a data string. You save the address of this character in the next element of the pointer array. As you find each comma, you should be identifying the next field of the record at the same time.

The other character to watch for is the double quotes (''). These surround text attributes. They always come in pairs. The first one tells you to start looking for the

```
#define  NUMBER_OF_FIELDS        10
#define  BL_NAME                  0
#define  BL_X                     1
#define  BL_Y                     2
#define  BL_LAYER                 3
#define  BL_ORIENT                4
#define  BL_XSCALE                5
#define  BL_YSCALE                6
#define  STOCK_NUMBER             7
#define  FABRIC_STYLE             8
#define  FABRIC_COLOR             9
```

Listing 6-3. Defining indexes.

```
char           *attribs[NUMBER_OF_FIELDS];
char           in_buf[1024];
```

Listing 6-4. Variables for finding attributes.

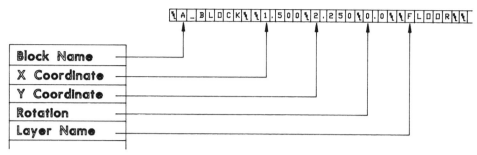

Fig. 6-4. Establishing references to attribute record.

second one. Replace the first quote with a **NUL** character and bump the corresponding pointer in the array to the first character of the string. Replace the second quote with a **NUL.** There is no more to do for the second quote since it has terminated the string. When you return to your normal hunt for commas, everything is in good shape. There may be a newline character at the end of the line. Replace it with a **NUL** character.

Stop the search when you reach the **NUL** character at the end of the line. If you have been keeping track of your addresses and pointers, you should have a list of pointers to strings of attribute information.

The first field starts in the first character of the input buffer. Pretend that there was a comma in the byte before it. Listing 6-7 shows the separation process.

Once the program has completed the separations, it is a matter of following the pointers to the data fields. These data fields are all strings. With further processing and inquiry, you may use conversion software on the numeric fields for better computation. Listing 6-8 shows a simple output process for displaying the results of the separation.

You must do something with the data in the input buffer before you read the next record. The next read operation flushes the data from the input buffer and invalidates the pointers.

```
while there are input records
   read a single attribute extraction record
   separate the individual fields
   establish pointers to each field
   process the record using the pointers to get data
```
Listing 6-5. Attribute retrieval strategy.

```
void read_attributes(fi)
FILE    *fi;
{
char        in_buf[1024]; /* your choice -- local or global */

    while (fgets(in_buf,1023,fi) != NULL)
      {
        separate_fields(in_buf);
        process_findings(in_buf);
      }
}
```
Listing 6-6. Reading the attribute file.

```
void separate_fields(b)
char        *b;
{
int         i;
char        *s;

  /* establish pointer to the first attribute */
  i = 0;
  attribs[i] = b;
  s = b;
  while (*s)  /* for all characters in the buffer */
   {
    switch(*s)
     {
       case ','  : *s++ = '\0';  /* replace with NUL */
                   attribs[++i] = s;  /* next address to table */
                   break;
       case '\n' : *s++ = '\0'; /* replace with NUL */
                   break;
       case '\"' : *s++ = '\0';   /* replace with NUL */
                   attribs[i]++;  /* bump pointer past quotes */
                   /* look for other quote */
                   while (*s && (*s != '\"')) s++;
                   /* replace second quote with NUL */
                   if (*s) *s++ = '\0';
                   break;
       default    : s++;     /* do nothing */
                    break;

     }
   }
}
```

Listing 6-7. Separating the attribute fields.

Using the attribute extraction method for gathering attribute data implies that you trust the user to define attribute values that fit the type and size of the template. It also implies that nobody ever tampers with the order or contents of the template file. Knowing that these events can never happen, **ATTEXT** provides the cleanest and easiest (for the program) method to gather attribute data.

Since I have used **ATTEXT** for application data preparation, I can speak from experience when I say that you can't assume that this fantasy world exists. Oh, sure, most users will automatically follow the guidelines because the template fits their work style. But, there are a few mavericks who require just a little different approach to the problem at hand. Their data has to be alphanumeric where the rest of society is numeric. They need

```
printf("Block Name : %s\n",attribs[BL_NAME]);
printf("Insert Point : %s,%s\n",attribs[BL_X],attribs[BL_Y]);
printf("Stock Number : %s\n",attribs[STOCK_NUMBER]);
```

Listing 6-8. Using attribute information.

floating point numbers to count oranges instead of integers. You can count on it happening. Extracting attribute information from the DXF file bypasses the template file by delivering the raw data directly to you. All of the data in the **DXF** file is alphanumeric **ASCII** characters. There are no commas (unless there are in the text). There are no quotes. All you have to do is parse the **DXF** and save attribute values when you encounter them. Moan and groan. "All you have to do is parse ... the ... **D** ... **X** ... **F**." Look, if you are going to get squeamish about this, go back to attribute extraction. Real Programmers Use **DXF** Files, (and really sadistic ones use **DWG** files).

In the **DXF** file, you gather attribute information from two sources. The first source is the attribute definition **(ATTDEF)** entity in the block definition section. The second source is the attribute **(ATTRIB)** entity which follows the block's **INSERT** entity. There should be an attribute entity for every variable (non-constant) attribute definition.

THE ATTRIBUTE DEFINITION

The Attribute Definition entity is found only in the blocks section of the **DXF** file. It is an entity to be found in and amongst the lines and circles defining a particular block. There is no requirement that definitions appear at the beginning or end of the other entities.

The attribute definition structure is very similar to the structure of the text entity (and with good reason). Both denote position, orientation, size, font, and content of text. If these qualities have a place in your program, you know how to pick them up — see Chapter five. What makes the attribute definition (and the attribute) different is the three fields ruling the text content of the attribute definition. The fields of interest are:

- Attribute Tag or Name
- Prompt
- Default Value
- Attribute Flags

The attribute tag field gives the attribute its name. This field is fixed and carries no other information other than identifying the attribute. The name gets repeated in the inserted block's attributes entities. In the **DXF** file, the attribute tag's numeric tag is 2.

The prompt field appears only in attribute definitions with variable (non-constant) attributes. The value of the variable attribute is satisfied when an instance of its block is inserted into the drawing. Shielding the user from the intricacies of the attribute process, AutoCAD presents the prompt to the user to signal that an appropriate input is needed. When looking through the **DXF** file, don't confuse the prompt with the attribute tag value. Attribute tags should be unique (I don't know what happens if they aren't!). Prompts do not need to be unique. However, it certainly helps the user in deciding upon their proper response if kept unique. The **DXF** tag for the prompt is 3.

The default value field holds the value of the attribute. This is the site of the data extracted by **ATTEXT.** In a constant attribute, this is the constant value. No attribute **(ATTRIB)** entity exists for constant attribute definitions. For variable attributes, this field defines the default value for the attribute. That is, should the user choose to enter no response to the attribute prompt, this default value becomes the value of the attribute. The **DXF** tag for the attribute default value is 1. Listing 6-9 illustrates a typical **DXF** attribute definition entity. We'll use this example in working through the program segments.

```
   0
ATTDEF
   8
0
  10
1.2345
  20
2.3456
  40
0.125
   1
Statue of Liberty
   3
Enter Name of Monument
   2
Monument
  70
0
  50
90.0
   7
HELVETIC
```

Listing 6-9. Typical DXF attribute definition sequence.

THE ATTRIBUTE ENTITY

The attribute entity follows the instantiation (love that word) of a block though an **INSERT** command. The **INSERT** entity contains a flag value which indicates the presence of following attributes. This is the 66 tag. The value for the 66 tag is always one. If there are no attribute following an **INSERT** entity, the 66 tag is not present.

Like the attribute definition entity, the attribute entity is similar to text. The location, font, text height, and rotation values are all present. However, unlike the definition entity, only the attribute tag or name and attribute values are present. No longer are the prompt or default values required. The attribute tag is the link back to the attribute definition. Actually, the insert entity identifies the basic block declaration. and the attribute tag identities the corresponding attribute definitions. The **ATTDEF** is attached to the basic block. Since the same attribute tag can be attached to several block definitions, (How many ways can you say "Stock Number?") — it is imperative that you identify the block before trying to match an attribute to its definition. Like I said, the most important items in the attribute entity are:

- Attribute Tag or Name
- Attribute Value

```
struct
  {
  char      *att_tag;
  char      *att_value;
  }         att_entry;
```

Listing 6-10. Basic attribute structure.

```
#define   REAL      1
#define   STRING    2
#define   INTEGER   3

struct
 {
  char      *att_tag;
  int        att_type; /* REAL, STRING or INTEGER */
  char      *att_value;
 }           att_entry;
```
Listing 6-11. Internal attribute structure with type definition.

The Attribute tag or name identifies the attribute. This field is the logical connection back to the attribute definition.

Use the block name in the insert entity to find the block. Use the attribute tag to find the definition. Like the **ATTDEF** entity, the **DXF** tab for this field is 2. The reasons for all of the rambling is to find the specific attribute value assigned to the instance of a block. The value is either the one entered by the user, an application program or the default value. The **DXF** tab for the attribute value is 1.

Now that I have identified these pieces in the **DXF** attribute puzzle, we can look at how to use them. The following discussion revolves around a technique that works well for me. It provides a well structured environment for dealing with attribute information. Yet it is open and general enough to fit into most any situation. The techniques fall back on the fact that you only need to collect the attribute tag and its value in most circumstances. Some strange situations call for an extra piece of information, the data type. Listing 6-10 shows a basic data structure.

Since both the tag and value are **ASCII** characters, their values (of variable length) can be stored in the string table. The only values in the structure are pointers to the actual values in the table.

If a data type entry becomes a necessity, it can be added to the structure. An enum would be a good choice here or #define constants. Listing 6-11 is the same attribute data structure with the type definition field. A list of these structures provides a nice table containing all of the pertinent attribute information available.

If you've been following all of this stuff, you've seen that all of the attribute information has been strings extracted from the **DXF** file. So, how come there are mentions of

Block Name	STRING
Insertion Point	REAL
Rotation Angle	REAL
Scale Factor X	REAL
Scale Factor Y	REAL
Layer Name	STRING

Table 6-4. Predefined Attribute Data Types.

REAL and **INTEGER** numbers? There are some internal attributes provided by AutoCAD that don't show up in attribute entities. These attributes are not necessarily character strings. Table 6-4 illustrates the AutoCAD internal attributes and their natural data types. Include enough space in the attribute table that you build for internal values as you see fit.

What I propose to show is the construction of a table which holds the identification and value of all required attributes for a block. This table is an array of the type att_entry. The number of elements in the table depends entirely upon the number of attribute definitions in the block and the number of internal attribute that you wish to add. For the sake of the discussion, we'll use all of the internal attributes except **BL: LEVEL**. **BL:LEVEL** refers to the nesting level at which the resident block was referenced. This calls for some recursive programming and resizing of the table in a dynamic fashion. Since I don't want to get into that level of complexity (Yes, I have done it.) here, we'll stay at the first level of processing.

Here is what we will do:

1. Form a template of the attribute definitions and attach it to the block definition node.
2. Copy the template into a working memory block when an inserted block is found.
3. Fill in the attribute values from the **INSERT** entity and attendant attribute entities.
4. Return the table to calling routine for processing.

There are two times in the processing of the **BLOCKS** section of the **DXF** file when it makes sense to build the templates. The first time is at the termination of the block definition. Instead of simply leaving the finite state machine loop when finding the **ENDBLK** entity, perform the template building procedure before leaving the loop. The other time is at the end of the **BLOCKS** section. In a loop that goes through each block entry in the block definition chain. construct a template for each block in the chain.

Regardless of the sequence that you chose to construct the template, the procedure is the same, Given a pointer to a block definition, construct and attach the template to the block definition.

```
int count_attdef(b)
block_node     *b;
{
int            count;
generic        *e;

  count = 0;
  e = b->ent;
  while(e)
    {
      if (e->ident == ATTDEF) count++;
      e = e->next;
    }
  return count;
}
```
Listing 6-12. Counting the attribute definitions.

```
void get_template(b)
block_node      *b;
{
int       n;

  n = count_attdef(b) + 7 + 1;
  b->template = (att_entry *)calloc(n,sizeof(att_entry));
}
```
Listing 6-13. Attaching a template to a block.

The first thing to do in constructing a table template is to allocate enough memory to hold the template. Count the number of attribute definitions attached to the block and add the number of desired internal attributes to that value. Add one more entry as a termination value. Listing 6-12 shows a function, count_attdef, that returns the number of attribute definitions in a block.

Listing 6-13 shows the summation of attribute definitions, the internal attributes and the terminating **NULL** entry. The calloc function returns the properly sized and cleared

BL:NAME	BL:XSCALE
BL:X	BL:YSCALE
BL:Y	BL:LAYER
BL:ORIENT	

Table 6-5. The Predefined Attributes.

```
void set_internal_attributes(b)
block_node      *b;
{
 b->template[BL_NAME].att_tag = locate("BL:NAME");
 b->template[BL_NAME].att_type = STRING;
 b->template[BL_NAME].att_value = NULL;
 b->template[BL_X].att_tag = locate("BL:X");
 b->template[BL_X].att_type = REAL;
 b->template[BL_X].att_value = NULL;
 b->template[BL_Y].att_tag = locate("BL:Y");
 b->template[BL_Y].att_type = REAL;
 b->template[BL_Y].att_value = NULL;
 b->template[BL_ORIENT].att_tag = locate("BL:ORIENT");
 b->template[BL_ORIENT].att_type = REAL;
 b->template[BL_ORIENT].att_value = NULL;
 b->template[BL_XSCALE].att_tag = locate("BL:XSCALE");
 b->template[BL_XSCALE].att_type = REAL;
 b->template[BL_XSCALE].att_value = NULL;
 b->template[BL_YSCALE].att_tag = locate("BL:YSCALE");
 b->template[BL_YSCALE].att_type = REAL;
 b->template[BL_YSCALE].att_value = NULL;
 b->template[BL_LAYER].att_tag = locate("BL:LAYER");
 b->template[BL_LAYER].att_type = STRING;
 b->template[BL_LAYER].att_value = NULL;
}
```
Listing 6-14. Initializing the internal attributes.

146

```
void add_attdefs(b)
block_node      *b;
{
generic         *e;
int              next_att;

   next_att = 7;
   e = b->ent;
   while(e)
     {
      if (e->ident == ATTDEF)
        {
         b->template[next_att].att_tag = locate(e->name);
         b->template[next_att].att_type = STRING;
         b->template[next_att++].att_value = locate(e->value);
        }
      e = e->next;
     }
}
```

Listing 6-15. Adding the attribute definitions.

block of memory for the template table. The summation could be made inside of the calloc reference, but for purposes of example, it is kept separate.

The next step is to fill in the internal attribute tags or names in the template. There are seven of them in our example. These initializations are best done separately. The names of the internal attributes is rather arbitrary since they will be handled internally in a consistent manner throughout the program (Aren't they?). I will use the names from the **ATTEXT** section so that you can follow what I do. For your convenience, these fields are listed again in Table 6-5.

To make the following code easier to read, I will use the defined constants in Listing 6-3 through the remaining listings. Listing 6-14 shows the initialization process for the internal attributes. No actual values are assigned in this sequence. You may add default values.

This leaves the other table entries for receiving data from the attribute definitions in the block definitions chain. The procedure examines each entity. If the entity is an **ATTDEF,** it places the attribute tag and the default values into the next location in the table. The type of the attribute is **ALWAYS** string. You can experiment with mixed data types if you wish. Listing 6-15 illustrates the procedure.

Figure 6-5 shows the constructed table. The last entry is empty to indicate the terminating position. The table waits for use until the program reads the **ENTITIES** Section.

The concerns of this discussion spring back into life when the program reaches an **INSERT** entity. With the **INSERT** entity comes the promise of attributes and realized preparations. But, we must do first things first. If there is a template for the attributes, we must set up a block of memory for the instance of the block. We need to copy the template into a working block. That means that we have to find the block references and get its pointer to its template. Listing 6-16 fetches the pointer to the template. From the **INSERT** entity, we get the name of the block. With the block name, we can get a pointer to the reference, The reference nodes yields the pointer to the template. With the template

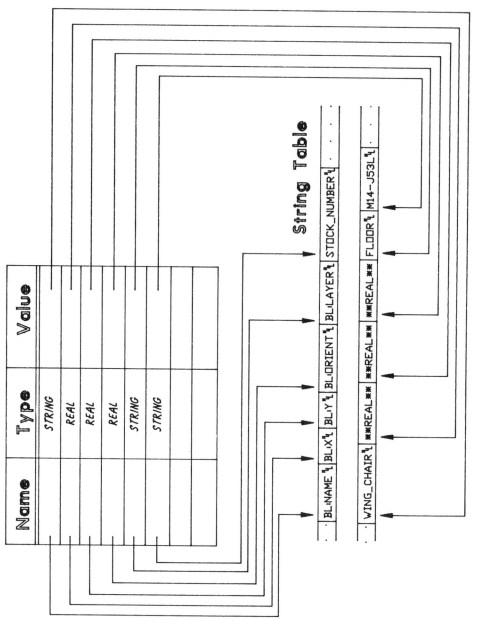

Fig. 6-5. DXF attribute structure.

```
b = find_block(e->block_name);
tmplt = b->template;
```

Listing 6-16. Acquiring a pointer to the referenced template.

securely fastened, we can easily plug in the values for the internal attributes. These values all come from the **INSERT** entity,.

There is one tricky place here. Some of the internal attributes are not strings. They are **REAL** and **INTEGER.** Now putting an **INTEGER** with its 16 bits into the table where a 32 bit pointer goes is no problem. But, putting a 64 bit floating point number into a 32 bit field is a real squeeze job.

Instead of squishing, stretching, and squeezing, I suggest that you go with the prevailing structure and use a pointer to the **INTEGER** and **REAL** numbers. This being the case, where do the values go? You can't leave them as local variables because that area disappears as soon as the procedure returns to its parent and releases the stack. You can't shove them off on global variables because another **INSERT** may come along and write right over them with new values. How about putting these numeric values into the string table? It's a static area that isn't going to be overwritten once the next_word pointer is changed. I wouldn't recommend hashing the floating point numbers; that's going too far. I do recommend that the values be placed in the next available location and the pointer bumped by the size of the variable. This brings us to two routines: put_int and put_double. Listings 6-17 and 6-18 show these routines. If you believe in separate compilation of functional groups, these routines belong with locate and hash. Having the point to the template in variable tmplt and a means of placing all manner of data into the template, we proceed.

```
char *put_int(n)
int      n;
{
char      *p;

    p = next_word;
    next_word += sizeof(int);
    *(int *)p = n;
    return n;
}
```

Listing 6-17. The put_int function.

```
char *put_double(n)
double      n;
{
char         *p;

  p = next_word;
  next_word += sizeof(double);
  *(double *)p = n;
  return p;
}
```

Listing 6-18. The put_double function.

The next operation is to get a working copy of the template with the same size and contents as the original template.

First, we get the size. There are several ways to get the size of the template block. One way is to save the size in the block definitions node when the template was created in the first place. The number of attribute definitions entity found by our little count routine would be enough information for you to save and calculate the size later.

Another way to find the size of the template is a bit marginal when you are looking for a portable solution. Some **C** compilers (notably, Microsoft **C**) include a function called _msize. Given a pointer to a block, _msize returns the number of bytes in the block. Since this feature is not in all compiler libraries and it is not an **ANSI** routine, it is best left out of these example programs. A third sizing method would be to recount the attribute definitions in the block. The code is already available and easy to use.

Another alternative would be to count the elements in the template itself. At this time, the attribute names are completely filled in. The last name is a **NULL** pointer. It is the terminator in the list. To find the total size, count the non-**NULL** pointers and add one to account for the **NULL.** Listing 6-19 shows you what I mean.

With the number of elements in the template table (or the number of bytes), get a block of memory. Listing 6-20 shows you how this is done. Now we copy the template into the working copy. This gives us the attribute names, data types and the attribute constant and default values already in place.

You might be able to write a more efficient routine than the C language memcpy (memory copy) function, but why bother? This routine copies a given number of bytes from one location to another. Listing 6-21 shows the transfer of information from the template to the working copy. memcpy requires a byte count, so it is supplied from previous computations. If you tend toward obscure code, Listing 6-22 should be to your liking.

Nevertheless, we end up with two pointers referencing two identical blocks of memory. The template has done its job so we can forget it for now. Don't throw it away

```
count = 0;
s = tmplt;
while (s->att_tag)
  {
  count++;
  s++;
  }
count++;
```
Listing 6-19. Counting the template elements.

```
work = (att_entry *) calloc(count,sizeof(att_entry));
```
Listing 6-20. Getting the working template.

```
memcpy(work,tmplt,count*sizeof(att_entry));
```
Listing 6-21. Copying the template to the working copy.

```
work = memcpy(malloc(_msize(tmplt)),tmplt,_msize(tmplt));
```
Listing 6-22. Doing the same thing in an obscure manner.

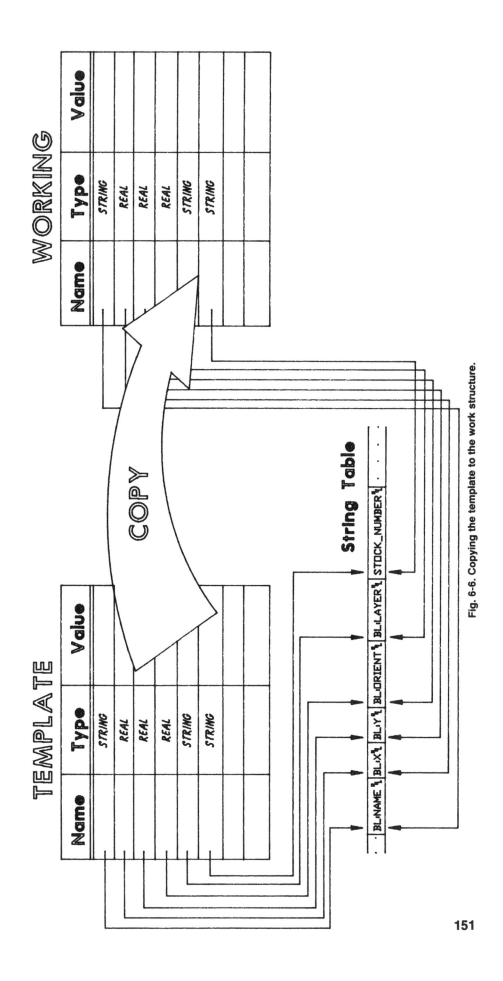

Fig. 6-6. Copying the template to the work structure.

151

```
work[BL_NAME].att_value = locate(e->block_name);
work[BL_X].att_value = put_double(e->x);
work[BL_Y].att_value = put_double(e->y);
work[BL_ORIENT].att_value = put_double(e->orient);
work[BL_XSCALE].att_value = put_double(e->xscale);
work[BL_YSCALE].att_value = put_double(e->yscale);
work[BL_LAYER].att_value = locate(e->lyr);
```

Listing 6-23. Fetching the internal attribute values.

since it will be needed for every instance of the block. Figure 6-6 relates what we have done.

From the **INSERT** entity we collect the internal attributes. These are ready for us in the parsed **INSERT** entity node. All we have to do is to move the values to the working block. Listing 6-23 illustrates this movement. For the remainder of the process, we will be filling in the values of the real attributes.

If an **INSERT** entity has attributes following it, you will find a 66 tag in the **DXF** file for the entity itself and a **SEQEND** entity at the end of the associated attributes. The **SEQEND** is your signal to stop looking for attributes and to send the pointer of the working attribute block to its processor. The only entities that immediately follow an **INSERT** entity with attributes are **ATTRIB** and **SEQEND** entities.

```
case ATTDEF     :
case ATTRIB     :
case TEXT       : text_processor(en);
                  break;
case SHAPE      : shape_processor(en);
                  break;
case INSERT     : insert_processor(en);
                  break;
case DIMENSION  : dimen_processor(en);
                    break;
case SEQEND     : if (en) pline_processor(en);
                  break;
```

Listing 6-24. The entity parser revisited.

```
case ATTRIB     : attribute_processor(en,templt);
                  break;
case INSERT     : templt = insert_processor(en);
                  break;
case SEQEND     : if (en) pline_processor(en);
                  if (templt)
                   {
                     process_template(templt);
                     free(templt);
                     templt = NULL;
                   }
                  break;
```

Listing 6-25. The entity parser updated.

The discussion about entity parsers in Chapter five may have been a wee-bit vague as to what to do with attributes. This is because I don't know what you want to do with them. I still don't. However, I can get more detailed about the entity parser for attributes and inserted blocks. Listing 6-24 is a part of Listing 5-56, the entity parser. This listing shows only the calls to the insert and attribute processors.

Listing 6-25 shows the replacement code for these calls when you use attribute processing such as described here. The insert processor returns a pointer to the working copy of the template. The attribute processor uses this pointer to the table as its input. Inside the processor, the table gets updated for the value of the found attribute. The sequence-end processor triggers the mechanism for dealing with the filled table.

Let's take a look at how simple the attribute processor is. Since the attribute processor can't be triggered until the program has successfully found a complete **ATTRIB** entity, we know that we are getting a completed entity structure. This structure contains two things of interest to us, the attribute tag and the attribute value. **ALL** other fields could have been overlooked if our goal was to find only these two things. With the name of the attribute, we can find the entry in the table. With the value of the attribute, we can assign a value to the correct table entry. That's simple. Listing 6-26 shows the attribute processor. Since both the attribute name in the **ATTRIB** entity and the int attribute table got their pointer values from the locate function, they should be equal. We could find a match by comparing the values of the pointers. However, just in case you didn't use the locate function, the listing shows the comparison being made with the strcmp function. When the **SEQEND** rolls around, you will have a completed table.

One of the benefits of doing things in this manner is that you don't have to worry about default and constant values. Constant values never show up with an **ATTRIB** entity, so their original value is carried to the working copy by the copying process. The attribute processor does not touch it. The same goes for the default value with no **ATTRIB** entity or no response to a prompt. Detecting the sign of no input — a **NULL** pointer — you simply return from the processor with no substitutions.

```
void attribute_processor(e,w)
att_entity    *e;
att_entry     *w;
{
att_entry     *p;

   /* no entry -- leave as default */
   if (e->att_value == NULL) return;

   p = w;
   while (p->att_tag)
     {
      if (strcmp(e->att_name,p->att_tag) == 0)
        {
         p->att_value = locate(e->att_value);
         return;
        }
      p++;
     }
}
```

Listing 6-26. The attribute processor.

```
void print_attributes(w)
att_entry      *w;
{
att_entry       *p;

  p = w;
  while (p->att_tag)
   {
    printf("%s  ",p->att_tag);
    switch(p->att_type)
      {
      case INTEGER  : printf("%d\n",*(int *)p->att_value);
                       break;
      case REAL     : printf("%f\n",*(double *)p->att_value);
                       break;
      case STRING   : printf("%s\n",p->att_value);
                       break;
      }
    p++;
    }
}
```

Listing 6-27. Printing the attribute values.

Now that you have this stuff, what are you going to do with it? I haven't a clue, but I feel that I have to do something. Listing 6-27 prints the names and value of the found attributes.

This brings us to the end of the discussion about attributes. We have seen how attributes play a part in AutoCAD drawings to provide additional non-graphical information to a drawing. We have also seen two ways to gather this information to put it to use in an application program.

7

Driving AutoCAD with Script Files

I**T IS TIME TO LOOK AT HOW OUR PROGRAMS CAN GENERATE INSTRUCTIONS FOR DRIVING** AutoCAD. It certainly made sense to use AutoCAD drawings as a source of data for analysis, synthesis, or database creation. With the results of these programs, perhaps it is reasonable to let AutoCAD prepare graphic presentations of the analysis or synthesis. In my own work with AutoCAD, programs calculate how a working drawing should appear and then tell AutoCAD how to draw the completed structure.

These next two chapters discuss the preparation of drawing data for use in an AutoCAD drawing. This chapter discusses the use of script files. The next chapter covers the generation of **DXF** and **DXB** files for input.

SCRIPT FILE INTRODUCTION

The AutoCAD script file is an **ASCII** file containing AutoCAD commands in the same format as commands typed from the keyboard. When AutoCAD reads a script file, it suspends input from the keyboard and digitizer until the script file is finished or interrupted (the one exception to keyboard suspension).

You may interrupt the reading of a script file by pressing the backspace key. You can have AutoCAD continue reading the script file by entering the **RESUME** command from the keyboard. Using other drawing and environmental commands between the interruption and the resumption does not effect the status of the script file. During this time, AutoCAD reads the script file and follows the commands as if they were being typed from the keyboard.

The script file may not sound like such a great feat, yet it is a feature that makes third party applications easier to implement in AutoCAD than any other **PC**-based **CAD** system I know.

STARTING THE SCRIPT FILE

You can start a script file in several ways. The easiest way to start a script file is to start it at the same time that you start AutoCAD. This is done at the **DOS** command prompt. Normally, you would name the drawing you wish to edit on the command line as shown in Listing 7-1.

AutoCAD starts, and after some loading and kerchunking, it presents you with the main menu. For drawing editing, you choose menu item one (new drawing) or two (edit old

```
ACAD my_dwg
```
Listing 7-1. Command line to start AutoCAD.

drawing). Next AutoCAD asks for the name of the drawing. Although you've already told it the name of the drawing, it still wants to know. Your drawing name is the default. Pressing enter uses the default name.

A script file can automate this process. Certainly, script files can be more complicated than this, but it is a comfortable place to start.

First, the **DOS** command line changes. After the name of your drawing, add the name of the script file. Listing 7-2 illustrates the new command line. When AutoCAD starts (using the example), it will look for a file called old_dwg.scr. Not finding the script file, if it is missing, AutoCAD gets upset and quits.

```
ACAD my_dwg old_dwg
```
Listing 7-2. Command line with script filename.

Just what is in old_dwg.scr? Since it is a script file, it is the normal things that you would enter from the keyboard. Your first entry is a two to edit an existing drawing. Your second is a carriage return to indicate the default drawing name. Listing 7-3 shows old_dwg.scr. There is an extra line in the example. Since it is difficult to show a blank line (carriage return) as the last line in a listing, I've added a **REDRAW** command. This isn't necessary except to show the blank line.

If there is a script file for starting an old drawing, there might as well be a script file for a new drawing. The only difference between the two is the AutoCAD main menu selection item. For a new drawing, use selection one. Listing 7-4 shows the new_dwg.scr script file.

I'll be the first person to admit that the extra typing on the command line hardly justifies pressing the 1 or 2 and a couple of **ENTER**s. However, we are one step away from setting up a batch file that will eliminate the need to do any of this excessive typing or menu selecting.

Here's what we're going to do. **MS-DOS** can check for the existence of a particular file (a drawing file in our case). Based on the existence of a file, **MS-DOS** can choose different paths through the batch file. It can start AutoCAD with the old_dwg script file if a drawing exists. It can start AutoCAD with the new_dwg script file if the drawing does not exist.

Listing 7-5 is the AutoCAD starting batch file. You can pick just about any name for this batch file. There is one to avoid, however, and that name is **ACAD**. Using **ACAD** for a batch file name can create conflicts with other batch files. Other batch files may use the name **ACAD** with the intent of starting the AutoCAD program. Instead of starting

```
2
```

```
redraw
```
Listing 7-3. The old_dwg script file.

```
1
```

```
redraw
```
Listing 7-4. The new_dwg script file.

```
echo off
if exist %1.dwg goto old
acad %1 new_dwg
goto join
:old
acad %1 old_dwg
:join
cls
echo on
```

Listing 7-5. Batch file for starting AutoCAD.

AutoCAD directly and resuming the execution of the batch file when the session is done, the first batch file could start the **ACAD** batch file. In this case, when the AutoCAD session is over, the **ACAD** batch file ends the sequence and the processing stream of the first batch file would be lost.

In the batch file, the %1 notation causes **MS-DOS** to substitute the first parameter in the activating command line for the %1. Suppose we call the batch file **CAD.BAT**. Listing 7-6 shows how to start AutoCAD with the batch file.

The **MS-DOS** batch processor substitutes the name that you use at the invocation of the batch file for the %1 symbol in the batch file. The batch file requests a test for the existence of a drawing file. This request applies to the drawing file name that you used. If the file exists, the old_dwg script file starts the AutoCAD editor. If the file does not exist, AutoCAD initiates a new drawing with the name that you entered.

There is a second way to start a script file. You may start a script file from within AutoCAD. In AutoCAD the **SCRIPT** command starts a script file. From the AutoCAD command prompt, enter:

SCRIPT

AutoCAD will respond with the prompt:

Script file:

You enter the name of the script file. It is not necessary to use the .scr suffix. When invoking a script file from within AutoCAD, your script file should contain only AutoCAD editing commands. The leading menu selection entries cause errors in the editor.

If an error occurs during the script reading, AutoCAD will stop the script and return to normal manual input. If the error is small, such as a typo or missing data, the script can be restarted with the **RESUME** command.

Errors that occur in the middle of a **LINE** command or **LAYER** command stop the script in the middle of these commands (and others). Using the **RESUME** command here, asks AutoCAD to read a coordinate or **LAYER** command argument. These won't be valid commands and AutoCAD will stop again. Pressing **ENTER** causes AutoCAD to repeat the last command, **RESUME**. The script input starts again. If it keeps failing, keep pressing **ENTER** to wade through the problem area.

```
CAD my_dwg
```

Listing 7-6. Using the start up batch file.

157

GENERATING SCRIPT FILES

Making a little start-up script file is a nice exercise for getting to know the ways of the script file. However, the real power is in the construction of a script file that directs the actions of AutoCAD to the point of building a new drawing—from the ground up.

Programs that generate script files of complicated drawing elements become a very useful tool to the professional designer. Instead of entering large amounts of drawing data by hand or menu, a program can automate certain facets of the design cycle.

Now, you can't expect a program to do the creative work of a human, but it can do enough of the rote and tedious work to put a designer at a position in his work to fully use his creative powers. I usually split the activity of generating a script files into two parts.

The first script generating activity involves setting up the AutoCAD drawing environment. This is usually a static piece of program. Once you have an environment to your liking (or the users's liking), the code can be copied into other programs. Setting the environment includes:

- Creating Layers
- Setting Layer Colors
- Setting Layer Linetypes
- Creating Text Styles
- Setting Drawing Limits
- Setting Snap and Grid Sizes
- Toggling Modes (Ortho, Snap and Coords)
- Drawing Page Borders
- Reading a Menu
- Zooming to show the drawing area

The example listing (Listing 7-7) doesn't do all of these things. Yet, it shows code involved in the production of a script file for initializing the working environment.

One minor point of style arises in the generation of script files. AutoCAD recognizes both the space and the linefeed as separators of commands and parameters. It is quite conceivable to produce a script file of one line where you use only spaces as delimiters.

On a more realistic level, you could use spaces as separators for a single command and its list of parameters with a linefeed at the end of the list. This is the most natural form of output.

```
fprintf(SCR_file,"LIMITS 0,0 12,12\n");
fprintf(SCR_file,"SNAP 0.125\n");
fprintf(SCR_file,"GRID 0.250\n");
fprintf(SCR_file,"ORTHO ON\n");
fprintf(SCR_file,"LAYER\n");
fprintf(SCR_file,"NEW FLOOR,WALL,SURFACE\n");
fprintf(SCR_file,"COLOR RED FLOOR\n");
fprintf(SCR_file,"COLOR BLUE WALL\n");
fprintf(SCR_file,"COLOR GREEN SURFACE\n");
fprintf(SCR_file,"ON *\n");
fprintf(SCR_file,"SET FLOOR\n\n");
fprintf(SCR_file,"ZOOM ALL\n");
```

Listing 7-7. Initializing the script file.

However, on some commands, notably the polyline and line commands, a list of parameters or coordinates can stretch for some length. In these cases, it may become difficult to edit the script file (this happens on occasion) with simple editors. For commands that have a variable number of parameters, it is good style to separate parameters or coordinate pairs with a linefeed so you can easily inspect the script file.

One of the most important things about generating script files is to remember the format of the various commands. Several AutoCAD commands end with an extra carriage return. The **LAYER** command is the prime example of this. Listing 7-8 shows a script file for creating and setting a layer called **FLOOR,** colored **BLUE.** The AutoCAD layer processor accepts input until it encounters the empty line (linefeed or extra space). Notice the extra linefeed in the source code listing (Listing 7-7) to overcome this potential trouble spot. Once again the **REDRAW** command appears to show the presence of a blank line in the script file. The second part of the script file deals with the mechanics of the drawing. Here we call the drawing commands into play.

```
LAYER NEW FLOOR
COLOR BLUE FLOOR
SET FLOOR

REDRAW
```
Listing 7-8. Creating layer FLOOR.

Non-English AutoCAD

One of the objectives of the Autodesk founders was to make AutoCAD an international product. With founders from several countries, expertise for this objective was readily available. AutoCAD is available in English, French, German, Spanish, and Italian. Rumors and news carry word of Chinese and Russian versions. In these various language versions, the commands and prompts are displayed in the native language. Other versions, Swedish and Japanese, for example, have prompts in the native language, yet use English for the command language.

Therefore, it is possible to make your program into an international product by having the hooks for various languages, and this section tells you how to do it.

The various language versions of AutoCAD differ only in the spelling of commands and responses. The structure of the commands, and of course, numbers are the same throughout all AutoCAD versions. The only thing that we have to do is to change the spelling of each of the commands.

Here is the basis for doing this. Listing 7-9 shows a short program segment for

```
output_line(scr,x1,y1,x2,y2)
FILE        *scr;
double      x1;
double      y1;
double      x2;
double      y2;
{
   fprintf(scr,"LINE %f,%f %f,%f\n\n",x1,y1,x2,y2);
}
```
Listing 7-9. Simple script output for LINE.

writing an AutoCAD **LINE** command. The function writes the word **LINE** to the script file and follows it with the coordinate pairs of the line segment. Please notice that the fprintf format argument ends with two linefeeds. The second linefeed terminates the **LINE** command. There isn't much to this listing, but it illustrates the principles used in multi-lingual outputs.

The one big thing that makes this script instruction English-only is the hard coding of the word **LINE** in the output statement. But, it is not necessary to do this. It could be an argument to the output format. So, let's try it again. Listing 7-10 moves the word **LINE** outside of the fprintf format argument.

One more pass over this code takes the English **LINE** completely out of the picture. Listing 7-11 substitutes the literal **LINE** for a #define constant of the same name. During compilation, the string **LINE** replaces the name **LINE** in the output statement.

It is now a simple matter to change the English **LINE** to the French **LIGNE.** Upon recompilation, the output statement speaks French instead of English. Listing 7-12 is the French script generator for the line command.

Now, do you want to settle it, once and for all? By adding some preprocessor switches, we can change languages with the flick of the switch. As shown in Listing 7-13, we can generate English AutoCAD scripts if we define **ENGLISH** before compiling this routine. Likewise, defining the value **FRENCH** before compiling gets a French AutoCAD output. Most compilers allow you to predefine values from the **DOS** command line. For instance, Microsoft **C** uses the command line switch **"-D"** to set definitions.

Compiling for English would use this command:

cl -c **-DENGLISH** line_out.c

```
output_line(scr,x1,y1,x2,y2)
FILE        *scr;
double      x1;
double      y1;
double      x2;
double      y2;
{
   fprintf(scr,"%s %f,%f %f,%f\n\n","LINE",x1,y1,x2,y2);
}
```
Listing 7-10. Second script output for LINE.

```
#define LINE    "LINE"

output_line(scr,x1,y1,x2,y2)
FILE        *scr;
double      x1;
double      y1;
double      x2;
double      y2;
{
   fprintf(scr,"%s %f,%f %f,%f\n\n",LINE,x1,y1,x2,:
}
```
Listing 7-11. Simple script output for LINE.

```
#define LINE    "LIGNE"

output_line(scr,x1,y1,x2,y2)
FILE        *scr;
double      x1;
double      y1;
double      x2;
double      y2;
{
   fprintf(scr,"%s %f,%f %f,%f\n\n",LINE,x1,y1,x2,y2);
}
```

Listing 7-12. French script output for LINE.

```
#ifdef ENGLISH
#define LINE    "LINE"
#endif
#ifdef FRENCH
#define LINE    "LIGNE"
#endif

output_line(scr,x1,y1,x2,y2)
FILE        *scr;
double      x1;
double      y1;
double      x2;
double      y2;
{
   fprintf(scr,"%s %f,%f %f,%f\n\n",LINE,x1,y1,x2,y2);
}
```

Listing 7-13. Two language script output for LINE.

Compiling for French would use this command:

cl -c **-DFRENCH** line_out.c

Object code modules for these two compilations should be kept separated (You know how well the English and the French get along.) in their own directories. When linked with other modules calling the script generator, you get the appropriate version for the language that you want.

Appendix A is a listing of a header file for creating AutoCAD scripts in the various languages. On my system, the header file is called lang.h. I leave it in the same directory (\include) as the normal **C** header files such as stdio.h, stdlib.h and ctype.h. In the program, include the following line so that the header file is read:

#include <lang.h>

As for setting the **ENGLISH, FRENCH, ITALIAN, SPANISH** and **GERMAN** definitions, I have specific batch files and **MAKE** files that use the -Dname format in the compiler command line. All of the language translations are from official AutoCAD Reference Manuals of the various languages.

Generating Scripts With an Editor

The primary reason for this chapter is to demonstrate how to develop a script file for driving AutoCAD. The emphasis is on using a program to generate the file. However, using a text editor and following the suggestions of this discussion, you should be able to write a script file by hand. Let's look at that concept for a moment. Hand generated script files have some powerful uses. I use hand generated script files for the formation of symbol libraries.

For me, script files offer two benefits. The first benefit is a minor one to me, but it is a major one to the customers. I can offer source code to the libraries. If someone wants to see how I make a symbol or wants to radically change a symbol, they have a standard outline from which to follow the action.

The major reason for hand generated symbols is the consistency that they afford. When I am building several library parts, there is often a relationship between each one. I use this relationship to my advantage. This relationship usually involves a small drawing difference from symbol to symbol. It might be the length of the main structure, a different number of extensions of the position of a label. Whatever the case, I develop the first symbol in a script file. I can plan to a hair's breadth where a line will go. There is no guessing with snaps and grids. Everything is exact. I let AutoCAD draw the symbol from the script file. Is the drawing okay? Does it look good? Is the text in the right location? Is it the right size?

Returning to the script file and the text editor, I make the required adjustments. I repeat the AutoCAD and text editor cycle until I am happy with the symbol's appearance.

If the symbol contains attributes, I will insert it into a dummy drawing to check the prompts and placement of the attribute values. If you have ever tried to modify an attribute with AutoCAD, you know that it can be a frustrating experience. AutoCAD is not mindful of ordered attributes. If your attribute prompts must appear in a certain order, modifying a block with attributes can ruin the order. The order is always preserved when you control the block structure yourself. By the way, attributes generated by a script file are **LIFO** (last-in-first-out).

This may be a major undertaking for one symbol, but I started this by saying that I wanted several symbols. Here is where the payoff occurs. Already having one symbol in script form, it is a simple matter (Being rather lazy — but not slothfully lazy — I look for the simple and easy ways to do repetitive work.) to duplicate the working symbol any number of times. Use the **COPY** command or **CUT** and **PASTE** commands of your text editor to do this. With a working template, you make the small changes that create the various parts. Remember that the symbols have to be similar for maximum benefit. Just getting the attributes in the correct order for unrelated symbols might be enough justification for using this method.

I am now going to take another side trip before we get too involved in programming. There is usually a single program that generates the script files. Sometimes there are several. There should be some arrangement for selecting a name for the script file. This name must be known so that it can be presented to AutoCAD for input. The easiest way to do this is to have a fixed name. Listing 7-14 shows a batch file with a fixed name script file.

The program generating the script file must be aware of the convention so that it can open the necessary file. Listing 7-15 shows the appropriate file opening sequence.

Now, there is the %1 filename in the batch file with which to deal. When the batch file starts, the batch file processor in **DOS** substitutes a user introduced name in place of the

```
my_prog
acad %1 a_script
```
Listing 7-14. Fixed name script file.


```
FILE       *fo;

fo = fopen("a_script.scr","w");
```
Listing 7-15. Opening the fixed name script file.


```
my_prog %1
acad %1 %1
```
Listing 7-16. Using the same name for the drawing and script files.

%1 symbol. Furthermore, it substitutes other user names for other % symbols. The second name goes to %2 while the third goes to %3. When you start the batch file in the example above, you would add the name of the drawing so that **DOS** may substitute it for the %1 and activate AutoCAD for that drawing.

Playing to this notion, another possibility in picking script file names is to name the script file with the same name as the drawing. The name of the drawing can also be used as a parameter for the script file generator program. Here it is used to name the script file. Listing 7-16 shows the new batch file. Listing 7-17 is the new open sequence in the program. Using these sequences in your batch files and in your programs, you can tie the drawing and script filenames together.

The program code shows the letter "w" in the fopen command. This informs the file management system that the program will be writing to the file. The file manager resets its internal file position pointer to the beginning of the file. If a script file exists with the same name that you have pasted together, you lose the previous contents. Most of the time, this is perfectly acceptable. However, if you have several programs that write to the script file, you want all of the script information in the file and not just the output of the last program. In this case, use the "w" in the fopen command for the first program in the operation and the letter "a" in all of the others. Using the letter "a" in the fopen tells the file manager to position its file pointer to the end of the file so that you can append to the file.

Meanwhile, back at the main subject . . . There is nothing to keep you from jumping into a script file frenzy and generating commands in a near random sequence. It might work. Just the same, I will direct this discussion toward an orderly approach of creating script files. The **DXF** file (and for that matter, the **DWG** file) exhibits a certain logical drawing organization. This organization divides the drawing into several sections.

> Header (Drawing Environment)
> Tables
>> Linetypes
>> Layers
>> Styles
>> Views
> Blocks
> Entities

```
int         debug;
int         quiet;
FILE        *fo;

main(argc,argv)
int         argc;
char        *argv[];
{
char        basename[80];
char        filename[80];
int         i;

  if (argc == 1)
   {
    printf("No file name on command line\n");
    printf("Usage: \n");
    printf("    my_prog script-name\n");
    exit(1);
   }

  for (i=0;i<=argc;i++)
  /* check for command line switches */
   if (*argv[i] == '-')
     switch(toupper(*(argv[i]+1)))
      {
        case 'D'  : debug = TRUE;
                    printf("Debug is ON\n");
                    break;
        case 'Q'  : quiet = TRUE;
                    printf("Quiet is ON\n");
                    break;
      }
   else  /* no hyphen -- must be filename */
     strcpy(basename,argv[i]);

    /* create and open script file name */
    strcpy(filename,basename);
    strcat(filename,".scr");
    fo = fopen(filename,"w");
```

Listing 7-17. Retrieving script file name from the command line.

If we were to organize the script file along the same outline, we would find that required settings would be in place when we get to where we need them. The script file will also be easier to read.

Our main interest is putting AutoCAD commands into an **ASCII** file. There are several ways to do this. Most of these ways are out of the mainstream of normal programming. Some may involve chanting and having unclean thoughts. I'll stick with the practical world and suggest two approaches. Both methods require that you have the outgoing data ready. These are output techniques.

The first approach is the more sensible method in most cases. This method is to centralize the writing to the file to individual routines. This lets all outputs of a single type to pass through a single routine. To draw a line, you call the line drawing routine with the endpoints. To draw a circle, you call the circle drawing routine with the center and the radius. You could get fancy and send a code and a predetermined number of floating point numbers to the circle command. The code would indicate which of the many ways to draw a circle should be implemented with the numbers. See Chapter 3 for more details on drawing a circle.

The second approach is to write the script file at whatever point you need to write it. This method sprinkles write commands (fprintf, in our examples) throughout the program. They are highly visible. This strikes me as the quick way to do things; the way that you might use to get something going quickly without worrying about efficiency or elegance. If you use this method and there are numerous writes of the same kind (such as, generating **LINE** commands) you are being frightfully wasteful of resources. However, it makes very good sense for one-of-a-kind items as you would find in the header section. There is no need for an elaborate subroutine to set the snap or grid.

Actually a blended method is the most satisfactory approach. I will use individual writes where it is a one-of-a-kind situation and the centralized output for commands.

To give the one-of-a-kind situations a consistent look with regard to the rest of the script writing routines, I wrote #define macros for them. They are shown within the listing of each section.

The Header Section

The header establishes the working environment of the drawing. Not only for the script file that follows, but also for the user. The designer should be able to start using the generated drawing without having to reset everything to his liking. Since everyone has their own way of doing things, This may be difficult to do.

One way around the dilemma of second guessing the designer (and guessing wrong) is to ask what their preferences are. Now I've never found it to be completely satisfying to carry on a long question and answer time with a computer. I don't like to write the code and I don't like to be on the answering end. For this reason, I like preference files.

Preference files are **ASCII,** text editor generated files with a simple mechanism for stating preferences. The only settings that the designer needs to enter are those that differ from the default values already in the program. If the designer likes the default values (Don't count on it.), then there are no problems and there is no preference file.

Listing 7-18 shows a typical preference file. The values on the left represent various parameters of the program. The values on the right represent the designers preferences for these parameters. Several parameters represent the names of layers that the program generates. The corresponding response is the color of the layer.

You can get very creative with your preferences. The designer could designate certain text styles for dimensions, notes, cautions, warning and signatures (by their

```
ORTHO = ON
SNAP  = 0.125
GRID  = 0.25
BASE  = WHITE
LEVEL1 = RED
LEVEL2 = BLUE
```

Listing 7-18. Typical preference file.

internal use); and at the same time specify the colors for these same items (by layer). You can allow this flexibility with some creative energy. Inside you program you need a procedure for reading this preference file. Here is what you do.

In the data portion of your program, you need four things.

1. The actual variables which represent the parameters in the preference file. These should be set to their advertised default values.
2. An array of acceptable parameter names. If you want to accept variations in the spelling of these names, make sure that they are all in the list.
3. As a part of the parameter names or as a separate list, the address of the variable that corresponds to each parameter name. They must be in the exact same order as the spelling list.
4. The type of the data. If there are mixed data types, you will have to know how to cope with each one. Since all data are **ASCII** at the beginning, you do not need this entry if you retain all information in its **ASCII** form.

Listing 7-19 shows a sample of this set up with four individual structures. Listing 7-20 combines the last three items into a single structure. Listing 7-21 narrates the strategy for finding and setting a preference. Listing 7-22 shows the code for reading the preference file using the data structure of Listing 7-19. Likewise, Listing 7-23 is the code for the preference file using the data structure of Listing 7-20.

No matter how you arrive at the values for the drawing values, you must get them into the script file. Using the variable names in these last examples as a source of values, Listing 7-24 generates the environment for our script files. This is considered to be a new drawing, so the initial lines set AutoCAD to receive a new drawing script.

The Tables Section

The thoroughness of any aspect of a program generated script file depends upon the requirements of the drawing entities. In my programs, layers are very important. Yet, I rarely get into linetypes and never into views. The AutoCAD defaults are usually enough for my needs. Declare whatever you need. You don't need to declare everything.

```
#define CHAR            1
#define INTEGER          2
#define REAL            3
#define STRNG           4
#define YN              5

char                *ortho = ON;
double                   *snap = 0.500;
double                   *grid = 1.000;
char                *base_color = WHITE;
char                *lyr_color[] = {WHITE,
                                    RED,
                                    BLUE,
                                    YELLOW,
                                    GREEN,
                                    MAGENTA,
                                    CYAN,
                                    WHITE,
                                    WHITE,
```

```
                                        WHITE,
                                        WHITE};
        char             param_name[] = {"ORTHO",
                                         "SNAP",
                                         "GRID",
                                         "BASE",
                                         "LEVEL0",
                                         "LEVEL1",
                                         "LEVEL2",
                                         "LEVEL3",
                                         "LEVEL4",
                                         "LEVEL5",
                                         "LEVEL6",
                                         "LEVEL7",
                                         "LEVEL8",
                                         "LEVEL9",
                                         "LEVEL10",
                                         NULL};

        int              params_type[] = {STRNG,
                                          REAL,
                                          REAL,
                                          STRNG,
                                          STRNG,
                                          STRNG,
                                          STRNG,
                                          STRNG,
                                          STRNG,
                                          STRNG,
                                          STRNG,
                                          STRNG,
                                          STRNG,
                                          STRNG,
                                          STRNG,
                                          0};

        void             *param_value[] = {&ortho,
                                           &snap,
                                           &grid,
                                           &base_color,
                                           &lyr_color[0],
                                           &lyr_color[1],
                                           &lyr_color[2],
                                           &lyr_color[3],
                                           &lyr_color[4],
                                           &lyr_color[5],
                                           &lyr_color[6],
                                           &lyr_color[7],
                                           &lyr_color[8],
                                           &lyr_color[9],
                                           &lyr_color[10],
                                           NULL};
```

Listing 7-19. Separate parameter parser lists.

```
#define CHAR          1
#define INTEGER        2
#define REAL          3
#define STRNG         4
#define YN            5

typedef
  struct param
    {
      char              *param_name;
      short              param_type;
      void              **param_value;
    }                   param;

char              *ortho = ON;
double               *snap = 0.500;
double               *grid = 1.000;
char              *base_color = WHITE;
char              *lyr_color[] = {WHITE,
                                  RED,
                                  BLUE,
                                  YELLOW,
                                  GREEN,
                                  MAGENTA,
                                  CYAN,
                                  WHITE,
                                  WHITE,
                                  WHITE,
                                  WHITE};

param              params[] = {{"ORTHO",STRNG,&ortho},
                               {"SNAP",REAL,&snap},
                               {"GRID",REAL,&grid},
                               {"BASE",STRNG,&base_color},
                               {"LAYER0",STRNG,&lyr_color[0]},
                               {"LAYER1",STRNG,&lyr_color[1]},
                               {"LAYER2",STRNG,&lyr_color[2]},
                               {"LAYER3",STRNG,&lyr_color[3]},
                               {"LAYER4",STRNG,&lyr_color[4]},
                               {"LAYER5",STRNG,&lyr_color[5]},
                               {"LAYER6",STRNG,&lyr_color[6]},
                               {"LAYER7",STRNG,&lyr_color[7]},
                               {"LAYER8",STRNG,&lyr_color[8]},
                               {"LAYER9",STRNG,&lyr_color[9]},
                               {"LAYER10",STRNG,&lyr_color[10]},
                               {NULL,0,NULL}};
```

Listing 7-20. Combined parameter parser lists.

To set a preference:

>   Read preference line from preference file
>   Find parameter name in the list of recognized names Issue
>   warning if the name is not found
>   Get the data type of preference (same index as name) Convert
>   preference value to proper data type
>   Store value in designated variable

Listing 7-21. Preference parser strategy.

```
void set_params (f)
FILE    *f;
{
short       quit;
short       i;
short       state;
char        w[20];
int         *v;
double              *d;
char        *c;

  printf("\nReading parameter file\n");
  quit = FALSE;
  state = 1;
  while (!quit)
    {
    if (fscanf (f,"%s",w) == EOF)  state = 0;
    strupr(w);
    switch (state)
      {
      case  0 : quit = TRUE;
                break;
      case  1 :
                i = 0;
                /* search for word -- establish ptr to variable */
                /* for each entry in the table */
                while (param_name[i])
                  {
                  /* is this the word?  */
                  if (!strcmp(param_name[i],w))
                    {
                    /* change to state 2 if a match */
                    state = 2;
                    break;
                    }
                  ++i;
                  }
                /* no matches -- notify user in case of misspelling */
                if (!p) printf ("Expecting parameter name, found %s\n",w
                break;
```

```
     case   2 :
     case   3 :
            /* pass over = signs  */
            if (w[0] == '=') break;
            state = 1;
            /* get type for table of matchee  */
            /* copy value to variable by type */
            switch(param_type[i])
              {
                case CHAR     : c = (char *) param_value[i];
                                *c = toupper(w[0]);
                                break;

                case INTEGER : v = (int *) param_value[i];
                                *v = atoi(w);
                                break;

                case REAL     : d = (double *)param_value[i];
                                *d = atof(w);
                                break;

                case STRNG    : *(param_value[i]) = locate(w);
                                break;

                /* this case detects YES and NO responses  */
                case YN       : v = (int *) param_value[i];
                                *v = (toupper(w[0]) == 'Y')?TRUE:FALSE;
                                break;
              }
            break;
        default : break;
      }
    }
}
```

Listing 7-22. Preference parser using separate lists.

Linetypes

Following the example of the **DXF** file, the next item is the linetype. The **DXF** file described the linetype entries in great detail. You could actually invent a linetype in the **DXF.** You could create a new linetype in a script file. Although I'm not sure whether this is the proper place to do so.

There are four options in the linetype. Only three are useful in a script file. The fourth, the linetype query, lists the linetypes available. There isn't much that you can do with such a list from within a script file. The other three: **CREATE, LOAD,** and **SET,** can be useful. We'll look at the **SET** option later — we use it in controlling entities.

The **CREATE** option lets us define our own linetypes. To create a linetype, we'll need:

• A linetype name
• A linetype filename

```c
void set_params (f)
FILE    *f;
{
short       quit;
short       state;
char        w[20];
param    *p;
int         *v;
double              *d;
char        *c;

  printf("\nReading parameter file\n");
  quit = FALSE;
  state = 1;
  while (!quit)
    {
     if (fscanf (f,"%s",w) == EOF)  state = 0;
     strupr(w);
     switch (state)
       {
       case  0 : quit = TRUE;
                 break;
       /* search for word -- establish ptr to variable */
       /* for each entry in the table */
       case  1 :
                 p = param;
                 while (p->param_name)
                   {
                    /* is this the word?  */
                    if (!strcmp(p->param_name,w))
                      {
                       /* change to state 2 if a match */
                       state = 2;
                       break;
                      }
                    p++;
                   }
                 /* no matches -- notify user in case of misspelling */
                 if (!p) printf ("Expecting parameter name, found %s\n",w
                 break;
       case  2 :
       case  3 :
                 /* pass over = signs  */
                 if (w[0] == '=') break;
                 state = 1;
                 /* get type for table of matchee  */
                 /* copy value to variable by type */
                 switch(p->param_type)
                   {
                    case CHAR     : c = (char *) p->param_value;
                                    *c = toupper(w[0]);
                                    break;
```

```
                    case INTEGER : v = (int *) p->param_value;
                                   *v = atoi(w);
                                   break;

                    case REAL    : d = (double *)p->param_value;
                                   *d = atof(w);
                                   break;

                    case STRNG   : *(p->param_value) = locate(w);
                                   break;

                    /* this case detects YES and NO responses  */
                    case YN      : v = (int *) p->param_value;
                                   *v = (toupper(w[0]) == 'Y')?TRUE:FALSE;
                                   break;
                }
            break;
          default : break;
        }
      }
}
```

Listing 7-23. Preference parser using combined lists.

```
printf("Initializing Script File\n");

fprintf(SCR_file,"%s %s\n",ZOOM,ALL);
fprintf(SCR_file,"%s %f\n",GRID,grid);
fprintf(SCR_file,"%s %s\n",ORTHO,ortho);
fprintf(SCR_file,"%s\n",LAYER);
fprintf(SCR_file,"%s %s 0\n",COLOR,lyr_color[0]);
fprintf(SCR_file,"%s BASE %s %s BASE\n",NEW,,COLOR,base_color);
for(i=1;i<11;i++);
   fprintf(SCR_file,"%s LEVEL%d %s %s LEVEL%d\n",
                    NEW,i,COLOR,lyr_color[i],i);
fprintf(SCR_file,"\n");
```

Listing 7-24. Generating the drawing environment.

- A brief (less than 80 characters) **ASCII** description
· • A mathematical description

The **ASCII** description is a visual description of what the linetype looks like. Listing 7-25 shows some examples of linetype descriptions.

The mathematical description is a list of lengths, detailing the definition of the line. Positive values in this description are visible line lengths. Negative values are invisible lengths. A zero indicates a point or dot. Dots do not cause line length progression.

A dotted line may have a mathematical description of

$$A,0,-0.25,0,-0.25,0,-0.25,0,-0.25$$

The initial letter **"A"** is for alignment purposes. There are no other options for its

```
.   .   .   .   .   .   .
._._._._._._._._
.  __  .  __  .  __  .
__ __ __ __ __ __
```
Listing 7-25. Linetype descriptions.

```
void create_linetype(SCR_file,ltype_name,ltype_file,
                     ASCII_desription,math_description)
FILE          *SCR_file;
char          *ltype_name;
char          *ltype_file;
char          *ASCII_description;
char          *math_description;
{
  fprintf(SCR_file,"%s %s %s\n",LINETYPE,CREATE,ltype_name);
  fprintf(SCR_file,"%s\n",ltype_file);
  fprintf(SCR_file,"%s\n",ASCII_description);
  fprintf(SCR_file,"A,%s\n",math_description);
}
```
Listing 7-26. Creating a linetype.

```
LINETYPE C my_sos
my_lines
...  ___  ___  ___  ...
A,0,-.25,0,-.25,0,-.25,.25,-.25,.25,-.25,.25,0,-.25,0,-.25,0
```
Listing 7-27. Linetype creation script.

```
void load_linetype(SCR_file,ltype_name,ltype_file)
FILE         *SCR_file;
char         *ltype_name;
char         *ltype_file;
{
  fprintf(SCR_file,"%s %s %s\n",LINETYPE,SET,ltype_name);
  fprintf(SCR_file,"%s\n",ltype_file);
}
```
Listing 7-28. Loading a linetype.

```
LINETYPE S my_sos
my_lines
```
Listing 7-29. Linetype loading script.

value. Listing 7-26 shows the code to create a new linetype. Listing 7-27 shows the resulting script file.

It's easier to load a known linetype. The script includes the linetype and the linetype filename. Listing 7-28 shows the code for loading a known filetype from a standard file. Listing 7-29 shows the resulting script file.

Layers

Computer generated layer assignments are more common than any of the other table items. Looking over the material on the layer command in Chapter 3, you will notice that

173

there are several options to the layer command. You can construct code to whatever complexity you like to define layers to suit your needs.

The listings in this section illustrate the #define macro approach of generating script files. The layer commands can be short and sweet and plugged into the program at any point. As I mentioned before, this may increase the size of your program with all of the expanded macros. If this is a problem, converting the macros to routines is a matter of defining the argument types and adding some braces around the output statements.

The macros of Listing 7-30 belong in the defines.h file. They define the basic macros for the program. The statements only appear when you reference one of them. Make sure that the language flag is set so that the macros produce the proper AutoCAD language. Listing 7-31 shows the use of the macros. Listing 7-32 shows the resulting script file segment.

```
#define NEW_LAYER(f,n)  fprintf(f,"%s %s %s\n\n",LAYER,NEW,n)
#define SET_LAYER(f,n)  fprintf(f,"%s %s %s\n\n",LAYER,SET,n)
#define SET_COLOR(f,c,n) fprintf(f,"%s %s %s %s\n\n",LAYER,COLOR,c,n)
#define SET_LTYPE(f,l,n) fprintf(f,"%s %s %s %s\n\n",LAYER,LTYPE,l,n)
#define LAYER_ON(f,n) fprintf(f,"%s %s %s\n\n",LAYER,ON,n)
#define LAYER_OFF(f,n) fprintf(f,"%s %s %s\n\n",LAYER,OFF,n)
#define MAKE_LAYER(f,n) fprintf(f,"%s %s %s\n\n",LAYER,MAKE,n)
#define FREEZE(f,n) fprintf(f,"%s %s %s\n\n",LAYER,FREEZE,n)
#define THAW_LAYER(f,n) fprintf(f,"%s %s %s\n\n",LAYER,THAW,n)
```
Listing 7-30. Layer command macros.

```
NEW_LAYER(SCR_file,"FLOOR");
NEW_LAYER(SCR_file,"SURFACE");
SET_COLOR(SCR_file,"RED","FLOOR");
SET_COLOR(SCR_file,"13","SURFACE");
LAYER_ON(SCR_file,"*");
SET_LAYER(SCR_file,"FLOOR");
fprintf(SCR_file,"%s\n",REDRAW);
```
Listing 7-31. Using the layer macros.

```
LAYER NEW FLOOR

LAYER NEW SURFACE

LAYER COLOR RED FLOOR

LAYER COLOR 13 SURFACE

LAYER ON *

LAYER SET FLOOR

REDRAW
```
Listing 7-32. Layer command script.

Text Style

Establishing a text style from the script file is one of the most orderly operations available. AutoCAD wants a fixed amount of data in a known fashion and you supply it.

To create a text style, you must have the following data:

- Name of the Text Style
- Name of the Defining Font File **(.SHX)**
- Text Height (0 = not a fixed height)
- Width Factor (to make condensed type faces)
- Obliquing Angle (for the slanted look)
- Backwards? (a **YES** or **NO** question)
- Upside-Down (a **YES** or **NO** question)
- Vertical (a **YES** or **NO** question)

With this battery of information at your disposal, you can create the script commands to define a new style. The program code is simple enough. It starts the **STYLE** command and pumps all of the data to AutoCAD. Listing 7-33 shows a routine to handle this highly demanding task. Listing 7-34 shows a typical script file segment.

```
void create_text_style(SCR_file,style_name,font_name,
                       height,width,oblique,
                       backwards,upside_down)
FILE        *SCR_file;
char        *style_name;
char        *font_name;
double       height;
double       width;
double       oblique;
int          backwards;
int          upside_down;
{

  fprintf(SCR_file,"%s %s\n",STYLE,style_name);
  fprintf(SCR_file,"%s\n",font_name);
  fprintf(SCR_file,"%f\n",height);
  fprintf(SCR_file,"%f\n",width);
  fprintf(SCR_file,"%f\n",oblique);
  fprintf(SCR_file,"%s\n",(backwards)?YES:NO);
  fprintf(SCR_file,"%s\n",(upside_down)?YES:NO);
}
```
Listing 7-33. Creating a text style.

```
STYLE MY_FONT
TXT
0.0
0.75
0.0
NO
NO
```
Listing 7-34. Text style creation script.

```
void create_view(SCR_file,x,y,z,view_name)
FILE      *SCR_file;
double    x;
double    y;
double    z;
char      *view_name;
{
  fprintf(SCR_file,"%s %f,%f,f\n",VPOINT,x,y,z);
  fprintf(SCR_file,"%s %s %s\n",VIEW,SAVE,view_name);
  fprintf(SCR_file,"%s 0.0,0.0,1.0\n",VPOINT);
}
```
Listing 7-35. Creating a view.

```
VPOINT 2.4,1.3,2.5
VIEW SAVE NICE_VIEW
VPOINT 0.0,0.0,1.0
```
Listing 7-36. View creation script.

View

Setting a view in AutoCAD is actually a two step task. First the desired view must be produced. Establishing a view point makes this possible. Second, use the **VIEW** command to name this particular view. This isn't the sort of thing that is done from the mechanical confines of a script file, unless you are very sure of how the view will appear on the screen.

Your program can combine the operations of establishing and naming the view into one routine. To your program it would appear that a name and a view point are all that is needed. Listing 7-35 shows the routine. Listing 7-36 shows the resulting script file from the use of the routine.

The Entities and Blocks Section

There doesn't seem to be much need in skirting the inevitable. The blocks and entities sections remains so similar that it makes sense to combine the two sections in this discussion. We handle both groups of drawing entities identically. Having assembled the entities that create a symbol, it is simply a matter of using a **BLOCK** or **WBLOCK** command to turn the entities into a block.

In the introduction to this section, we looked at two approaches to generating script files. These approaches involved centralizing the output statements or scattering the output statements. The scattering method works well for headers and tables to some degree. However, it isn't a very good idea for entities. With headers, you write a **LIMITS** statement only once. With entities, you write a **LINE** statement any number of times. You centralize these output commands for easier management and efficiency. This discussion dwells on the development of these output routines.

Which output commands you use and what the data values are that use these commands is your domain. This chapter gets your data into a script file. You are going to see an almost identical treatment of the entities section two more times in Chapter 8. In those discussions, the output format will be different, but the presentation of your data to the output commands is the same. You'll excuse me if I copy everything here into the next chapter and modify it to fit the circumstances.

At this point in your script writing program, you have established the working environment, the declaration of linetypes, layers, styles, and views that you reference in the creation of blocks and entities. Now is the time to make some pixels appear on the screen.

But first, let's tie up some loose ends. Throughout the tables section I set aside the use of the **SET** commands for linetypes, layers, styles, and views. I deferred these items to this point because they aren't used until this point in the program. The most important of these **SET** commands are for layers and styles. Linetypes should be set in the layer declaration. It doesn't make much sense to reset the linetype for the entire layer when you are halfway through the drawing. Setting the view is something that I think the designer should perform. Oh, I can see where you might construct something on the screen and use the views to control a slideshow performance; but I don't think that this is appropriate when you are trying to aid designers in increasing their productivity. Constructing the views is fine, using them is not. Listing 7-37 through Listing 7-40 show the script file sequences for each of the **SET** commands. The **REDRAW** command appears to show the end of blank lines indicating default values or terminating lines. Listing 7-41 through Listing 7-44 shows the program code to create these script file lines. The frequency of use

```
LINETYPE SET DASHED
```
Listing 7-37. The linetype SET.

```
LAYER SET LAYER_1
```

```
REDRAW
```
Listing 7-38. The layer SET.

```
STYLE HELVETIC

        (default filename)

        (default height)

        (default width factor)

        (default oblique)

        (default backwards)

        (default upside-down)

        (default vertical)

REDRAW
```
Listing 7-39. The style SET.

```
VIEW R VISTA
```
Listing 7-40. The view SET.

```
#define SET_LINETYPE(f,l)   fprintf(f,"%s %s %s\n",LINETYPE,SET,l)
```
Listing 7-41. The linetype SET code.

```
#define SET_LAYER(f,l) fprintf(f,"%s %s %s\n\n",LAYER,SET,l);
```
Listing 7-42. The layer SET code.

```
void set_style(dxf,stylename)
FILE         *dxf;
char         *stylename;
{
  fprintf(f,"%s %s\n",STYLE,stylename);
  fprintf(f,"\n\n\n\n\n\n\n");
}
```
Listing 7-43. The style SET code.

```
#define SET_VIEW(f,n)    fprintf(f,"%s %s %s\n",VIEW,V_R,n);
```
Listing 7-44. The view SET code.

of these commands determines the style of the output method. You will notice that the techniques are varied in these listings.

Using the AutoCAD **CHANGE** command, you can change the layer, linetype, elevation or thickness of certain entities. This command has so many paths, gotcha's and variations that I'm not going to spend any time with it. If you know exactly what you want to change, have a way to specify the exact entities to be changed and can use the **CHANGE** command in real life, you stand a good chance of utilizing this command. It really is an interactive editing command. We now dedicate the rest of this discussion to program listings for generating script files for drawing entities.

All of the listings include a layer check. Assume that there is a global variable with the current layer. If there is a layer name passed to the script routine and it is different than the current layer, the routine sets the layer and resets the current layer to the new layer.

Arguments to these script generating routines feature primitive data types. That is, coordinates appear as separate floating point numbers. The code takes the course of using these arguments in the proper order to provide a meaningful script file.

There is a second technique that you may wish to explore. In the earlier chapter on **DXF** files, the code placed data into well-defined structures. The flow of control through the program brought about the movement of these structures to the other procedures in the program. Instead of passing several values in the form of individual coordinates and angles, the only argument value was a pointer to the structure. What I would suggest to you is that you pass a structure reference to the script generating routines, instead of several numerical arguments. This provides a certain continuity of logic and structure in your programs if you are linking ideas from various chapters into a working program. Pushing a single pointer onto the program stack is faster than stacking several floating point numbers. On the other hand, I show several techniques in these discussions so that you see the variety of approaches available to you.

LINE	Listing 7-45
POINT	Listing 7-46
CIRCLE	Listing 7-47
ARC	Listing 7-48
TRACE	Listing 7-49
SOLID	Listing 7-50
TEXT	Listing 7-51
SHAPE	Listing 7-52
INSERT	Listing 7-53
ATTDEF	Listing 7-54
POLYLINE	Listing 7-55
BLOCK	Listing 7-56
WBLOCK	Listing 7-57

Table 7-1. Entity Listing Guide.

Table 7-1 lists the drawing entities covered by this discussion and the corresponding script file output source code listing. If an entity is not listed and you need it, check out the command requirements in the AutoCAD reference manual. Follow the style of the routines presented here and create your own routine. The comments in the code will guide you through the operations. You will not find such entities as: **DIMENSION, DONUT, POLYGON** or **ELLIPSE** in these listings.

```
void write_line (SCR_file,from_x,from_y,to_x,to_y,layer)
FILE          *SCR_file;
double         from_x;
double         from_y;
double         to_x;
double         to_y;
char          *layer;
{
   /* check for current layer                      */

   if (strcmp(layer,current_layer))
    {
     set_layer(SCR_file,layer);
     current_layer = layer;
    }

   /* the script file allows any number of line    */
   /* coordinates in a LINE -- the termination      */
   /* is an extra linefeed. There is no difference */
   /* in the DWG file -- LINE entities all have     */
   /* only the two end points                       */
   /* There is no lose in DWG efficiency here.      */

   fprintf(SCR_file,"%s %f,%f %f,%f\n\n",LINE,
                    from_x, from_y, to_x, to_y);
}
```

Listing 7-45. Writing the script file for a LINE.

```
void write_point (SCR_file,x,y,layer)
FILE          *SCR_file;
double         x;
double         y;
char          *layer;
{
    /* check for current layer  */

    if (strcmp(layer,current_layer))
      {
       set_layer(SCR_file,layer);
       current_layer = layer;
      }

    fprintf(SCR_file,"%s %f,%f\n",POINT,x,y);
  }
```

Listing 7-46. Writing the script file for a POINT.

Why a Script File?

Is it truly necessary to go through all of the work to generate a script file, remembering command structures, preparing the data correctly, and switching between languages? Wouldn't it be easier to just generate a **DXF** file for the parts that you want? I've had this discussion any number of times and I want to give you some pros and cons of using script files and **DXF** files. Both file formats have their place and benefits. Understanding the strengths and weaknesses of both formats will let you pick the best one for the occasion.

This chapter has covered the script file format. The next chapter deals with **DXF** as an input format. In this chapter, I will discuss the benefits of the script file. In the next chapter, I will discuss the benefits of the **DXF** file format. There isn't always conflict between the formats, but if there is an opposing view, I will try to express it.

A script file is easier to generate. A script file is easier to read and modify. A script file can insert unknown blocks. A script file in a native language is more readily accepted. A script file makes continuous slide shows or demonstrations easy. A script file with a batch file assist can create, modify and save a drawing without human intervention.

```
#define CENTER_RADIUS          1
#define CENTER_DIAMETER        2
#define CIRCLE_3_POINTS        3
#define CIRCLE_2_POINTS        4

void write_circle (SCR_file,code,a,b,c,d,e,f,layer)
FILE          *SCR_file;
int           code;
double        a;
double        b;
double        c;
double        d;
double        e;
double        f;
char          *layer;
{
   /* check for current layer                    */

   if (strcmp(layer,current_layer))
    {
     set_layer(SCR_file,layer);
     current_layer = layer;
    }

   /* there are four decent ways to generate a    */
   /* circle in the script -- the activating      */
   /* routine should include a code stating the   */
   /* method to use -- the #define lines above    */
   /* give numeric values to the methods          */
   /* the values of the arguments take different  */
   /* meanings depending upon usage               */

   switch(code)
    {
     case CENTER_RADIUS   : fprintf(SCR_file,"%s %f,%f
            %f\n",CIRCLE,a,b,c); break;
     case CENTER_DIAMETER :
            fprintf(SCR_file,"%s %s %f,%f %f\n",
                              CIRCLE,DIAMETER,a,b,c);
            break;
     case CIRCLE_3_POINTS :
            fprintf(SCR_file,"%s %s %f,%f %f,%f %f,%f\n",
                              CIRCLE,3P,a,b,c,d,e,f);
            break;
     case CIRCLE_2_POINTS :
            fprintf(SCR_file,"%s %s %f,%f %f,%f\n",
                              CIRCLE,2P,a,b,c,d);
            break;
    }
}
```

Listing 7-47. Writing the script file for a CIRCLE #define.

```
#define ARC_3_POINTS          1
#define ARC_SCE               2
#define ARC_SCA               3
#define ARC_SCL               4
#define ARC_SER               5
#define ARC_SEA               6
#define ARC_SED               7
#define ARC_CONTINUE          8

void write_arc (SCR_file,code,a,b,c,d,e,f,layer)
FILE            *SCR_file;
int             code;
double          a;
double          b;
double          c;
double          d;
double          e;
double          f;
char            *layer;
{
   /* check for current layer                            */

   if (strcmp(layer,current_layer))
    {
     set_layer(SCR_file,layer);
     current_layer = layer;
    }

   /* there are eight decent ways to generate an    */
   /* arc in the script -- the activating           */
   /* routine should include a code stating the     */
   /* method to use -- the #define lines above      */
   /* give numeric values to the methods            */
   /* the values of the arguments take different    */
   /* meanings depending upon usage                 */

   switch(code)
    {
     case ARC_3_POINTS    :    /* 3 points on an arc */
             fprintf(SCR_file,"%s %f,%f %f,%f %f,%f\n",ARC,
                             a,b,c,d,e,f);
             break;
     case ARC_SCE         :    /* Start Center End points */
             fprintf(SCR_file,"%s %f,%f %s %f,%f %f,%f\n",
                             ARC,a,b,ARC_C,c,d,e,f):
             break;
     case ARC_SCA         :    /* Start Center Angle */
             fprintf(SCR_file,"%s %f,%f %s %f,%f %s %f\n",
                             ARC,a,b,ARC_C,c,d,ARC_A,e);
             break;
     case ARC_SCL         :    /* Start Center Length */
             fprintf(SCR_file,"%s %f,%f %s %f,%f %s %f\n",
                             ARC,a,b,ARC_C,c,d,ARC_L,e;;
             break;
```

```
    case ARC_SER          :     /* Start End Radius */
            fprintf(SCR_file,"%s %f,%f %s %f,%f %s %f\n',
                            ARC,a,b,ARC_E,c,d,ARC_R,e);
            break;
    case ARC_SEA          :     /* Start End Angle */
            fprintf(SCR_file,"%s %f,%f %s %f,%f %s %f\n",
                            ARC,a,b,ARC_E,c,d,ARC_A,e);
            break;
    case ARC_SED          :     /* Start End Direction */
            fprintf(SCR_file,"%s %f,%f %s %f,%f %s %f\n",
                            ARC,a,b,ARC_E,c,d,ARC_D,e);
            break;
    case ARC_CONTINUE     :     /* Continuation */
            fprintf(SCR_file,"%s\n%f,%f\n",ARC,a,b); break;
    }
}
```

Listing 7-48. Writing the script file for a ARC.

```
typedef
  struct coord
    {
      double    x;
      double    y;
    }           coord;

/*                                                          */
/* polylines and traces require a continuous flow of  */
/* coordinates so that connectivity and beveling may  */
/* occur properly                                     */
/* the code for TRACE and POLYLINE expects the vertex */
/* endpoints to be in a table of type COORD           */
/* the code also expects a count of the number of     */
/* vertices in the table                              */
/* you could use this arrangement for LINE also       */

int              xy_count = 0;
coord            *xy[100];  /* you pick a size */

void write_trace (SCR_file,xy,n,width,layer)
FILE             *SCR_file;
coord            xy[];
int              n;
double           width;
char             *layer;
{
int              i;

    /* check for current layer       */

    if (strcmp(layer,current_layer))
      {
        set_layer(SCR_file,layer);
        current_layer = layer;
      }
    fprintf(SCR_file,"%s %f\n",TRACE,width);
    for(i=0;i<n;i++)
      fprintf(SCR_file,"%f,%f\n",xy[i].x,xy[i].y);
    fprintf(SCR_file,"\n"); /* terminating linefeed */
  }
```

Listing 7-49. Writing the script file for a TRACE.

```
void write_solid (SCR_file,x1,y1,x2,y2,x3,y3,x4,y4,layer)
FILE          *SCR_file;
double         x1;
double         y1;
double         x2;
double         y2;
double         x3;
double         y3;
double         x4;
double         y4;
char          *layer;
{

   /* check for current layer          */

   if (strcmp(layer,current_layer))
    {
     set_layer(SCR_file,layer);
     current_layer = layer;
    }

   fprintf(SCR_file,"%s %f,%f %f,%f\n",SOLID,x1,y1,x2,y2);
   fprintf(SCR_file,"%f,%f %f,%f\n\n",x3,y3,x4,y4);
}
```

Listing 7-50. Writing the script file for a SOLID.

```
#define LEFT_JUSTIFY        1
#define CENTER_JUSTIFY      2
#define MIDDLE_JUSTIFY      3
#define RIGHT_JUSTIFY       4
#define ALIGN_JUSTIFY       5
#define FIT_JUSTIFY         6
#define CONTINUE_TEXT       7

void write_text (SCR_file,justify,x1,y1,x2,y2,ht,angle,
                 txt,style,layer)
FILE          *SCR_file;
int            justify;
double         x1;
double         y1;
double         x2;
double         y2;
double         ht;
double         angle;
char          *txt;
char          *style;
char          *layer;
{
```

```
/* check for current layer        */
if (strcmp(layer,current_layer))
 {
  set_layer(SCR_file,layer);
  current_layer = layer;
 }

if (justify == CONTINUE_TEXT)
  fprintf(SCR_file"\n");
else
 {
  fprintf(SCR_file"%s ",TEXT);
  if (style) fprintf(SCR_file,"%s %s\n",TEXT_S,style);
 }

switch(justify)
 {
  case LEFT_JUSTIFY    :
          fprintf(SCR_file,"%f,%f %f %f\n",
                          x1,y1,ht,angle);
          break;
  case CENTER_JUSTIFY :
          fprintf(SCR_file,"%s %f,%f %f %f\n",TEXT_C,
                          x1,y1,ht,angle);
          break;
  case MIDDLE_JUSTIFY :
          fprintf(SCR_file,"%s %f,%f %f %f\n",TEXT_M,
                          x1,y1,ht,angle);
          break;
  case RIGHT_JUSTIFY  :
          fprintf(SCR_file,"%s %f,%f %f %f\n",TEXT_R,
                          x1,y1,ht,angle);
          break;
  case ALIGN_JUSTIFY  :
          fprintf(SCR_file,"%s %f,%f %f %f\n",TEXT_A,
                          x1,y1,x2,y2);
          break;
  case FIT_JUSTIFY    :
          fprintf(SCR_file,"%s %f,%f %f %f\n",TEXT_F,
                          x1,y1,x2,y2,ht);
          break;
  case CONTINUE_TEXT  : fprintf(SCR_file,"\n");
          break;
 }
 fprintf(SCR_file,"%s\n",txt);
}
```

Listing 7-51. Writing the script file for a TEXT.

```
void write_shape (SCR_file,shape,x1,y1,ht,angle,layer)
FILE          *SCR_file;
char          *shape;
double         x1;
double         y1;
double         ht;
double         angle;
char          *layer;
{

    /* check for current layer        */
    if (strcmp(layer,current_layer))
     {
      set_layer(SCR_file,layer);
      current_layer = layer;
     }

    fprintf(SCR_file"%s %s %f,%f %f %f\n",
                    SHAPE,shape,x1,y1,ht,angle);
}
```

Listing 7-52. Writing the script file for a SHAPE.

```
void write_insert (SCR_file,name,x1,y1,
                    xscale,yscale,angle,layer)
FILE          *SCR_file;
char          *name;
double         x1;
double         y1;
double         xscale;
double         yscale;
double         angle;
char          *layer;
{

    /* check for current layer        */
    if (strcmp(layer,current_layer))
     {
      set_layer(SCR_file,layer);
      current_layer = layer;
     }

    fprintf(SCR_file"%s %s %f,%f %f %f %f\n",INSERT,
                    name,x1,y1,xscale,yscale,angle);
}
```

Listing 7-53. Writing the script file for an INSERT.

```
void write_attrib (SCR_file,txt)
FILE         *SCR_file;
char         *txt;
{
    /* there is no check for current layer   */
    /* layer information comes from attdef    */
    /* or insert commands                     */

    fprintf(SCR_file,"%s\n",txt);

    /* this routine must follow directly after */
    /* the write_insert to give values to the  */
    /* defined attributes -- this is block      */
    /* dependent                                */
}
```
Listing 7-54. Writing the script file for an ATTRIBUTE.

```
typedef
  struct coord
    {
    double      x;
    double      y;
    double      sw;  /* starting width */
    double      ew;  /* starting width */
    }           coord;

/*                                                      */
/* polylines and traces require a continuous flow of    */
/* coordinates so that connectivity and beveling may    */
/* occur properly                                       */
/* the code for TRACE and POLYLINE expects the vertex   */
/* endpoints to be in a table of type COORD             */
/* the code also expects a count of the number of       */
/* vertices in the table                                */
/* you could use this arrangement for LINE also         */
/*                                                      */
/* you need to add more fields to the COORD type to     */
/* use the polyline facilities of ARC. added fields     */
/* include angles, second points or overriding center   */
/* points                                               */
/*                                                      */
/* you will also need a field to tell you what action   */
/* to take (LINE, ARC, ARC with CENTER, etc.)           */
/*                                                      */

int             xy_count = 0;
coord           *xy[100];  /* you pick a size */

void write_pline (SCR_file,xy,n,width,layer)
FILE            *SCR_file;
coord           xy[];
int             n;
char            *layer;
{
int             i;

    /* check for current layer        */

    if (strcmp(layer,current_layer))
      {
      set_layer(SCR_file,layer);
      current_layer = layer;
      }

    fprintf(SCR_file,"%s %f,%f %s %f %f\n",PLINE,
              xy[0].x,xy[0].y,WIDTH,xy[0].sw,xy[0 ].ew);
    for(i=1;i<n;i++)
      {
      if (xy[i].sw || xy[i].ew)
          fprintf(SCR_file,"%s %f %f\n",
```

189

```
                            WIDTH,xy[i].sw,xy[i].ew);
    fprintf(SCR_file,"%f,%f\n",xy[i].x,xy[i].y);
    }
  fprintf(SCR_file,"\n"); /* terminating linefeed */
}
```
Listing 7-55. Writing the script file for a POLYLINE.

```
#define BLK_WINDOW    1
#define BLK_LAST      2

void write_block (SCR_file,name,ix,iy,action,x1,y1,x2,y2)
FILE          *SCR_file;
char          *name;
double         ix;
double         iy;
int           action;
double         x1;
double         y1;
double         x2;
double         y2;
{

   fprintf(SCR_file"%s %s %f,%f\n",BLOCK,name,ix,iy);

   /* we need to generate a selection set to determine */
   /* which entities are in the block                  */
   /* the first method is to grow a window around the  */
   /* the block -- this is the most satifactory method */
   /* the other method is to take the last entity      */
   /* this isn't quite as inclusive                    */

   switch(action)
     {
     case BLK_WINDOW : fprintf(SCR_file,"%s %f,%f %f,%f\n\n",
                                   WINDOW,x1,y1,x2, y2);
                       break;
     case BLK_LAST   : fprintf(SCR_file,"%s\n\n",LAST);
                       break;
     }
}
```
Listing 7-56. Writing the script file for a BLOCK.

190

```
#define BLK_WINDOW    1
#define BLK_LAST      2

void write_wblock (SCR_file,name,ix,iy,action,x1,y1,x2,y2)
FILE          *SCR_file;
char          *name;
double        ix;
double        iy;
int           action;
double        x1;
double        y1;
double        x2;
double        y2;
{

    fprintf(SCR_file"%s %s\n\n%f,%f\n",WBLOCK,name,ix,iy);

    /* we need to generate a selection set to determine */
    /* which entities are in the block                  */
    /* the first method is to grow a window around the  */
    /* the block -- this is the most satifactory method */
    /* the other method is to take the last entity      */
    /* this isn't quite as inclusive                    */

    switch(action)
      {
      case BLK_WINDOW : fprintf(SCR_file,"%s %f,%f %f,%f\n\n",
                                        WINDOW,x1,y1,x2, y2);
                        break;
      case BLK_LAST   : fprintf(SCR_file,"%s\n\n",LAST);
                        break;
      }
}
```

Listing 7-57. Writing the script file for a WBLOCK.

8

DXF and DXB File Input

THE SCRIPT FILE FORMAT IS NOT THE ONLY WAY FOR AN EXTERNAL PROGRAM TO DICTATE the operations of AutoCAD. The repertoire of AutoCAD commands includes a means of reading two types of **DXF** files. This chapter deals with the management of these file formats.

PARTIAL DXF GENERATION

When AutoCAD generates a **DXF** file, it includes all pertinent information in the file. This is necessary for the full expression of the drawing details. Quite to the contrary, when AutoCAD reads a **DXF** file, AutoCAD requires that the **DXF** contain only the bare minimum of information to express the drawing. This lets us off the hook from generating the immense volume of **DXF** details to which AutoCAD holds itself. Rather, we can generate as much or little as we see fit.

The structure of the application generated **DXF** file must follow some of the aspects of the AutoCAD generated **DXF** file. If it does not follow some general structure, Auto-CAD will not know how to interpret what you have. We'll follow the **DXF**'s input structure in much the same manner as we did for the output structure. Required fields will be emphasized. Let's cover the mandatory items first.

You must properly terminate the **DXF** file. That sounds like a great place to start. Listing 8-1 shows the last lines of the generated **DXF** file. These are the **ONLY** lines **ABSOLUTELY** required to be a proper **DXF** file.

Listing 8-2 illustrates a very short function for closing the **DXF** file. The routine is so brief that you might want to use only the file output statement (fprintf) where it is needed in your program. Everything past the **EOF** makes the **DXF** file a little more complicated.

If you need a sequence of code to guide you through the use of the **EOF** function and the others that we will discuss, Listing 8-3 shows the order of calling the various functions for writing the **DXF** file.

All sections of the **DXF** are strictly optional. AutoCAD is pretty good about covering for you when you choose to leave out a section. For instance, if you do not need to define fancy settings for your layers (exotic linetypes or colors), you can omit the layer table from the **TABLES** section. However, if you refer to a layer in the entities section which has not been defined, AutoCAD creates the layer and sets the linetype to **CONTINUOUS** and the color to **WHITE**. Still we will look at the generation of each section.

```
    0
EOF
```
Listing 8-1. Terminating the DXF file.


```
void generate_eof(dxf)
FILE       *dxf;
{
    fprintf(dxf,"   0\nEOF\n");
}
```


```
void generate_eof(dxf)
FIle       *dxf;
{
    fprintf(dxf,"%3d\nEOF\n",0);
}
```
Listing 8-2. Function for generating DXF EOF.


```
dxf = fopen(dxf_name,"w");
generate_header(dxf);
generate_tables(dxf);
generate_blocks(dxf);
generate_entities(dxf);
generate_eof(dxf);
fclose(dxf);
```
Listing 8-3. General control for DXF generation.

HEADER SECTION

The Header section of the **DXF** file contains all kinds of parametric information. Some of it is useful to the outside program, some of it is excess baggage. Finding the limits to a drawing so that plotting or calculating scaling factors makes good sense. Using the toggled settings of dimensional values makes little sense.

Why should an outside program cater to all of these header values if they are completely irrelevant to the program? The good news is that you don't have to generate any value that you do not use.

The general structure of the **HEADER** section is shown in Listing 8-4. This structure is generated by the source code in Listing 8-5. If the **HEADER** section is used, there are certain entries in the **DXF** file that must be made. Since the header section is a full-fledged section, the section must be opened (so to speak) and named. Once opened, the section must be correctly closed. This closing signals AutoCAD to prepare for the arrival of another section. Recalling the discussions of the finite state machine for reading the **DXF** file, we are now on the other end of the stick and AutoCAD is the program with the finite state machine figuring out what we have.

You'll note that the header generator procedure uses another function called write_DXF. This very useful function localizes and condenses the file writing activity to

```
0
SECTION
2
HEADER
. . . . .
0
ENDSEC
```

Listing 8-4. Header section structure.

```
void generate_header(dxf)
FILE      *dxf;
{
  write_DXF(dxf,0,"SECTION");
  write_DXF(dxf,2,"HEADER");
  /* program code for generating DXF Header */
  write_DXF(dxf,0,"ENDSEC");
  }
```

Listing 8-5. Code to produce DXF header structure.

one function. The arguments to this function are a file descriptor, a tag and its associated value. To accommodate the multitude of data types written to the **DXF** file, the third argument to the write_**DXF** file is a pointer to the value. This keeps the size of the argument constant. The argument declaration show us that the type of the pointer is void. This gives us some flexibility in using this pointer. Before we can use this pointer, regardless of how flexible it is, we have to cast it to a specific type. And, where do we get the type? The **DXF** tag tells us how the referenced value appears. It gives it a type. Recall the discussion in Chapter 2 how certain tag values determined the type of the associated data? The write_**DXF** routine uses that same association. Sifting out the type of the data through cascading if-then-else statements, the tag value determines the type of the pointer. The properly de-referenced value gets written to the **DXF** file behind its faithful tag. Listing 8-6 shows the details of the write_**DXF** function.

The first file output line in this listing has the notation of "%3d" for its output format. The tag appears in the **DXF** file as a **FORTRAN I3** integer. The format in the listing

```
void write_DXF(dxf,tag,value)
FILE      *dxf;
int        tag;
void       *value;
{
  fprintf(dxf,"%3d\n",tag);
  if (tag <= 9)
    fprintf(dxf,"%s\n",(char *)value);
  else
    if (tag <= 59)
      fprintf(dxf,"%f\n",*(double *)value);
    else
      fprintf(dxf,"%d\n",*(int *)value);
}
```

Listing 8-6. The write_DXF function.

creates the same format. This format is not really required by AutoCAD, but may be expected by other application programs.

In Chapter five we used a finite state machine and a token recognizer to determine the identity of the **HEADER** values. Pointers to target variables place the resulting values into the correct variables. In this chapter we will use another method of relating to the **DXF** file. The thrust of the discussion will be aimed at writing the **DXF,** but the structure could be turned around and used for parsing the **DXF** file. Since we will not require a complete header section, we write only the names and values found in this table. This table, shown in its entirety in Appendix B, contained the following fields:

1. AutoCAD **HEADER** Name
2. Data type of value
3. Pointer to variable receiving (containing) value.

Listing 8-7 shows the type structure for this table and a couple of lines of the table itself. I wouldn't want you to be flipping pages back and forth to keep up with this.

Dumping header values by using this table is actually easier than parsing the **DXF** file. All of the information that we need is here. It is just a matter of giving it to write_**DXF** to get it to the disk. Listing 8-8 is a narrative of the procedure for dumping the **HEADER** section of a **DXF.** Listing 8-9 implements this design in a nice and neat fashion.

```c
#define COORDX        1
#define COORDY        2
#define CORRDZ        3
#define ANGLE         4
#define INTEGER       5
#define STRING        6
#define LAYER         7

typedef
  struct
  {
    char        *name;
    int          type;
    void        *value;
  }             header_entry;

double          extminx;
double          extminy;
double          extmaxx;
double          extmaxy;

header_entry    header_table[] = { {"$EXTMIN",COORDX,&extminx},
                     { NULL,     COORDY,&extminy},
                     {"$EXTMAX",COORDX,&extmaxx},
                     { NULL,     COORDY,&extmaxy},
                     { NULL,     0, NULL}};
```

Listing 8-7. Definitions of header table.

```
Write SECTION record
Write HEADER record
For every entry in header table
   Write Name of entry with a tag of 9
   In the case of DATA TYPE:
      COORD     Write X,Y and Z coordinates
                     with proper tags
      INTEGER   Write value with tag of 70
      ANGLE     Write value with tag of 50
      STRING    Write value with tag of 1
      LAYER
      etc.
   Write ENDSEC record
```
Listing 8-8. HEADER generation strategy.

```
generate_header(dxf)
FILE       *dxf;
{
header_entry        *h;

   write_DXF(dxf,0,"SECTION");
   write_DXF(dxf,2,"HEADER");
   h = header_table;
   while (h->value)
     {
      if (h->name) write_DXF(dxf,9,h->name);
      switch(h->type)
        {
         case COORDX   : write_DXF(dxf,10,h->value);
                         break;
         case COORDY   : write_DXF(dxf,20,h->value);
                         break;
         case COORDZ   : write_DXF(dxf,30,h->value);
                         break;
         case ANGLE    : write_DXF(dxf,50,h->value);
                         break;
         case INTEGER  : write_DXF(dxf,70,h->value);
                         break;
         case STRING   : write_DXF(dxf,1,h->value);
                         break;
         case LAYER    : write_DXF(dxf,8,h->value);
        }
      h++;
     }
   write_DXF(0,"ENDSEC");
}
```
Listing 8-9. The complete generate_header function.

```
double          limmin_x;
double          limmin_y;
double          limmax_x;
double          limmax_y;
double          extmin_x;
double          extmin_y;
double          extmax_x;
double          extmax_y;

void generate_header(dxf)
FILE       *dxf;
{
  write_DXF(dxf,0,"SECTION");
  write_DXF(dxf,2,"HEADER");
  write_DXF(dxf,9,"$LIMMIN");
  write_DXF(dxf,10,&limmin_x);
  write_DXF(dxf,20,&limmin_y);
  write_DXF(dxf,9,"$LIMMAX");
  write_DXF(dxf,10,&limmax_x);
  write_DXF(dxf,20,&limmax_y);
  write_DXF(dxf,9,"$EXTMIN");
  write_DXF(dxf,10,&extmin_x);
  write_DXF(dxf,20,&extmin_y);
  write_DXF(dxf,9,"$EXTMAX");
  write_DXF(dxf,10,&extmax_x);
  write_DXF(dxf,20,&extmax_y);
  write_DXF(dxf,0,"ENDSEC");
}
```

Listing 8-10. Generating a partial header section.

It is certainly not beyond our grasp to generate the **DXF** header in a more deliberate manner. If you were wanting to write only a few entries, hardly enough to rationalize the construction of a driver table, you could build a function that methodically writes each field. Listing 8-10 shows just such a function. This function writes the values of the calculated drawing extents and limits. This section has covered the ways for generating the **HEADER** section of the **DXF** file. Look back at Chapter five for more information concerning the structure of the header table. The complete listing for this table is in Appendix B.

TABLES SECTION

Like the **HEADER** section, you only need to generate the **TABLES** section if it is required. If you do not require anything out of the ordinary, you can bypass the **TABLES.**

- If you use fonts other than **STANDARD** —
- If you use linetypes other than **CONTINUOUS** —
- If you create layers of various colors —
- If you construct viewpoints —

you will have to generate a **TABLES** section.

```
generate_tables(dxf)
FILE        *dxf;
{
  write_DXF(dxf,0,"SECTION");
  write_DXF(dxf,2,"TABLES");
  generate_styles(dxf);
  generate_linetypes(dxf);
  generate_layers(dxf);
  generate_views(dxf);
  write_DXF(dxf,0,"ENDSEC");
}
```

Listing 8-11. Central table control.

The top level function for generating the **TABLES** section is purely administrative. The example listing (Listing 8-11) shows all tables being written. Well, you have to show them in the example, but they don't have to be there in your application. If you write the **TABLES** section, the **SECTION, TABLES,** and **ENDSEC** records are required. The order of the various tables is semi-critical. The best example is: you must define linetypes before they can be referenced. Therefore, the linetypes generator must precede the layers generator.

All of the table generators must include specific identification sequences. Just as the sections must properly start and finish, the tables must do the same. Listing 8-12 shows the form of the identification.

Notice that the value for the 2 tag is **TABLE** (singular). The section name is **TABLES** (plural). The maximum number of allowed entries is shown (70 tag) following the name of

```
0
TABLE
2
table name
70
maximum item count
.....
0
ENDTAB
```

Listing 8-12. Required TABLE entries.

```
Count entries on linked list
  If there are entries
    Write TABLE record (tag 0)
    Write table type record (tag 2)
    Write entry count record (tag 70)
    For each table entry
      Write the table type (tag 0)
      Write the name of the table (tag 2)
      Write special flags (tag 70)
      Write specific table values
    Write ENDTAB record (tag 0)
```

Listing 8-13. Table generator strategy.

198

Table 8-1. DXF Tables Listing Guide.

the table. This is not necessarily the number of items in the **DXF** table, but it must be greater than or equal to the number of entries in your **DXF** file. However, you will help out AutoCAD and conserve memory by setting the value to the exact number of items in the table.

For our examples here, I'll assume that you have organized the tables in a manner similar to the structure shown in Chapter five. In those structures, there are anchors for each table, pointing to a linked list of entries. A basic strategy can be applied to all table generators when this structure is used. Listing 8-13 narrates the strategy. There isn't much need to fool around with explanations. The following listings show the implementation of the narrative for each of the table types. Table 8-1 shows the **DXF** tables and the corresponding listing.

BLOCKS Generation

Drawing entities and blocks are very similar in the **DXF** file. The only difference is the declaration of the blocks. All drawing information is exactly the same. With this in mind, I will delay the discussion about the generation of the drawing details of a block. We'll look at entity **DXF** generation in the **ENTITIES** section. Since this is a section of the **DXF,** a section must be started and finished. Within the blocks section, each block is identified and defined. These blocks also have a starting point and an ending point. Listing 8-18 shows the outer shells of the **BLOCKS** section. Each individual block is enclosed within a **BLOCK** and **ENDBLK** pair. Since these will make more sense later, they receive attention at the end of the discussion about entities.

Admittedly, I left the output of entity information to the next section. In the **ENTITY** section we will see the code for writing each of the various entities. The block definition node includes a pointer to a string of entities. Presumably, these were attached at an earlier time. Perhaps when another **DXF** file was read or the program synthesized it.

ENTITY Section

Building entities in the **DXF** file is the reverse of parsing the file. Having the elements that compose the definition of the entity, it is the job of the output routines to produce the proper tag and value pairs. With the rest of your program dedicated to the origination of the drawing specifics (I'm not telling you how to do this—that's your problem.), the output section can concentrate on the output techniques.

This section deals with the creation of **DXF** formatted entities. I've named the routines in the following listings by the same routine names found in the script file chapter.

```
typedef
  struct           ln
    {
     struct ln        *next;
     char              flags;
     char              name[32];
     char              describe[48];
     unsigned char     align;
     unsigned char     dash_count;
     double            pattern_length;
     double            dashes[16];
    }                  line_node;

line_node             *line_anchor;

void generate_ltypes(dxf)
FILE      *dxf;
{
int          i;
int          k;
int          cnt;
line_node    *l;

    if ((l = line_anchor) != NULL)
     {
      cnt = 0;
      while (l)
        {
         cnt++;
         l = l->next;
        }
     }
    write_DXF(dxf,0,"TABLE");
    write_DXF(dxf,2,"LTYPE");
    write_DXF(dxf,70,&cnt);
    l = line_anchor;
    while (l)
     {
      write_DXF(dxf,0,"LTYPE");
      write_DXF(dxf,2,l->name);
      l->flags |= 64;
      write_DXF(dxf,70,&l->flags);
      write_DXF(dxf,3,l->describe);
      write_DXF(dxf,72,&l->align);
      write_DXF(dxf,73,&l->dash_count);
      write_DXF(dxf,40,&l->pattern_length);
      for (k=0;k<l->dash_count;k++)
         write_DXF(dxf,49,&l->dashes[k]);
      l = l->next;
     }
    write_DXF(dxf,0,"ENDTAB");
}
```

Listing 8-14. Writing the linetype table to DXF.

```
typedef
  struct layer_node
    {
     struct layer_node      *next;
     char                   *name;
     int                     flags;
     int                     color;
     char                   *linetype;
    }                        layer_node;

layer_node                   *layer_anchor;


void generate_layers(dxf)
FILE          *dxf;
{
layer_node      *l;
int              cnt;

   if ((l = layer_anchor) != NULL)
    {
     cnt = 0;
     while (l)
       {
         cnt++;
         l = l->next;
       }
     write_DXF(dxf,0,"TABLE");
     write_DXF(dxf,2,"LAYER");
     write_DXF(dxf,70,&cnt);
     l = layer_anchor;
     while (l)
       {
        write_DXF(dxf,0,"LAYER");
        write_DXF(dxf,2,l->name);
        write_DXF(dxf,70,&l->flags);
        write_DXF(dxf,62,&l->color);
        write_DXF(dxf,6,l->linetype);
        l = l->next;
       }
     write_DXF(dxf,0,"ENDTAB");
    }
}
```

Listing 8-15. Writing the layer table to DXF.

```
typedef
  struct          st
    {
    struct st   *next;
    shape_entry  *shape_index;
    char          flags;
    char          name[32];
    double        txt_height;
    double        txt_scale;
    double        oblique;
    char          gen_flags;
    double        last_height;
    char          font[32];
    char          bigfont[32];
    }            style_node;

style_node       *sty_anchor;

void generate_styles(dxf)
FILE        *dxf;
{
int          i;
style_node   *sty;

    if ((sty = sty_anchor) != NULL)
      {
      cnt = 0;
      while (sty)
        {
        cnt++;
        sty = sty->next;
        }
      }
    write_DXF(dxf,0,"TABLE");
    write_DXF(dxf,2,"STYLE");
    write_DXF(dxf,70,&cnt);
    sty = sty_anchor;
    while (sty)
      {
      write_DXF(dxf,0,"STYLE");
      write_DXF(dxf,2,sty->name);
      sty->flags |= 64;
      write_DXF(dxf,70,&sty->flags);
      write_DXF(dxf,40,&sty->txt_height);
      write_DXF(dxf,41,&sty->txt_scale);
      write_DXF(dxf,50,&sty->oblique);
      write_DXF(dxf,71,&sty->gen_flags);
      write_DXF(dxf,42,&sty->last_height);
      write_DXF(dxf,3,sty->font);
      write_DXF(dxf,4,sty->bigfont);
      sty = sty->next;
      }
    write_DXF(dxf,0,"ENDTAB");
}
```

Listing 8-16. Writing the style table to DXF.

```
typedef
  struct          vw
    {
     struct vw   *next;
     char         flags;
     char         name[32];
     double       vw_height;
     double       vw_ctr_x;
     double       vw_ctr_y;
     double       vw_width;
     double       vw_dir_x;
     double       vw_dir_y;
     double       vw_dir_z;
    }             view_node;

view_node         *vw_anchor;

write_views(dxf)
FILE    *dxf;
{
int            i;
view_node      *v;

    if ((v = vw_anchor) != NULL)
      {
       cnt = 0;
       while (v)
         {
          cnt++;
          v = v->next;
         }
      }

    write_DXF(dxf,0,"TABLE");
    write_DXF(dxf,2,"VIEW");
    write_DXF(dxf,70,&cnt);
    v = vw_anchor;
    while (v)
      {
       write_DXF(dxf,0,"VIEW");
       write_DXF(dxf,2,v->name);
       write_DXF(dxf,70,&v->flags);
       write_DXF(dxf,40,&v->vw_height);
       write_DXF(dxf,10,&v->vw_ctr_x);
       write_DXF(dxf,20,&v->vw_ctr_y);
       write_DXF(dxf,41,&v->vw_width);
       write_DXF(dxf,11,&v->vw_dir_x);
       write_DXF(dxf,21,&v->vw_dir_y);
       write_DXF(dxf,31,&v->vw_dir_z);
       v = v->next;
      }
    write_DXF(dxf,0,"ENDTAB");
}
```

Listing 8-17. Writing the view table to DXF.

```
   0
SECTION
   2
BLOCKS
   0
BLOCK
   2
name of block
.....
   0
ENDBLK
more blocks
   0
ENDSEC
```
Listing 8-18. BLOCK section structure.

This demonstrates the flexibility that you can build into your programs with some standard names. By simply changing the object code module references in your link file, you could change the output characteristics of your program with a single linking process.

In fact, you could rewrite these routines to allow a global variable to control the form of the output. With a switch/case or if-then-else statement, you could combine the script and **DXF** operations into a single routine. By setting the variable through the value of a command line argument to one output form or the other, the individual routines can route the control to the proper output statements.

As in all other sections in the **DXF** file, the **ENTITIES** section has an enveloping shell structure. Listing 8-19 shows this shell structure. These are required lines when you introduce individual entities to the drawing. Listing 8-20 shows the code for generating these lines. Notice that the ubiquitous procedure write_**DXF** is the central player in this sequence.

The entities in the **DXF** each exhibit different structures. This is intuitively obvious since a line and text are quite different. However, the **DXF** entities do share some similar structural details. Two structural members appear in all entities. There are also several optional members.

First and foremost is the identity of the entity. You identify the entity by a zero tag and the name of the entity. Listing 8-21 shows the **DXF** file for the identification of a line entity. Review the tables in Chapter five for the names of the other entities. Using the useful write_**DXF** routine, you can write the DXF identification sequence in one statement. Listing 8-22 shows that one line in action.

The other structural member that needs to show up in each entity is the layer name. In the script and **DXB** file formats, it is necessary to change the layer whenever it is convenient in the flow of instructions. To this end, the output routines check the entity's layer against the currently active layer. There is no need to do anything if they are the same. Being different, you issue the command sequence to change the layer.

To the contrary, there is no active layer in the **DXF** file. Each entity has its own resident layer. This layer appears with each entity. You specify a layer with an eight (8) tag and the name of the layer. Listing 8-23 shows the layer declaration in the **DXF** file. Listing 8-24 shows the code for generating this **DXF** segment. Remember that the layer name is one of the arguments in our standard output routine.

```
   0
SECTION
   2
ENTITIES
   :
   :
   0
ENDSEC
```
Listing 8-19. The structure of the ENTITIES section.


```
write_DXF(dxf,0,"SECTION");
write_DXF(dxf,2,"ENTITIES");
/* write entity information here */
write_DXF(dxf,0,"ENDSEC");
```
Listing 8-20. Generating the ENTITIES structure.


```
   0
LINE
```
Listing 8-21. The LINE entity identification.


```
write_DXF(dxf,0,"LINE");
```
Listing 8-22. Generating the identification entry.


```
   8
LAYER_1
```
Listing 8-23. Layer definition in the DXF file.


```
write_DXF(dxf,8,layer);
```
Listing 8-24. Generating the layer definition.

There are four other structural members that you may add to your entities. These members are entity modifiers and may not be relevant for some entities. These modifiers are:

- **COLOR**
- **LINETYPE**
- **ELEVATION**
- **THICKNESS**

The **COLOR** modifier allows you to override the default color of the entity's layer. The **COLOR** modifier has a tag value of 62. The value of the pair is a number between 1 and 255. A color of zero may generate undefined results. Besides, a zero color has its uses in other ways. A value of 255 sets the color to **BYBLOCK** where the entity color tracks the color of the block or its inserted layer. Listing 8-25 shows the appearance of the color modifier in the **DXF** file. Listing 8-26 shows the code for generating these **DXF** lines.

```
62
1
```
Listing 8-25. The COLOR modifier in the DXF file (RED = 1).

Since the entity modifiers are not arguments to our standard output routines, you will need to add a mechanism for getting the data to the output routine. By far the easiest method of doing this is by adding the arguments to the output routine parameter list. A zero value means that there is no override. The listing assumes the presence of the **COLOR** argument. Here is an example of using the zero color to mean that there is no color override. (Listing 8-26.)

```
if (color) write_DXF(dxf,62,&color);
```
Listing 8-26. Generating the COLOR modifier.

The **LINETYPE** modifier allows you to override the default linetype of the layer. The **LINETYPE** modifier has a tag value of 6. The value of the pair is the name of the **LINETYPE** as established by a linetype table entry. Listing 8-27 shows the appearance of the **DXF** file for a **LINETYPE** modifier. Listing 8-28 is the code for generating this modifier.

```
6
DASHED
```
Listing 8-27. The LINETYPE modifier in the DXF file.

```
if (linetype) write_DXF(dxf,6,linetype);
```
Listing 8-28. Generating the LINETYPE modifier.

The **ELEVATION** modifiers allow you to specify a Z coordinate to some entities. The **ELEVATION** modifier has a tag value of 38. The value of the pair is a floating point number representing the Z value of the entity. Listing 8-29 shows the appearance of an **ELEVATION** modifier in the **DXF** file. Listing 8-30 is the code for generating this modifier.

The **THICKNESS** modifiers allow you to specify a Z coordinate for extending a surface using the entity as a base. The **THICKNESS** modifier has a tag value of 39. The value of the pair is a floating point number representing the Z value of the extended portion of the entity. Listing 8-31 shows the appearance of a **THICKNESS** modifier in the **DXF** file. Listing 8-32 is the code for generating this modifier.

```
38
2.125
```
Listing 8-29. The ELEVATION modifier in the DXF file.

```
if (elevation) write_DXF(dxf,38,&elevation);
```
Listing 8-30. Generating the ELEVATION modifier.

```
39
12.345
```
Listing 8-31. The THICKNESS modifier in the DXF file.

```
if (thickness) write_DXF(dxf,39,&thickness);
```
Listing 8-32. Generating the THICKNESS modifier.

The rest of the **DXF** file generation is quite straight-forward. Refer to the tables in Chapter five for the tags and associated values for each entity. Defaulted entries need not appear in the entity declaration unless you use a value other than the default.

Table 8-2 is your guide to the listings for the **DXF** output routines. You may substitute a single structure for the individual parameter arguments. You may add more arguments to cover the modifiers. These routines represent a starting point for further development.

Block definitions also contain entities. The entities in a block are structurally identical to those found outside of the block. You may use the same routines to write the entities. There are only differences in the environment of the entities. Block related entities appear in the **BLOCKS** section of the **DXF** file. A **BLOCK** definition and **ENDBLK** entry completely surround the entities.

The **BLOCK** definition contains the name of the block, some block flags and its base point (or insertion point). Listing 8-47 shows the structure of the **DXF** file for a block definition. I've removed the entities within the block definition to show the basis of the shell. The **ENDBLK** entry terminates the list of entities comprising the block's structure.

Listing 8-48 shows the code for generating the block definition. We are back to the form of structure where the block definition within the program contains a pointer to a string of entity definitions. We pass this pointer to an entity handler which generates the corresponding **DXF** lines. Never code today what you can put off to a subroutine.

```
void write_line (DXF_file,from_x,from_y,to_x,to_y,layer)
FILE         *DXF_file;
double       from_x;
double       from_y;
double       to_x;
double       to_y;
char         *layer;
{
  write_dxf(DXF_file,0,"LINE");
  write_dxf(DXF_file,8,layer);
  write_dxf(DXF_file,10,&from_x);
  write_dxf(DXF_file,20,&from_y);
  write_dxf(DXF_file,11,&to_x);
  write_dxf(DXF_file,21,&to_y);
}
```
Listing 8-33. Writing the DXF file for a line.

```
void write_point (DXF_file,x,y,layer)
FILE            *DXF_file;
double          x;
double          y;
char            *layer;
{
   write_dxf(DXF_file,0,"POINT");
   write_dxf(DXF_file,8,layer);
   write_dxf(DXF_file,10,&x);
   write_dxf(DXF_file,20,&y);
}
```
Listing 8-34. Writing the DXF file for a POINT.

```
void write_circle (DXF_file,x,y,r,layer)
FILE            *DXF_file;
double          x;
double          y;
double          r;
char            *layer;
{
   write_dxf(DXF_file,0,"CIRCLE");
   write_dxf(DXF_file,8,layer);
   write_dxf(DXF_file,10,&x);
   write_dxf(DXF_file,20,&y);
   write_dxf(DXF_file,40,&r);
}
```
Listing 8-35. Writing the DXF file for a CIRCLE.

```
void write_arc (DXF_file,cx,cy,r,sa,ea,layer)
FILE            *DXF_file;
double          cx;
double          cy;
double          f;
double          sa;
double          ea;
char            *layer;
{
   write_dxf(DXF_file,0,"ARC");
   write_dxf(DXF_file,8,layer);
   write_dxf(DXF_file,10,&cx);
   write_dxf(DXF_file,20,&cy);
   write_dxf(DXF_file,40,&r);
   write_dxf(DXF_file,50,&sa);
   write_dxf(DXF_file,51,&ea);
}
```
Listing 8-36. Writing the DXF file for a ARC.

```
void write_trace (DXF_file,x1,y1,x2,y2,x3,y3,x4,y4,layer)
FILE          *DXF_file;
double        x1;
double        y1;
double        x2;
double        y2;
double        x3;
double        y3;
double        x4;
double        y4;
char          *layer;
{
    /* once inside AutoCAD, TRACEs start looking like */
    /* SOLIDS -- the four points in the arguments are */
    /* the four corners of the area covered by the    */
    /* TRACE. Your input in script is the center line */
    /* and width -- these are changed to a beveled    */
    /* area                                           */
    /*      x1,y1                          x3,y3      */
    /*           _____  */
    /*          /                                  /   */
    /*         / ----- center line ------------- /    */
    /*        /_____/     */
    /*      x2,y2                          x4,y4      */
    /*                                               */

    write_dxf(DXF_file,0,"TRACE");
    write_dxf(DXF_file,8,layer);
    write_dxf(DXF_file,10,&x1);
    write_dxf(DXF_file,20,&y1);
    write_dxf(DXF_file,11,&x2);
    write_dxf(DXF_file,21,&y2);
    write_dxf(DXF_file,12,&x3);
    write_dxf(DXF_file,22,&y3);
    write_dxf(DXF_file,13,&x4);
    write_dxf(DXF_file,23,&y4);
}
```

Listing 8-37. Writing the DXF file for a TRACE.

```
void write_solid (DXF_file,x1,y1,x2,y2,x3,y3,x4,y4,layer)
FILE            *DXF_file;
double          x1;
double          y1;
double          x2;
double          y2;
double          x3;
double          y3;
double          x4;
double          y4;
char            *layer;
{
   write_dxf(DXF_file,0,"SOLID");
   write_dxf(DXF_file,8,layer);
   write_dxf(DXF_file,10,&x1);
   write_dxf(DXF_file,20,&y1);
   write_dxf(DXF_file,11,&x2);
   write_dxf(DXF_file,21,&y2);
   write_dxf(DXF_file,12,&x3);
   write_dxf(DXF_file,22,&y3);
   write_dxf(DXF_file,13,&x4);
   write_dxf(DXF_file,23,&y4);
}
```

Listing 8-38. Writing the DXF file for a SOLID.

```
void write_text (DXF_file,justify,x1,y1,xscale,
                 ht,angle,oblique,txt,style,layer)
FILE            *DXF_file;
double          x1;
double          y1;
double          xscale;    /* scale factor */
double          ht;
double          angle;
double          oblique;   /* oblique angle */
char            *txt;
char            *style;
char            *layer;
{
  /* The DXF format for the TEXT entity needs a few */
  /* parameters not found in the SCRIPT environment */
  /* this makes the argument list somewhat changed  */

  write_DXF(DXF_file,0,"TEXT");
  write_DXF(DXF_file,8,layer);
  write_DXF(DXF_file,10,&x1);
  write_DXF(DXF_file,20,&y1);
  write_DXF(DXF_file,40,&ht);
  write_DXF(DXF_file,1,txt);
  if (angle) write_DXF(DXF_file,50,&angle);
  if (x2 != 1.0) write_DXF(DXF_file,41,&xscale);
  if (oblique) write_DXF(DXF_file,51,oblique);
  if (style) write_DXF(DXF_file,7,style);
}
```

Listing 8-39. Writing the DXF file for a TEXT.

210

```
void write_shape (DXF_file,shape,x1,y1,ht,angle,xscale,oblique,layer)
FILE          *DXF_file;
char          *shape;
double         x1;
double         y1;
double         ht;
double         angle;
double         xscale;
double         oblique;
char          *layer;
{
  write_DXF(DXF_file,0,"SHAPE");
  write_DXF(DXF_file,8,layer);
  write_DXF(DXF_file,10,&x1);
  write_DXF(DXF_file,20,&y1);
  write_DXF(DXF_file,40,&ht);
  write_DXF(DXF_file,2,shape);
  if (angle) write_DXF(DXF_file,50,&angle);
  if (xscale != 1.0) write_DXF(DXF_file,41,xscale);
  if (oblique) write_DXF(DXF_file,51,oblique);
}
```

Listing 8-40. Writing the DXF file for a SHAPE.

```
void write_insert (DXF_file,name,x1,y1,xscale,yscale,angle,
                    attribs,layer)
FILE          *DXF_file;
char          *name;
double         x1;
double         y1;
double         xscale;
double         yscale;
double         angle;
char          *layer;
{
int            i;

  i = 1;
  write_DXF(DXF_file,0,"INSERT");
  write_DXF(DXF_file,8,layer);
  /*                                                       */
  /* if attribute entities follow this INSERT entity */
  /* you must declare a complex entity with the 66   */
  /* flag -- end the sequence with an SEQEND         */
  /*                                                       */
  if (attribs) write_DXF(DXF_file,66,&1); write_DXF(DXF_file,2,name);
  write_DXF(DXF_file,10,&x1);
  write_DXF(DXF_file,20,&x2);
  if (xscale != 1.0) write_DXF(DXF_file,41,&xscale);
  if (yscale != 1.0) write_DXF(DXF_file,42,&yscale);
  if (angle) write_DXF(DXF_file,50,&angle);
}
```

Listing 8-41. Writing the DXF file for an INSERT.

```
void write_attrib (DXF_file,justify,x1,y1,xscale,ht,
                    angle,oblique,txt,name,style,layer)
FILE          *DXF_file;
double         x1;
double         y1;
double         xscale;    /* scale factor */
double         ht;
double         angle;
double         oblique;   /* oblique angle */
char          *txt;       /* attribute value */
char          *name;      /* attribute name */
char          *style;
char          *layer;
{
  /* The DXF format for the ATTRIB entity needs a few */
  /* parameters not found in the SCRIPT environment   */
  /* this makes the argument list somewhat changed    */

  write_DXF(DXF_file,0,"ATTRIB");
  write_DXF(DXF_file,8,layer);
  write_DXF(DXF_file,10,&x1);
  write_DXF(DXF_file,20,&y1);
  write_DXF(DXF_file,40,&ht);
  write_DXF(DXF_file,1,txt);
  write_DXF(DXF_file,2,name);
  if (angle) write_DXF(DXF_file,50,&angle);
  if (x2 != 1.0) write_DXF(DXF_file,41,&xscale);
  if (oblique) write_DXF(DXF_file,51,&oblique);
  if (style) write_DXF(DXF_file,7,style);
}
```

Listing 8-42. Writing the DXF file for an ATTRIBUTE.

```
void write_attdef (DXF_file,justify,x1,y1,xscale,ht,flags,
                    angle,oblique,txt,name,prompt,style,layer)
FILE          *DXF_file;
double         x1;
double         y1;
double         xscale;    /* scale factor */
double         ht;
int            flags;
double         angle;
double         oblique;   /* oblique angle */
char          *txt;       /* attribute default value */
char          *name;      /* attribute name */
char          *prompt;    /* user prompt */
char          *style;
char          *layer;
{
  /* The DXF format for the ATTDEF entity needs a few */
  /* parameters not found in the SCRIPT environment   */
```

```
/* this makes the argument list somewhat changed    */

write_DXF(DXF_file,0,"ATTDEF");
write_DXF(DXF_file,8,layer);
write_DXF(DXF_file,10,&x1);
write_DXF(DXF_file,20,&y1);
write_DXF(DXF_file,40,&ht);
write_DXF(DXF_file,1,txt);
write_DXF(DXF_file,3,prompt);
write_DXF(DXF_file,2,name);

/*   The Attribute Flags are bit settings:         */
/*    1 (bit 0)   invisible text                    */
/*    2 (bit 1)   constant value (no ATTRIB)        */
/*    4 (bit 2)   verify input                      */

write_DXF(DXF_file,70,&flags);
if (angle) write_DXF(DXF_file,50,&angle);
if (x2 != 1.0) write_DXF(DXF_file,41,&xscale);
if (oblique) write_DXF(DXF_file,51,&oblique);
if (style) write_DXF(DXF_file,7,style);
}
```

Listing 8-43. Writing the DXF file for a ATTDEF.

```
void write_pline (DXF_file,flags,width1,width2,layer)
FILE         *DXF_file;
int           flags;
double        width1;
double        width2;
char         *layer;
{
int           i;

  write_DXF(DXF_file,0,"POLYLINE");
  write_DXF(DXF_file,8,layer);

  /* The polyline flag is set by bits    */
  /* the values are:                     */
  /* 1 (bit 0) closed polyline           */
  /* 2 (bit 1) curve fit data included   */

  write_DXF(DXF_file,70,&flags);

  /* a polyline is a complex entity that */
  /* must be terminated with the SEQEND  */

  i = 1;
  write_DXF(DXF_file,66,&i);
  write_DXF(DXF_file,40,&width1);
  write_DXF(DXF_file,41,&width2);
}
```

Listing 8-44. Writing the DXF file for a POLYLINE.

```
void write_vertex(DXF_file,x,y,width1,width2,bulge,layer)
FILE            *DXF_file;
double          x;
double          y;
double          width1;
double          width2;
double          bulge;
char            *layer;
{
   write_DXF(DXF_file,0,"VERTEX");
   write_DXF(DXF_file,8,layer);
   write_DXF(DXF_file,10,&x);
   write_DXF(DXF_file,20,&y);
   if (width1) write_DXF(DXF_file,40,&width1);
   if (width2) write_DXF(DXF_file,41,&width2);
   if (bulge) write_DXF(DXF_file,42,&bulge);
}
```

Listing 8-45. Writing the DXF file for a VERTEX.

```
void write_seqend(DXF_file,layer)
FILE            *DXF_file;
char            *layer;
{
  write_DXF(DXF_file,0,"SEQEND");
  write_DXF(DXF_file,8,layer);
}
```

Listing 8-46. Writing the DXF file for a SEQEND.

```
   0
BLOCK
   8
0
   2
A_BLOCK
  10
0.0
  20
0.0
   :
ENTITIES HERE
   :
   0
ENDBLK
   8
0
```

Listing 8-47. BLOCK structure in the DXF file.

214

Table 8-2. DXF Output Routine Listing Guide.

```
typedef
  struct block_node
    {
    struct block_node        *next;
    char                     *name;
    char                     *layer;
    int                       flags;
    double                    base_x;
    double                    base_y;
    void                     *entities;
    }                         block_node;

block_node                   *block_anchor;

generate_blocks(dxf)
FILE      *dxf;
{
block_node      *b;
entity_node     *e; /* generic header */
  if ((b = block_anchor) != NULL)
```

```
{
  write_DXF(dxf,0,"SECTION");
  write_DXF(dxf,2,"BLOCKS");
  while (b)
   {
    write_DXF(dxf,0,"BLOCK");
    write_DXF(dxf,8,b->layer);
    write_DXF(dxf,2,b->name);
    write_DXF(dxf,70,&b->flags);
    write_DXF(dxf,10,&b->base_x);
    write_DXF(dxf,20,&b->base_y);
    e = (entity_node *)b->entities;
    while (e)
     {
      write_entity(dxf,e);
      e = e->next;
     }
    write_DXF(dxf,0,"ENDBLK);
    b = b->next;
   }
  write_DXF(dxf,0,"ENDSEC");
 }
}
```

Listing 8-48. Generating DXF blocks.

MODIFYING THE DXFOUT TO BE A DXFIN FILE

Perhaps easier to write than to describe is another method of generating a **DXF** file. This methods uses an existing **DXF** file to create a **DXF** file.

The main strategy is this; Read a **DXF** file and look for specific items, if you don't find the item, write the original line. If you find the item, modify the data and write the updated information.

In the printed circuit package from The Great SoftWestern Company, Inc., the Auto-Board System, two drawings share associated information. In this particular case, it is the names of electronic components. Each integrated circuit has a name. Each resistor has a name. All components have a unique identifier. As it happens, during the manufacturing phase of producing a printed circuit board, it is desirable to change the names of the components to better represent their position on the printed circuit board. However, changing the names on the printed circuit board invalidates the names created and used by the designer in the schematic diagrams.

What was needed was a program to update the schematic diagrams with the new names. The solution was to add an invisible attribute to all printed circuit board component drawings. The manufacturing engineer could not (or wasn't supposed to) change this attribute. This attribute was set to the name created by the original designer. A second attribute also carried the name created by the designer. However, this second attribute was visible and changeable.

On a modified board, both the old name and the modified names were available. There are two ways to get this list. The first way is to use the **ATTEXT** command when the drawing is in AutoCAD. With a template containing only the attributes of the name fields, the **ATTEXT** command delivers a nice list.

The second way is to write a program that scans the **DXF** file for the attribute information. The algorithms of Chapter five can be modified to perform this task. By one means or another, a list of old and new names is created.

Next, the user produces a **DXF** of the schematic diagram. The program for updating the schematic diagram quickly read and wrote the **HEADER, TABLES,** and **BLOCKS** sections of the **DXF** file. There was no pertinent information there. It was in the **ATTRI-BUTE** entities that the real information lurked. When a component name showed up in the appropriate attribute field, the new name was substituted and the field written. With the updated schematic in **DXF** form, the designer creates a new drawing using the **DXF** as its base. Listing 8-49 shows the major portion of the detection and substitution code.

```
void duplicate_dxf (fi,fo)
FILE    *fi;                         /* incoming DXF */
FILE    *fo;                         /* outgoing DXF */
{
char        quit;
int         state;
char        s[120];
char        b[120];
char        dev_name[120];
int         dev_here;
int         t;
int         stop_output;

  quit = FALSE;
  dev_here = FALSE;
  state = 1;
  stop_output = FALSE;
  while (!quit)
   {
    /* read a LINE from incoming DXF */
    fgets(b,120,fi);
    /* scan for 1st string -- TAG   */
    sscanf(b,"%s",s);
    /* convert TAG to token number   */
    t = get_token(s);
    /* all according to the current state */
    switch (state)
     {
      /* find a zero TAG to start */
      /* this handles start of sections */
      case 1:  if (t == ZERO) state = 2;
            break;
      /* continue looking for SECTION */
      /* this may be the name of a     */
      /* section TAG = 2                   */
      case 2:  state = 1;
               if (t == SECTION) state = 3;
               if (t == EOFILE) quit = TRUE;
               break;
```

217

```
case 3:  state = 1;
         if (t == TWO) state = 4;
         break;
/* we are looking for the    */
/* ENTITIES section          */
/* TAG ZERO is start of entity */
case 4:  state = 1;
         if (t == ENTITIES) state = 5;
         break;
case 5:  if (t == ZERO) state = 6;
/* TAG EIGHT is start of layer */
         if (t == EIGHT) state = 19;
         break;
/* process entities of interest */
case 6:  switch (t)
            {
             case EOFILE      : quit = TRUE;
                                break;
             case INSERT      : state = 7;
                                break;
             case ATTRIB      : state = 12;
                                break;
             case ENDSEC      : state = 1;
                                break;
             case ENDSEQ      : state = 5;
                                break;
             case EIGHT       : state = 18;
                                break;
             default          : state = 5;
                                break;
            }
         break;
case 7:  switch (t)
/* this is for INSERT     */
/* states go to nowhere   */
/* in this example, but   */
/* you could make changes */
/* to the DXF value if you */
/* wanted -- set up a state */
/* to do it when the right  */
/* tag is found             */
            {
             case ZERO   : state = 6;
                             break;
             case TWO    : state = 8;
                             break;
             case EIGHT  : state = 16;
                             break;
             case TEN    : state = 9;
                             break;
```

```
                case TWENTY  : state = 10;
                               break;
                case FIFTY   : state = 11;
                               break;
                case SIXTY6  : state = 16;
                               break;
                default      : state = 5;
                               break;
            }
        break;
case 16:
case  8:
case  9:
case 10:
case 11:
        state = 7;
        break;
/* this state is for ATTRIB    */
/* the parent program modifies */
/* the DXF attribute values    */
/* here is the tag for the     */
/* attribute value             */
case 12: switch (t)
            {
            case ZERO      : state = 6;
                             break;
            case ONE       : state = 14;
                             stop_output = TRUE;
                             break;
            case TWO       : state = 15;
                             break;
            case EIGHT     : state = 13;
                             break;
            case TEN       : state = 13;
                             break;
            case TWENTY    : state = 13;
                             break;
            case FORTY     : state = 13;
                             break;
            default        : state = 17;
                             break;
            }
        break;
case 13: state = 12;
        break;
case 14: state = 12;
/* given the value in the DXF  */
/* find the substitution value */
        strupr(s);
        strcpy(dev_name,find_new_name(s));
        break;
```

```
        case 15: state = 5;
        /* ATTRIB is finished -- write new value */
        /* to the DXF      */
            fprintf(fo,"1\n%s\n2\n",dev_name);
            stop_output = FALSE;
            break;
        case 17: state = 5;
            break;
        case 18: state = 6;
            break;
        case 19: state = 5;
            break;
     }
      /* unless done in state 15, echo */
      /* input line to outgoing DXF      */
     if (!stop_output) fprintf(fo,"%s\n",s);
   }
}
```

Listing 8-49. Using a DXF to generate a DXF file.

PGP and DXB Files

A **DXF** file is the full definition of a drawing in an **ASCII** format. This file is usually quite bulky with all of the tags, full names and the multiple characters that it takes to form a number. There is a more abbreviated form of file for preparing input data for AutoCAD. This file is a cross between the **DXF** and the **DWG** drawing file. The file is the **DXB** file. It contains only entity information about the drawing. It is in a pure binary format. You cannot read this file with the **DOS TYPE** command or a word processor.

The **DXB** format is a handy and quick method for reading partial drawing information prepared by an outside program. Program sequences to generate the **DXB** file follow this discussion. For the moment, I want to go over how you can start an external program which produces the **DXB.**

It is possible to leave the working environment of AutoCAD to run an external program. You are probably aware of the **SHELL** command in AutoCAD. The **SHELL** command is a dummy name that allows you to start and execute external programs. Why is it a dummy name? The **SHELL** command is simply an entry in the **ACAD.PGP** file. This file contains the names of commands which AutoCAD recognizes as requests for the execution of external programs.

If you look at the **PGP** file, you will find several external commands. Listing 8-50 shows the **PGP** file distributed with the AutoCAD program. All of the entries in this file start the referenced external program. You can add your own programs to this list and this is what I want to tell you about.

There are five entries in the **PGP** file record. Separate all fields with commas.

```
DEL,DEL,27000,File to delete: ,0
DIR,DIR,27000,File specification: ,0
FILECOPY,COPY,27000,*Filenames for COPY: ,0
EDLIN,EDLIN,42000,File to edit: ,0
SHELL,,127000,*DOS Command: ,0
TYPE,TYPE,27000,File to list: ,0
QSEE,QSEE,200000,*File to View : ,0
```

Listing 8-50. Typical PGP file.

1. The command name—This is the name of the command that you would like AutoCAD to recognize as a valid command. You saw that **SHELL** was just one of the entries in the **PGP.**
2. The program name—This is the name of the external program that AutoCAD sends to **DOS** as the program to start. Any special command line switches may be added to this name. If you do not want to designate a particular program name at this time, you may leave the field blank. Notice that there is no program name in the **SHELL** command. Other entries show the program name.
3. The memory size—This is the amount of memory that AutoCAD should release to the operating system **(MS-DOS)** so that your program has enough memory to run. In addition to your program, AutoCAD loads a copy of the **DOS** command processor (command.com). This is how AutoCAD and **DOS** manage to load and execute your program. When estimating the amount of memory needed for your program, allow an extra 24K for the command processor.
4. The command prompt—There may be extra command line parameters that your program needs. Sometimes merely running the program by only its name is not enough. The prompt is your method of asking for further arguments for your program. You may leave the field blank if there is no prompt. Normally, AutoCAD will accept a response to this prompt until it encounters a space or **ENTER.** You may instruct AutoCAD to accept spaces (for multiple arguments) by inserting an asterisk ("*") as the first character of the prompt.
5. The return code—This field indicates the action that AutoCAD should take when the external program finishes. It is a bit oriented value. From the descriptions that follow, add the numbers to form the desired action. A zero value for this field means that AutoCAD has no further processing. The request for a external program puts AutoCAD into **TEXT** mode (as opposed to **GRAPHICS** mode). A zero value leaves it in **TEXT** mode. The action values are:

   1 Load a **DXB** File. Your program should produce a **DXB** formatted file with "$cmd.dxb" as its filename. AutoCAD deletes this file for you.
   2 Construct a Block from the **DXB** file. Your program may construct the **DXB** details for a block. Using code 1 and code 2 (2+1=3), you can create custom blocks. The name of the block is the value entered by the response to the **PROMPT** entry. The name of the block must be new. You cannot redefine an existing block.
   4 Restore Text/Graphics Mode. As mentioned above, AutoCAD enters the text mode when it starts an external program. Adding this value to the **PGP** field value returns AutoCAD to the graphics mode.

Besides the **PGP** method of **DXB** input, there is a regular AutoCAD command for reading the **DXB.** This command is identical to the **DXFIN** command. It is the **DXBIN** command. Its use is also identical. Now that we know how to get **DXB** information into AutoCAD, let's look at the generation of **DXB** files.

There are two things to know to generate a **DXB** file. First, the **DXB** is a pure binary file. It is not **ASCII** and you cannot use the stream oriented **I/O** commands (fopen, fprintf, fputs and fclose) to create it. You must use the open, write and close statements. Second, you must have a name for the file. For programs started within AutoCAD, "$cmd.dxb" must be the name of the file. Listing 8-51 shows the code for opening the "$cmd.dxb" binary file. The language is Microsoft C. Your open statement may be slightly different.

The rest of your program should be dedicated to the production of drawing entities. The generating program will look very similar to the programs that generate **DXF** files.

```
int             DXB_file;


  DXB_file = open("$cmd.dxb", O_BINARY¦O_WRONLY¦O_CREAT,
                  I_SWRITE¦I_SREAD);
```

Listing 8-51. Opening the DXB file.

The only difference will be the output routines. The **DXF** output routines wrote several tag and value pairs to the **ASCII** output stream. The DXB output routines place entity parameters into binary structures and write the structures to the output file.

The calling sequences in the following code segments are identical to the **DXF** entity output routines. Therefore, modifying a program to write a **DXB** file should be fairly painless. There is one gotcha. In the **DXF** format, the file reference value was a pointer to the **FILE** structure. In the **DXB** format, the file reference value is an integer file handle.

First, we'll take a look at some the operational entries in the **DXB** and then we'll deliver a pile of listings to show the details of generating the individual entities. Listing 8-47 offers the #define values used in all of remaining listing. These are identification values used in the **DXB** structures.

The **DXB** file has a special heading. You must always include this heading. AutoCAD will not recognize your file if the heading is not properly constructed. Listing 8-52 shows the construction of the **DXB** header. The **DXB** file must end with a **NUL** character. I use several constants in the listings in this section to make the code more readable. Listing 8-53 is the list #define constants.

One of the interesting aspects of the **DXB** is that AutoCAD will read in either a floating point mode or an integer mode. Both modes have identical entries; they just have different data types. These modes affect coordinates and angles. Integers provide a more compact file structure using only 16 bits for each value. The floating point mode uses 64 bit values, but offers much greater accuracy in the drawing. You may elect to change modes throughout the creation of your file. Listing 8-54 shows two routines for changing the mode of the **DXB** mode.

Since there are two modes in the **DXB** and they affect the entities with coordinates and angles, some of the listings show two routines. One is in floating point mode and designated with the name "double." The other is the integer mode and has the "int" designation.

You can change layers in the **DXB**. As in the chapter on generating script files, we use a global value, current_layer, to indicate the name of the current layer. Should an entity be on another layer, we need to change the **DXB** layer and set a new current layer. Listing 8-55 shows a routine for adding a layer change to the **DXB** file. The name of the layer is an **ASCII** character string with a trailing **NUL** character. This is the normal string construction for the **C** language. You may have to be careful if you are programming in Pascal or other languages. The output must include the trailing **NUL,** so the program uses strlen to

```
void write_header(DXB_file)
int             DXB_file;
{
char            header[40];

  strcpy(header,"AutoCAD DXB 1.0\r\n\x1a");
  write(DXB_file,header,strlen(header)+1);
}
```

Listing 8-52. Generating the DXB header.

```
#define DXB_LINE            1
#define DXB_POINT           2
#define DXB_CIRCLE          3
#define DXB_ARC             8
#define DXB_TRACE           9
#define DXB_SOLID          11
#define DXB_SEQEND         17
#define DXB_POLYLINE       19
#define DXB_VERTEX         20
#define DXB_SCALE         128
#define DXB_LAYER         129
#define DXB_L_EXTEND      130
#define DXB_T_EXTEND      131
#define DXB_BLOCK         132
#define DXB_BULGE         133
#define DXB_WIDTH         134
#define DXB_MODE          135
#define DXB_INTEGER         0
#define DXB_DOUBLE          1
```

Listing 8-53. Constants used to write the DXB file.

```
void set_double(DXB_file);
int             DXB_file;
{
unsigned char       id;
int                 mode;

  id = DXB_MODE;
  mode = DXB_DOUBLE;
  write(DXB_file,(char *)&id,sizeof(id));
  write(DXB_file,(char *)&mode,sizeof(mode));
}



void set_integer(DXB_file);
int             DXB_file;
{
unsigned char       id;
int                 mode;

  id = DXB_MODE;
  mode = DXB_INTEGER;
  write(DXB_file,(char *)&id,sizeof(id));
  write(DXB_file,(char *)&mode,sizeof(mode));
}
```

Listing 8-54. Two routines for changing DXB numeric mode.

```
void write_layer(DXB_file,layer)
int             DXB_file;
char            *layer;
{
unsigned char       id;

  id = DXB_LAYER;
  write(DXB_file,(char *)&id,sizeof(id));
  write(DXB_file,layer,strlen(layer)+1);
}
```

Listing 8-55. Writing a LAYER to the DXB file.

get the length of the layer name and adds an addition space for the **NUL.** You may set a scale factor into your drawing data. I can think of two times that this may be handy. I might even use these techniques in future projects.

The first instance is to create a compact floating point file. Here is an example. If all of your entity values fall between -32.000 and 32.000 and only require three decimal places of accuracy, you could use integer values in the **DXB** file. This keeps it relatively compact. Using a scale factor of 0.001, AutoCAD scales all of your values to the proper domain.

The second instance is for units conversion. If you have a program that normally computes in feet and inches (especially, inches), but you need to meet the demands of a metric oriented market (as in the rest of the world). Add a scale factor to the beginning of the **DXB** that will bring your values into line with a metric drawing. Multiply your inches by 2.54 and you have centimeters. Multiply your inches by 25.4 and you have millimeters. You can go on computing in inches, write the **DXB** file in inches and make a metric world happy. An argument in the **PGP** file can tell your program whether to add or ignore the scale factor. Listing 8-56 shows the code for adding a scale factor to your **DXB** file. The numeric mode does not affect this routine.

One of the switches in the **PGP** structure tells AutoCAD to regard the incoming **DXB** file as a block definition. The first entity value in the **DXB** file for a block definition must be a **BLOCK** entry. This block entry establishes the base point of the block. This value affects the transformation of the coordinates of the defining entities upon insertion of the block. This base value is usually 0.0,0.0, but could be any other value. Listing 8-57 shows the routines for defining the base coordinates of the block.

```
void write_scale (DXB_file,factor)
int             DXB_file;
double          factor;
{
struct
  {
  unsigned char         id;
  double                scale_factor;
  }                     scaling;

  scaling.id = DXB_SCALE;
  scaling.scale_factor = factor;
  write(DXB_file,(char *)&scaling,sizeof(scaling));
}
```

Listing 8-56. Setting a SCALE FACTOR in the DXB file.

```
void write_block(DXB_file,x,y,layer)
int             DXB_file;
double          x;
double          y;
char            layer;
{
struct
  {
   unsigned char        id;
   double               x;
   double               y;
  }                     block_double;

   if (strcmp(layer,current_layer))
     {
      write_layer(DXB_file,layer);
      current_layer = layer;
     }

   block_double.id = DXB_BLOCK;
   block_double.x = x;
   block_double.y = y;
   write(DXB_file,(char *)&block_double,sizeof(block_double));
}



void write_block(DXB_file,x,y,layer)
int             DXB_file;
int          x;
int          y;
char            layer;
{
struct
  {
   unsigned char        id;
   int               x;
   int               y;
  }                     block_int;

   if (strcmp(layer,current_layer))
     {
      write_layer(DXB_file,layer);
      current_layer = layer;
     }

   block_int.id = DXB_BLOCK;
   block_int.x = x;
   block_int.y = y;
   write(DXB_file,(char *)&block_int,sizeof(block_int));
}
```

Listing 8-57. Two routines for writing a BLOCK to the DXB file.

The remainder of the code listings cover the entities of the **DXB** file. Most are quite similar to their **DXF** and script counterparts. They expect the same type data. I mentioned in the section about script entities that you may choose to use pointers to structures for getting data to the routines in place of individual arguments. The same suggestion holds here. The examples here are specifically designed to show the similarity in the calling sequences from one output form to the next. The form of the output has no bearing on the preparation. The major difference is the form in referencing the file.

The **LINE** and **TRACE** routines deserve a special comment. The normal **LINE** and **TRACE** routines generate records for a single line or trace segment. To ease the generation of continuous lines and the repeating of the previous segment's endpoint, AutoCAD offers line and trace extension records. These records allow you to generate a line with several vertices by only naming the next endpoints. You will see these routines in the listings as write_ext_line and write_ext_trace.

The polyline structure is fully disassembled in the **DXB.** You make individual entries for line width changes, arc bulges and vertex coordinates. The bulge factor is the ratio of the distance between the endpoints of the arc and the height of the arc at its midpoint. The routine in the listing asks for the distance and the height, calculating the ratio before placing it into the record. Polylines must end with a **SEQEND** record. Table 8-3 lists the **DXB** entities and their respective listing.

BLOCK	Listing 8-57
LINE	Listing 8-58
LINE EXTENSION	Listing 8-59
POINT	Listing 8-60
CIRCLE	Listing 8-61
ARC	Listing 8-62
TRACE	Listing 8-63
TRACE EXTENSION	Listing 8-64
SOLID	Listing 8-65
POLYLINE	Listing 8-66
VERTEX	Listing 8-67
WIDTH	Listing 8-68
BULGE	Listing 8-69
SEQEND	Listing 8-70

Table 8-3. DXB Output Routine Listing Guide.

```
void write_line (DXB_file,from_x,from_y,to_x,to_y,layer)
int          DXB_file;
double       from_x;
double       from_y;
double       to_x;
double       to_y;
char         *layer;
{
struct
  {
  unsigned char        id;
  double               from_x;
  double               from_y;
  double               to_x;
  double               to_y;
  }                    line_double;

  if (strcmp(layer,current_layer))
   {
    write_layer(DXB_file,layer);
    current_layer = layer;
   }

  line_double.id = DXB_LINE;
  line_double.from_x = from_x;
  line_double.from_y = from_y;
  line_double.to_x = to_x;
  line_double.to_y = to_y;
  write(DXB_file,(char *)&line_double,sizeof(line_double));
}


void write_line (DXB_file,from_x,from_y,to_x,to_y,layer)
int          DXB_file;
int          from_x;
int          from_y;
int          to_x;
int          to_y;
char         *layer;
{
struct
  {
  unsigned char        id;
  int                  from_x;
  int                  from_y;
  int                  to_x;
  int                  to_y;
  }                    line_int;

  if (strcmp(layer,current_layer))
   {
    write_layer(DXB_file,layer);
    current_layer = layer;
```

```
    }
  line_int.id = DXB_LINE;
  line_int.from_x = from_x;
  line_int.from_y = from_y;
  line_int.to_x = to_x;
  line_int.to_y = to_y;
  write(DXB_file,(char *)&line_int,sizeof(line_int));
}
```
Listing 8-58. Two routines for writing a LINE to the DXB file.

```
void write_ext_line (DXB_file,to_x,to_y)
int          DXB_file;
int          to_x;
int          to_y;
{
struct
 {
  unsigned char       id;
  double              to_x;
  double              to_y;
 }                    l_extend_double;

  l_extend_double.id = DXB_L_EXTEND;
  l_extend_double.to_x = to_x;
  l_extend_double.to_y = to_y;
  write(DXB_file,(char * )&l_extend_double,sizeof(l_extend_double));
}
```

```
void write_ext_line (DXB_file,to_x,to_y)
int          DXB_file;
int          to_x;
int          to_y;
{
struct
 {
  unsigned char       id;
  int                 to_x;
  int                 to_y;
 }                    l_extend_int;

  l_extend_int.id = DXB_L_EXTEND;
  l_extend_int.to_x = to_x;
  l_extend_int.to_y = to_y;
  write(DXB_file,(char *)&l_extend_int,sizeof(l_extend_int));
}
```
Listing 8-59. Two routines for extending a LINE in the DXB file.

228

```
void write_point (DXB_file,x,y,layer)
int            DXB_file;
double         x;
double         y;
char           *layer;
{
struct
 {
  unsigned char        id;
  double               point_x;
  double               point_y;
 }                     point_double;

  if (strcmp(layer,current_layer))
   {
    write_layer(DXB_file,layer);
    current_layer = layer;
    }

  point_double.id =  DXB_POINT;
  point_double.point_x =  x;
  point_double.point_y =  y;
  write(DXB_file,(char *)&point_double,sizeof(point_double));
}




void write_point (DXB_file,x,y,layer)
int            DXB_file;
int            x;
int            y;
char           *layer;
{
struct
 {
  unsigned char        id;
  int                  point_x;
  int                  point_y;
 }                     point_int;

  if (strcmp(layer,current_layer))
   {
    write_layer(DXB_file,layer);
    current_layer = layer;
    }

  point_int.id =  DXB_POINT;
  point_int.point_x =  x;
  point_int.point_y =  y;
  write(DXB_file,(char *)&point_int,sizeof(point_int));
}
```

Listing 8-60. Two routines for writing a POINT to the DXB file.

```
void write_circle (DXB_file,x,y,r,layer)
int          DXB_file;
double       x;
double       y;
double       r;
char         *layer;
{
struct
  {
  unsigned char        id;
  double               center_x;
  double               center_y;
  double               radius;
  }                    circle_double;

  if (strcmp(layer,current_layer))
    {
    write_layer(DXB_file,layer);
    current_layer = layer;
    }

  circle_double.id = DXB_CIRCLE;
  circle_double.center_x = x;
  circle_double.center_y = y;
  circle_double.radius = r;
  write(DXB_file,(char *)&circle_double,sizeof(circle_double));
}


void write_circle (DXB_file,x,y,r,layer)
int          DXB_file;
int          x;
int          y;
int          r;
char         *layer;
{
struct
  {
  unsigned char        id;
  int                  center_x;
  int                  center_y;
  int                  radius;
  }                    circle_int;

  if (strcmp(layer,current_layer))
    {
    write_layer(DXB_file,layer);
    current_layer = layer;
    }
```

```
      circle_int.id = DXB_CIRCLE;
      circle_int.center_x = x;
      circle_int.center_y = y;
      circle_int.radius = r;

      write(DXB_file,(char *)&circle_int,sizeof(circle_int));
}
```

Listing 8-61. Two routines for writing a CIRCLE to the DXB file.

```
void write_arc (DXB_file,cx,cy,r,sa,ea,layer)
int             DXB_file;
double          cx;
double          cy;
double          r;
double          sa;
double          ea;
char            *layer;
{
struct
  {
  unsigned char         id;
  double                center_x;
  double                center_y;
  double                radius;
  double                start_angle;
  double                end_angle;
  }                     arc_double;

  if (strcmp(layer,current_layer))
    {
    write_layer(DXB_file,layer);
    current_layer = layer;
    }

  arc_double.id = DXB_ARC;
  arc_double.center_x = x;
  arc_double.center_y = y;
  arc_double.radius = r;
  arc_double.start_angle = sa;
  arc_double.end_angle = ea;
  write(DXB_file,(char *)&arc_double,sizeof(arc_double));
}

void write_arc (DXB_file,cx,cy,r,sa,ea,layer)
int             DXB_file;
int             cx;
int             cy;
int             r;
int             sa;
```

231

```
int              ea;
char             *layer;
{
struct
  {
  unsigned char            id;
  int                      center_x;
  int                      center_y;
  int                      radius;
  int                      start_angle;
  int                      end_angle;
  }                        arc_int;


if (strcmp(layer,current_layer))
  {
  write_layer(DXB_file,layer);
  current_layer = layer;
  }

arc_int.id = DXB_ARC;
arc_int.center_x = x;
arc_int.center_y = y;
arc_int.radius = r;
arc_int.start_angle = sa;
arc_int.end_angle = ea;
write(DXB_file,(char *)&arc_int,sizeof(arc_int));
}
```

Listing 8-62. Two routines for writing an ARC to the DXB file.

```
void write_trace (DXB_file,x1,y1,x2,y2,x3,y3,x4,y4,layer)
int             DXB_file;
double          x1;
double          y1;
double          x2;
double          y2;
double          x3;
double          y3;
double          x4;
double          y4;
char            *layer;
{
struct
 {
  unsigned char         id;
  double                x1;
  double                y1;
  double                x2;
  double                y2;
  double                x3;
  double                y3;
  double                x4;
  double                y4;
 }                       trace_double;

  if (strcmp(layer,current_layer))
   {
    write_layer(DXB_file,layer);
    current_layer = layer;
   }

  trace_double.id = DXB_TRACE;
  trace_double.x1 = x1;
  trace_double.y1 = y1;
  trace_double.x2 = x2;
  trace_double.y2 = y2;
  trace_double.x3 = x3;
  trace_double.y3 = y3;
  trace_double.x4 = x4;
  trace_double.y4 = y4;
  write(DXB_file,(char *)&trace_double,sizeof(trace_double));
}
```

```
void write_trace (DXB_file,x1,y1,x2,y2,x3,y3,x4,y4,layer)
int          DXB_file;
int          x1;
int          y1;
int          x2;
int          y2;
int          x3;
int          y3;
int          x4;
int          y4;
char         *layer;
{
struct
  {
  unsigned char        id;
  int                  x1;
  int                  y1;
  int                  x2;
  int                  y2;
  int                  x3;
  int                  y3;
  int                  x4;
  int                  y4;
  }                    trace_int;

  if (strcmp(layer,current_layer))
    {
    write_layer(DXB_file,layer);
    current_layer = layer;
    }

  trace_int.id = DXB_TRACE;
  trace_int.x1 = x1;
  trace_int.y1 = y1;
  trace_int.x2 = x2;
  trace_int.y2 = y2;
  trace_int.x3 = x3;
  trace_int.y3 = y3;
  trace_int.x4 = x4;
  trace_int.y4 = y4;
  write(DXB_file,(char *)&trace_int,sizeof(trace_int));
}
```

Listing 8-63. Two routines for writing a TRACE to the DXB file.

```
void write_ext_trace (DXB_file,x3,y3,x4,y4)
int           DXB_file;
int           x3;
int           y3;
int           x4;
int           y4;
{
struct
  {
  unsigned char        id;
  double               new_x3;
  double               new_y3;
  double               new_x4;
  double               new_y4;
  }                    t_extend_double;

  t_extend_double.id = DXB_T_EXTEND;
  t_extend_double.new_x3 = x3;
  t_extend_double.new_y3 = y3;
  t_extend_double.new_x4 = x4;
  t_extend_double.new_y4 = y4;
  write(DXB_file,(char * )&t_extend_double,sizeof(t_extend_double));
}


void write_ext_trace (DXB_file,x3,y3,x4,y4)
int           DXB_file;
int           x3;
int           y3;
int           x4;
int           y4;
{
struct
  {
  unsigned char        id;
  int                  new_x3;
  int                  new_y3;
  int                  new_x4;
  int                  new_y4;
  }                    t_extend_int;

  t_extend_int.id = DXB_T_EXTEND;
  t_extend_int.new_x3 = x3;
  t_extend_int.new_y3 = y3;
  t_extend_int.new_x4 = x4;
  t_extend_int.new_y4 = y4;
  write(DXB_file,(char *)&t_extend_int,sizeof(t_extend_int));
}
```

Listing 8-64. Two routines for extending a TRACE in the DXB file.

```
void write_solid (DXB_file,x1,y1,x2,y2,x3,y3,x4,y4,layer)
int            DXB_file;
double         x1;
double         y1;
double         x2;
double         y2;
double         x3;
double         y3;
double         x4;
double         y4;
char           *layer;
{
struct
  {
   unsigned char        id;
   double               x1;
   double               y1;
   double               x2;
   double               y2;
   double               x3;
   double               y3;
   double               x4;
   double               y4;
  }                      solid_double;

  if (strcmp(layer,current_layer))
   {
    write_layer(DXB_file,layer);
    current_layer = layer;
   }

  solid_double.id = DXB_SOLID;
  solid_double.x1 = x1;
  solid_double.y1 = y1;
  solid_double.x2 = x2;
  solid_double.y2 = y2;
  solid_double.x3 = x3;
  solid_double.y3 = y3;
  solid_double.x4 = x4;
  solid_double.y4 = y4;
  write(DXB_file,(char *)&solid_double,sizeof(solid_double));
}


void write_solid (DXB_file,x1,y1,x2,y2,x3,y3,x4,y4,layer)
int            DXB_file;
int            x1;
int            y1;
int            x2;
```

```
int            y2;
int            x3;
int            y3;
int            x4;
int            y4;
char           *layer;
{
struct
 {
  unsigned char        id;
  int                  x1;
  int                  y1;
  int                  x2;
  int                  y2;
  int                  x3;
  int                  y3;
  int                  x4;
  int                  y4;
 }                     solid_int;

  if (strcmp(layer,current_layer))
   {
    write_layer(DXB_file,layer);
    current_layer = layer;
   }

  solid_int.id = DXB_SOLID;
  solid_int.x1 = x1;
  solid_int.y1 = y1;
  solid_int.x2 = x2;
  solid_int.y2 = y2;
  solid_int.x3 = x3;
  solid_int.y3 = y3;
  solid_int.x4 = x4;
  solid_int.y4 = y4;
  write(DXB_file,(char *)&solid_int,sizeof(solid_int));
}
```

Listing 8-65. Two routines for writing a SOLID to the DXB file.

```
void write_pline (DXB_file,closure,layer)
int          DXB_file;
int          closure;
char         *layer;
{
unsigned char    id;

  if (strcmp(layer,current_layer))
    {
     write_layer(DXB_file,layer);
     current_layer = layer;
    }

  id = DXB_POLYLINE;
  write(DXB_file,(char *)&id,sizeof(id));
  write(DXB_file,(char *)&closure,sizeof(closure));
}
```
Listing 8-66. Writing the DXB file for a POLYLINE.

```
void write_vertex (DXB_file,x,y)
int          DXB_file;
double       x;
double       y;
{
struct
  {
   unsigned char      id;
   double             x;
   double             y;
  }                   vertex_double;

  vertex_double.id = DXB_VERTEX;
  vertex_double.x = x;
  vertex_double.y = y;
  write(DXB_file,(char *)&vertex_double,sizeof(vertex_double));
}



void write_vertex (DXB_file,x,y)
int          DXB_file;
int          x;
int          y;
{
struct
  {
   unsigned char      id;
   int                x;
   int                y;
  }                   vertex_int;
```

```
  vertex_int.id = DXB_VERTEX;
  vertex_int.x = x;
  vertex_int.y = y;
  write(DXB_file,(char *)&vertex_int,sizeof(vertex_int));
}
```

Listing 8-67. Two routines for writing a polyline VERTEX to the DXB.

```
void write_width (DXB_file,sw,ew)
int          DXB_file;
double       sw;
double       ew;
{
struct
 {
  unsigned char        id;
  double               sw;
  double               ew;
 }                      width_double;

  width_double.id = DXB_VERTEX;
  width_double.sw = sw;
  width_double.ew = ew;
  write(DXB_file,(char *)&width_double,sizeof(width_double));
}


void write_width (DXB_file,sw,ew)
int          DXB_file;
int          sw;
int          ew;
{
struct
 {
  unsigned char        id;
  int                  sw;
  int                  ew;
 }                      width_int;

  width_int.id = DXB_VERTEX;
  width_int.sw = sw;
  width_int.ew = ew;
  write(DXB_file,(char *)&width_int,sizeof(width_int));
}
```

Listing 8-68. Two routines for writing a polyline WIDTH to the DXB.

```
void write_bulge (DXB_file,h,d)
int             DXB_file;
double          h;
double          d;
{
struct
  {
  unsigned char         id;
  float                 two_h_over_d;
  }                     bulge;

  bulge.id = DXB_BULGE;
  bulge.two_h_over_d = (h + h) / d;
  write(DXB_file,(char *)&bulge,sizeof(bulge));
}
```
Listing 8-69. Writing a polyline BULGE to the DXB.

```
void write_seqend (DXB_file)
int             DXB_file;
{
unsigned char    id;

  id = DXB_SEQEND;
  write(DXB_file,(char *)&id,sizeof(id));
}
```
Listing 8-70. Writing the DXB file for a SEQEND.

Appendix A
Multilingual AutoCAD

THE FOLLOWING LISTINGS COMPRISE THE LANGUAGE TRANSLATIONS OF ENGLISH AUTO-CAD commands to French, German, Italian, and Spanish. Included in your program as described in Chapter 7, you can write programs that can operate with any of the versions of AutoCAD. The listings are all portions of the **"LANG.H" INCLUDE** file.

Listing A-1 is the standard English listing. This is activated by defining the word **"ENGLISH"** in your C program. You can do this from the command line or inside your program with the #define command.

Listing A-2 is the French listing. This is activated by defining the word **"FRENCH"** in your C program.

Listing A-3 is the German listing. This is activated by defining the word **"GERMAN"** in your C program.

Listing A-4 is the Italian listing. This is activated by defining the word **"ITALIAN"** in your C program.

Listing A-5 is the Spanish listing. This is activated by defining the word **"SPANISH"** in your C program.

```
#ifdef ENGLISH
#define ALL         "A"
#define APERTURE    "APERTURE"
#define ARC         "ARC"
#define AREA        "AREA"
#define ARRAY       "ARRAY"
#define ATTDEF      "ATTDEF"
#define ATTDISP     "ATTDISP"
#define ATTEDIT     "ATTEDIT"
#define ATTEXT      "ATTEXT"
#define BASE        "BASE"
#define BLIPMODE    "BLIPMODE"
#define BLOCK       "BLOCK"
#define BLUE        "BLUE"
#define BREAK       "BREAK"
#define CHAMFER     "CHAMFER"
#define CHANGE      "CHANGE"
#define CIRCLE      "CIRCLE"
#define COLOR       "COLOR"
#define COPY        "COPY"
#define CYAN        "CYAN"
#define DBLIST      "DBLIST"
#define DELAY       "DELAY"
#define DIM         "DIM"
#define DIST        "DIST"
#define DIVIDE      "DIVIDE"
#define DONUT       "DONUT"
#define DOUGHNUT    "DOUGHNUT"
#define DRAGMODE    "DRAGMODE"
#define DTEXT       "DTEXT"
#define DXBIN       "DXBIN"
#define DXBOUT      "DXBOUT"
#define DXFIN       "DXFIN"
#define ELEV        "ELEV"
#define ELLIPSE     "ELLIPSE"
#define END         "END"
#define ERASE       "ERASE"
#define EXPLODE     "EXPLODE"
#define EXTEND      "EXTEND"
#define EXTENTS     "E"
#define FILES       "FILES"
#define FILL        "FILL"
#define FILLET      "FILLET"
#define GREEN       "GREEN"
#define GRID        "GRID"
#define HIDE        "HIDE"
#define ID          "ID"
#define IGESIN      "IGESIN"
#define IGESOUT     "IGESOUT"
#define INSERT      "INSERT"
```

```
#define ISOPLANE    "ISOPLANE"
#define LAST        "L"
#define LAYER       "LAYER"
#define LCHANGE     "L"
#define LIMITS      "LIMITS"
#define LINE        "LINE"
#define LINETYPE    "LINETYPE"
#define LIST        "LIST"
#define LOAD        "LOAD"
#define LTSCALE     "LTSCALE"
#define MAGENTA     "MAGENTA"
#define MEASURE     "MEASURE"
#define MENU        "MENU"
#define MINSERT     "MINSERT"
#define MIRROR      "MIRROR"
#define MOVE        "MOVE"
#define MSLIDE      "MSLIDE"
#define NEW         "NEW"
#define OFF         "OFF"
#define OFFSET      "OFFSET"
#define ON          "ON"
#define OOPS        "OOPS"
#define ORTHO       "ORTHO"
#define OSNAP       "OSNAP"
#define PAN         "PAN"
#define PEDIT       "PEDIT"
#define PLINE       "PLINE"
#define PLOT        "PLOT"
#define POINT       "POINT"
#define POLYGON     "POLYGON"
#define PRPLOT      "PRPLOT"
#define PURGE       "PURGE"
#define QTEXT       "QTEXT"
#define QUIT        "QUIT"
#define RED         "RED"
#define REDO        "REDO"
#define REDRAW      "REDRAW"
#define REGEN       "REGEN"
#define REGENAUTO   "REGENAUTO"
#define RENAME      "RENAME"
#define RESUME      "RESUME"
#define ROTATE      "ROTATE"
#define RSCRIPT     "RSCRIPT"
#define SAVE        "SAVE"
#define SCALE       "SCALE"
#define SCRIPT      "SCRIPT"
#define SELECT      "SELECT"
#define SET         "SET"
#define SETVAR      "SETVAR"
#define SH          "SH"
```

```
#define SHAPE       "SHAPE"
#define SHELL       "SHELL"
#define SKETCH      "SKETCH"
#define SNAP        "SNAP"
#define SOLID       "SOLID"
#define STATUS      "STATUS"
#define STRETCH     "STRETCH"
#define STYLE       "STYLE"
#define TABLET      "TABLET"
#define TEXT        "TEXT"
#define TIME        "TIME"
#define TRACE       "TRACE"
#define TRIM        "TRIM"
#define U           "U"
#define UNDO        "UNDO"
#define UNITS       "UNITS"
#define VIEW        "VIEW"
#define VIEWRES     "VIEWRES"
#define VPOINT      "VPOINT"
#define VSLIDE      "VSLIDE"
#define WBLOCK      "WBLOCK"
#define WHITE       "WHITE"
#define WIDTH       "W"
#define WINDOW      "W"
#define YELLOW      "YELLOW"
#define YES         "Y"
#define ZOOM        "ZOOM"
#endif
```
Listing A-1. The standard English commands.


```
#ifdef FRENCH
#define ALL         "T"
#define APERTURE    "OUVERTUR"
#define ARC         "ARC"
#define AREA        "AIRE"
#define ARRAY       "RESEAU"
#define ATTDEF      "ATTDEF"
#define ATTDISP     "ATTECRAN"
#define ATTEDIT     "ATTEDIT"
#define ATTEXT     "ATTEXTR"
#define BASE        "BASE"
#define BLIPMODE    "MARQUES"
#define BLOCK       "BLOC"
#define BLUE        "BLEU"
#define BREAK       "COUPURE"
#define CHAMFER     "CHNFREIN"
#define CHANGE      "CHANGER"
#define CIRCLE      "CERCLE"
#define COLOR       "COUL"
```

```
#define COPY       "COPIER
#define CYAN       "CYAN"
#define DBLIST     "DBLISTE"
#define DELAY      "DELAI"
#define DIM        "COTATION"
#define DIST       "DISTANCE"
#define DRAGMODE   "EVOLDYN"
#define DXBIN      "CHARGDXB"
#define DXFIN      "CHARGDXF"
#define ELEV       "ELEV"
#define END        "FIN"
#define ERASE      "EFFACER"
#define EXTENTS    "E"
#define FILES      "FICHIERS"
#define FILL       "REMPLIR"
#define FILLET     "RACCORD"
#define GREEN      "VERT"
#define GRID       "GRILLE"
#define HIDE       "CACHE"
#define ID         "ID"
#define INSERT     "INSERER"
#define ISOPLANE   "ISOMETR"
#define LAST       "D"
#define LAYER      "PLAN"
#define LCHANGE    "P"
#define LIMITS     "LIMITES"
#define LINE       "LIGNE"
#define LINETYPE   "TYPELIGN"
#define LIST       "LISTE"
#define LOAD       "CHARGER"
#define LTSCALE    "ECHLTP"
#define MAGENTA    "MAGENTA"
#define MENU       "MENU"
#define MIRROR     "MIROIR"
#define MOVE       "MOVE"
#define MSLIDE     "MEMCLICH"
#define NEW        "NOU"
#define OFF        "IN"
#define ON         "AC"
#define OOPS       "REPRISE"
#define ORTHO      "ORTHO"
#define OSNAP      "ACCROBJ"
#define PAN        "PAN"
#define PEDIT      "PEDIT"
#define PLINE      "POLYLIGN"
#define PLOT       "TRACEUR"
#define POINT      "POINT"
#define PRPLOT     "IMPGRAPH"
#define PURGE      "PURGER"
#define QTEXT      "RAPTEXTE"
```

```
#define QUIT        "QUITTER"
#define RED         "ROUGE"
#define REDRAW      "REDESS"
#define REGEN       "REGEN"
#define REGENAUTO   "REGNAUTO"
#define RENAME      "RENOMMER"
#define RESUME      "RESUMER"
#define RSCRIPT     "RSCRIPT"
#define SAVE        "SAUVEGRD"
#define SCRIPT      "SCRIPT"
#define SET         "MET"
#define SHAPE       "FORME"
#define SKETCH      "MAINLEV"
#define SNAP        "RESOL"
#define SOLID       "SOLIDE"
#define STATUS      "ETAT"
#define STYLE       "STYLE"
#define TABLET      "TABLETTE"
#define TEXT        "TEXTE"
#define TRACE       "TRACE"
#define UNITS       "UNITES"
#define VIEW        "VUES"
#define VPOINT      "POINTVUE"
#define VSLIDE      "AFFCLICH"
#define WBLOCK      "WBLOC"
#define WHITE       "BLANC"
#define WIDTH       "E"
#define WINDOW      "F"
#define YELLOW      "JAUNE"
#define YES         "O"
#define ZOOM        "ZOOM"
#endif
```

Listing A-2. English to French translations.

```
#ifdef GERMAN
#define ALL         "A"
#define APERTURE    "OEFFNUNG"
#define ARC         "BOGEN"
#define AREA        "FLAECHE"
#define ARRAY       "REIHE"
#define ATTDEF      "ATTDEF"
#define ATTDISP     "ATTZEIG"
#define ATTEDIT     "ATTEDIT"
#define ATTEXT      "ATTEXT"
#define BASE        "BASIS"
#define BLIPMODE    "KPMODUS"
#define BLOCK       "BLOCK"
#define BLUE        "BLAU"
#define BREAK       "BRUCH"
```

```
#define CHAMFER      "FACETTE"
#define CHANGE       "AENDERN"
#define CIRCLE       "KREIS"
#define COLOR        "FARBE"
#define COPY         "KOPIEREN"
#define CYAN         "CYAN"
#define DBLIST       "DBLISTE"
#define DELAY        "PAUSE"
#define DIM          "BEM"
#define DIST         "ABSTAND"
#define DIVIDE       "TEILEN"
#define DONUT        "RING"
#define DOUGHNUT     "RING"
#define DRAGMODE     "ZUGMODUS"
#define DXBIN        "DXBIN"
#define DXBOUT       "DXBOUT"
#define DXFIN        "DXFIN"
#define DXBOUT       "DXFOUT"
#define ELEV         "ERHEBUNG"
#define ELLIPSE      "ELLIPSE"
#define END          "ENDE"
#define ERASE        "LOESCHEN"
#define EXPLODE      "URSPRUNG"
#define EXTEND       "DEHNEN"
#define EXTENTS      "G"
#define FILES        "DATEIEN"
#define FILL         "FUELLEN"
#define FILLET       "ABRUNDEN"
#define GREEN        "GRUEN"
#define GRID         "RASTER"
#define HIDE         "VERDECKT"
#define ID           "ID"
#define IGESOUT      "IGESIN"
#define IGESOUT      "IGESOUT"
#define INSERT       "EINFUEGE"
#define ISOPLANE     "ISOBENE"
#define LAST         "L"
#define LAYER        "LAYER"
#define LCHANGE      "L"
#define LIMITS       "LIMITEN"
#define LINE         "LINIE"
#define LINETYPE     "LINIENTYP"
#define LIST         "LISTE"
#define LOAD         "LADEN"
#define LTSCALE      "LTFAKTOR"
#define MAGENTA      "MAGENTA"
#define MEASURE      "MESSEN"
#define MENU         "MENUE"
#define MINSERT      "MEINFUEG"
#define MIRROR       "SPIEGELN"
```

```
#define MOVE        "SCHIEBEN"
#define MSLIDE      "MACHDIA"
#define NEW         "NEU"
#define OFF         "AUS"
#define OFFSET      "VERSETZ"
#define ON          "EIN"
#define OOPS        "HOPPLA"
#define ORTHO       "ORTHO"
#define OSNAP       "OFANG"
#define PAN         "PAN"
#define PEDIT       "PEDIT"
#define PLINE       "PLINIE"
#define PLOT        "PLOT"
#define POINT       "PUNKT"
#define POLYGON     "POLYGON"
#define PRPLOT      "PRPLOT"
#define PURGE       "BEREINIG"
#define QTEXT       "QTEXT"
#define QUIT        "QUIT"
#define RED         "ROT"
#define REDO        "ZLOESCH"
#define REDRAW      "NEUZEICH"
#define REGEN       "REGEN"
#define REGENAUTO   "REGENAUTO"
#define RENAME      "UMBENENN"
#define RESUME      "RESUME"
#define ROTATE      "DREHEN"
#define RSCRIPT     "RSCRIPT"
#define SAVE        "SICHERN"
#define SCALE       "VARIA"
#define SCRIPT      "SCRIPT"
#define SELECT      "WAHL"
#define SET         "SETZ"
#define SHAPE       "SYMBOL"
#define SHELL       "SHELL"
#define SKETCH      "SKIZZE"
#define SNAP        "FANG"
#define SOLID       "SOLID"
#define STATUS      "STATUS"
#define STRETCH     "SKRECK"
#define STYLE       "STIL"
#define TABLET      "TABLETT"
#define TEXT        "TEXT"
#define TIME        "ZEIT"
#define TRACE       "BAND"
#define TRIM        "STUTZEN"
#define UNITS       "EINHEIT"
#define VIEW        "AUSSCHNT"
#define VIEWRES     "AUFLOES"
#define VPOINT      "APUNKT"
```

```
#define VSLIDE      "ZEIGDIA"
#define WBLOCK      "WBLOCK"
#define WHITE       "WEISS"
#define WIDTH       "B"
#define WINDOW      "F"
#define YELLOW      "GELB"
#define YES         "J"
#define ZOOM        "ZOOM"
#endif
```

Listing A-3. English to German translations.

```
#ifdef ITALIAN
#define ALL         "T"
#define APERTURE    "APERTURA"
#define ARC         "ARCO"
#define AREA        "AREA"
#define ARRAY       "SERIE"
#define ATTDEF      "DEFATT"
#define ATTDISP     "VISATT"
#define ATTEDIT     "EDITATT"
#define ATTEXT      "ESTRATT"
#define BASE        "BASE"
#define BLIPMODE    "PUNTINI"
#define BLOCK       "BLOCCO"
#define BLUE        "BLU"
#define BREAK       "SPEZZA"
#define CHAMFER     "SIMA"
#define CHANGE      "CAMBIA"
#define CIRCLE      "CERCHIO"
#define COLOR       "COLORE"
#define COPY        "COPIA"
#define CYAN        "AZZURRO"
#define DBLIST      "LISTABD"
#define DELAY       "PAUSA"
#define DIM         "DIM"
#define DIST        "DIST"
#define DRAGMODE    "TRASCINA"
#define DXBIN       "DXBIN"
#define DXFIN       "DXFIN"
#define ELEV        "ELEV"
#define END         "FINE"
#define ERASE       "CANCELLA"
#define EXTENTS     "E"
#define FILES       "FILE"
#define FILL        "RIEMPIE"
#define FILLET      "RACCORDO"
#define GREEN       "VERDE"
#define GRID        "GRIGLIA"
#define HIDE        "NASCONDE"
```

```
#define ID          "ID"
#define INSERT      "INSER"
#define ISOPLANE    "PIANOASS"
#define LAST        "P"
#define LAYER       "PIANO"
#define LCHANGE     "P"
#define LIMITS      "LIMITI"
#define LINE        "LINEA"
#define LINETYPE    "TLINEA"
#define LIST        "LISTA"
#define LOAD        "CARICA"
#define LTSCALE     "SCALATL"
#define MAGENTA     "MAGENTA"
#define MENU        "MENU"
#define MINSERT     "MINSERT"
#define MIRROR      "SPECCHIO"
#define MOVE        "SPOSTA"
#define MSLIDE      "GENDIA"
#define NEW         "NUOVO"
#define OFF         "OFF"
#define ON          "ON"
#define OOPS        "OOPS"
#define ORTHO       "ORTO"
#define OSNAP       "OSNAP"
#define PAN         "PAN"
#define PEDIT       "EDITPL"
#define PLINE       "PLINEA"
#define PLOT        "PLOT"
#define POINT       "PUNTO"
#define PRPLOT      "PLOTST"
#define PURGE       "ELIMINA"
#define QTEXT       "TESTOV"
#define QUIT        "USCIRE"
#define RED         "ROSSO"
#define REDRAW      "RIDIS"
#define REGEN       "RIGEN"
#define REGENAUTO   "RIGENAUTO"
#define RENAME      "RINOMINA"
#define RESUME      "RIPRENDE"
#define RSCRIPT     "RSCRIPT"
#define SAVE        "SALVA"
#define SCRIPT      "SCRIPT"
#define SET         "PIANOCOR"
#define SHAPE       "FORMA"
#define SHELL       "SHELL"
#define SKETCH      "SCHIZZO"
#define SNAP        "SNAP"
#define SOLID       "POLIGONO"
#define STATUS      "STATO"
#define STYLE       "STILE"
```

```
#define TABLET     "TAVOLET"
#define TEXT       "TESTO"
#define TRACE      "TRACCIA"
#define UNITS      "UNITA"
#define VIEW       "VISTA"
#define VPOINT     "PVISTA"
#define VSLIDE     "VISDIA"
#define WBLOCK     "MBLOCCO"
#define WHITE      "BIANCO"
#define WIDTH      "G"
#define WINDOW     "F"
#define YELLOW     "GIALLO"
#define YES        "S"
#define ZOOM       "ZOOM"
#endif
```

Listing A-4. English to Italian translations.

```
#ifdef SPANISH
#define ALL        "T"
#define APERTURE   "APERTURA"
#define ARC        "ARCO"
#define AREA       "AREA"
#define ARRAY      "MATRIZ"
#define ATTDEF     "DEFATR"
#define ATTDISP    "VISUATR"
#define ATTEDIT    "EDITATR"
#define ATTEXT     "EXTRATR"
#define BASE       "BASE"
#define BLIPMODE   "MARCAAUX"
#define BLOCK      "BLOQUE"
#define BLUE       "AZUL"
#define BREAK      "PARTE"
#define CHAMFER    "CHAFLAN"
#define CHANGE     "CAMBIA"
#define CIRCLE     "CIRCULO"
#define COLOR      "COLOR"
#define COPY       "COPIA"
#define CYAN       "CIANO"
#define DBLIST     "LISTBD"
#define DELAY      "RETARDA"
#define DIM        "ACOTA"
#define DIST       "DIST"
#define DRAGMODE   "ARRASTRE"
#define DXBIN      "CARGADXB"
#define DXFIN      "CARGADXF"
#define ELEV       "ELEV"
#define END        "FIN"
#define ERASE      "BORRA"
#define EXTENTS    "E"
```

```
#define FILES      "FICHEROS"
#define FILL       "RELLENA"
#define FILLET     "EMPALME"
#define GREEN      "VERDE"
#define GRID       "TRAMA"
#define HIDE       "OCULTA"
#define ID         "ID"
#define INSERT     "INSER"
#define ISOPLANE   "ISOPLANO"
#define LAST       "P"
#define LAYER      "CAPA"
#define LCHANGE    "C"
#define LIMITS     "LIMITES"
#define LINE       "LINEA"
#define LINETYPE   "TIPOLIN"
#define LIST       "LIST"
#define LOAD       "CARGA"
#define LTSCALE    "ESCALATL"
#define MAGENTA    "MAGENTA"
#define MENU       "MENU"
#define MIRROR     "SIMETRIA"
#define MOVE       "DESPLAZA"
#define MSLIDE     "SACAFOTO"
#define NEW        "CREA"
#define OFF        "DES"
#define ON         "ACT"
#define OOPS       "RECUPERA"
#define ORTHO      "ORTO"
#define OSNAP      "REFENT"
#define PAN        "ENCUADRE"
#define PEDIT      "EDITPOL"
#define PLINE      "POL"
#define PLOT       "SALTRAZ"
#define POINT      "PUNTO"
#define PRPLOT     "SALIMPR"
#define PURGE      "LIMPIA"
#define QTEXT      "LOCTEXTO"
#define QUIT       "QUITA"
#define RED        "ROJO"
#define REDRAW     "REDIBUJA"
#define REGEN      "REGEN"
#define REGENAUTO  "REGENAUTO"
#define RENAME     "RENOMBRA"
#define RESUME     "REANUDA"
#define RSCRIPT    "RELGUION"
#define SAVE       "SALVA"
#define SCRIPT     "GUION"
#define SET        "DEF"
#define SHAPE      "FORMA"
#define SHELL      "PROGREXT"
```

```
#define SKETCH    "BOCETO"
#define SNAP      "FORZCOOR"
#define SOLID     "SOLIDO"
#define STATUS    "ESTADO"
#define STYLE     "ESTILO"
#define TABLET    "TABLERO"
#define TEXT      "TEXTO"
#define TRACE     "TRAZO"
#define UNITS     "UNIDADES"
#define VIEW      "VISTA"
#define VPOINT    "PTOVISTA"
#define VSLIDE    "MIRAFOTO"
#define WBLOCK    "BLADISCO"
#define WHITE     "BLANCO"
#define WIDTH     "G"
#define WINDOW    "I"
#define YELLOW    "AMARILLO"
#define YES       "S"
#define ZOOM      "FOCAL"
#endif
```

Listing A-5. English to Spanish translations.

Appendix B
DXF Header Entries

TABLE B-1 LISTS THE ENTRIES FOUND IN A TYPICAL **DXF** file. Each name appears as it is spelled in the **DXF**. These name values have a tag value of 9. Following the name of the entry is the tag number for the entry's value. There is a short description of the entry following the tag number. Some descriptions contain appropriate values for the entry.

$ACADVER	1	AutoCAD Database Version
$ANGBASE	50	Angle 0 Direction
$ANGDIR	70	Direction of Angle Rotation
		0 = counterclockwise
		1 = clockwise
$ATTMODE	70	Attribute Visibility Mode
		0 = None Visible
		1 = Normal
		2 = All Visible
$AUNITS	70	Format for Angle from UNITS
		1 = Decimal degrees
		2 = Degrees/Minutes/Seconds
		3 = Grads
		4 = Radians
		5 = Surveyor's Units
$AUPREC	70	Format for Angle Fraction Precision
$AXISMODE	70	Axis Visibility (0 = OFF and 1 = ON)
$AXISUNIT	10	Axis Tick Spacing -- X Axis
	20	Axis Tick Spacing -- Y Axis
$BLIPMODE	70	Blip Display (0 = OFF and 1 = ON)
$CECOLOR	70	Current Entity Color (0 = BYBLOCK 256 = BYLAYER)
$CELTYPE	70	Current Linetype
$CLAYER	8	Name of Layer
$COORDS	70	Display Mode of Coordinates
		0 = Static Coordinates
		1 = Continuous Update
		2 = "d<a"
$DIMASZ	40	Arrow Size for Dimensions
$DIMBLK	1	Arrow Block Name
$DIMCEN	40	Size of Center Mark
$DIMDLE	40	Dimension Line Extension
$DIMDLI	40	Dimension Line Increment
$DIMEXE	40	Extension Line Extension
$DIMEXO	40	Extension Line Offset
$DIMLIM	70	Dimension Lines (0 = OFF and 1 = ON)
$DIMRND	40	Dimension Rounding Value
$DIMSCALE	40	Dimensioning Scale Factor
$DIMSE1	70	1st Extension Line Suppression (0 = OFF and 1 = ON)
$DIMSE2	70	2nd Extension Line Suppression (0 = OFF and 1 = ON)

$DIMTAD	70	Text ABOVE Dimension Line (0 = OFF and 1 = ON)
$DIMTIH	70	Text INSIDE Horizontal (0 = OFF and 1 = ON)
$DIMTM	40	Minus Tolerance
$DIMTOH	70	Text OUTSIDE Horizontal (0 = OFF and 1 = ON)
$DIMTOL	70	Dimension Tolerances (0 = OFF and 1 = ON)
$DIMTP	40	Plus Tolerance
$DIMTSZ	40	Dimension Tick Size
$DIMTXT	40	Dimensioning Text Height
$DIMZIN	70	Display ZERO Inches (0 = OFF and 1 = ON)

$DRAGMODE   70 Drag Mode Switch
                             0 = Off
                             1 = On
                             2 = Auto

$ELEVATION	40	Current Elevation

$EXTMAX   10 Drawing Extents -- Upper Right X Coordinate
                   20 Drawing Extents -- Upper Right Y Coordinate
                   30 Drawing Extents -- Upper Right Z Coordinate
                                   (if not 0.0)

$EXTMIN   10 Drawing Extents -- Lower Left X Coordinate
                   20 Drawing Extents -- Lower Left Y Coordinate
                   30 Drawing Extents -- Lower Left Z Coordinate
                                   (if not 0.0)

$FILLETRAD	40	Fillet Radius
$FILLMODE	70	Fill Mode (0 = OFF and 1 = ON)
$GRIDMODE	70	Grid Mode (0 = OFF and 1 = ON)

$GRIDUNIT   10 Grid X Spacing
                     20 Grid Y Spacing

$INSBASE   10 Insertion Base X coordinate
                    20 Insertion Base Y coordinate
                    30 Insertion Base Z coordinate (if not 0.0)

$LIMCHECK	70	Limits Checking (0 = OFF and 1 = ON)

$LIMMAX   10 Drawing Limits -- Upper Right X Coordinate
                   20 Drawing Limits -- Upper Right Y Coordinate

$LIMMIN   10 Drawing Limits -- Lower Left X Coordinate
                   20 Drawing Limits -- Lower Left X Coordinate

$LTSCALE	40	Linetype Scaling Factor

$LUNITS   70 Format for Coordinates and Distances
                           1 = Scientific
                           2 = Decimal
                           3 = Engineering
                           4 = Architectural

$LUPREC   70 Format for Coordinate and Distance Fractional
                       Precision

$MENU	1	Name of Current Menu File
$ORTHOMODE	70	ORTHO Mode Switch (0 = OFF and 1 = ON)
$OSMODE	70	Object Snap Mode
$PDMODE	70	Point Display Mode
$PDSIZE	40	Point Display Size
$PLINEWID	40	Current (default) Polyline Width
$QTEXTMODE	70	Quick Text Mode (0 = OFF and 1 = ON)
$REGENMODE	70	REGENAUTO Mode (0 = OFF and 1 = ON)
$SKETCHINC	40	Sketch Recording Increment
$SNAPANG	50	Snap Grid Rotation Angle
$SNAPBASE	10	Snap Grid Base X Coordinate
	20	Snap Grid Base Y Coordinate
$SNAPISOPAIR	70	Isometric Plane
		0 = Left
		1 = Top
		2 = Right
$SNAPMODE	70	SNAP Mode (0 = OFF and 1 = ON)
$SNAPSTYLE	70	Snap Style
		0 = Standard
		1 = Isometric
$SNAPUNIT	10	Snap Grid X Spacing
	20	Snap Grid Y Spacing
$TEXTSIZE	40	Current (default) Text Height
$THICKNESS	40	Current Thickness
$TRACEWID	40	Current Trace Width
$USERI1	70	Integer User Value
$USERI2	70	Integer User Value
$USERI3	70	Integer User Value
$USERI4	70	Integer User Value
$USERI5	70	Integer User Value
$USERR1	40	Floating Point User Value
$USERR2	40	Floating Point User Value
$USERR3	40	Floating Point User Value
$USERR4	40	Floating Point User Value
$USERR5	40	Floating Point User Value
$VIEWCTR	10	Screen Center of Current View -- X Coordinate
	20	Screen Center of Current View -- Y Coordinate
$VIEWDIR	10	Current View Point -- X Coordinate
	20	Current View Point -- Y Coordinate
	30	Current View Point -- Z Coordinate (if not 0.0)
$VIEWSIZE	40	Height of Current View on Screen

Table B-1. DXF Header Entries

Appendix C
DXF Header Data Structure

THE FOLLOWING LISTING IS THE EXPANDED DATA STRUCTURE USED TO GENERATE **DXF** header entries. Chapter 8 covers its use and implementation.

```
hdr_block           header[] =
    {{"$ACADVER",     STRING, (void *)acadver},
     {"$ANGBASE",     ANGLE,  (void *)&angbase},
     {"$ANGDIR",      INTEGER,(void *)&angdir},
     {"$AXISMODE",    INTEGER,(void *)&axismode},
     {"$AXISUNIT",    COORDX, (void *)&axisunitx},
     { NULL      ,    COORDY, (void *)&axisunity},
     {"$AUNITS",      INTEGER,(void *)&aunits},
     {"$AUPREC",      INTEGER,(void *)&auprec},
     {"$ATTMODE",     INTEGER,(void *)&attmode},
     {"$BLIPMODE",    INTEGER,(void *)&blipmode},
     {"$CLAYER",      LAYER,  (void *)&clayer},
     {"$COORDS",      INTEGER,(void *)&coords},
     {"$DIMASZ",      REAL,   (void *)&dimasz},
     {"$DIMBLK",      STRING, (void *)dimblk},
     {"$DIMDLI",      REAL,   (void *)&dimdli},
     {"$DIMEXE",      REAL,   (void *)&dimexe},
     {"$DIMEXO",      REAL,   (void *)&dimexo},
     {"$DIMCEN",      REAL,   (void *)&dimcen},
     {"$DIMDLE",      REAL,   (void *)&dimdle},
     {"$DIMLIM",      INTEGER,(void *)&dimlim},
     {"$DIMRND",      REAL,   (void *)&dimrnd},
     {"$DIMSCALE",    REAL,   (void *)&dimscale},
     {"$DIMSE1",      INTEGER,(void *)&dimse1},
     {"$DIMSE2",      INTEGER,(void *)&dimse2},
     {"$DIMTAD",      INTEGER,(void *)&dimtad},
     {"$DIMTIH",      INTEGER,(void *)&dimtih},
     {"$DIMTM",       REAL,   (void *)&dimtm},
     {"$DIMTOH",      INTEGER,(void *)&dimtoh},
     {"$DIMTOL",      INTEGER,(void *)&dimtol},
     {"$DIMTP",       REAL,   (void *)&dimtp},
     {"$DIMTSZ",      REAL,   (void *)&dimtsz},
     {"$DIMTXT",      REAL,   (void *)&dimtxt},
     {"$DIMZIN",      INTEGER,(void *)&dimzin},
     {"$DRAGMODE",    INTEGER,(void *)&dragmode},
     {"$ELEVATION",   REAL,   (void *)&elevation},
     {"$EXTMAX",      COORDX, (void *)&extmaxx},
     { NULL  ,        COORDY, (void *)&extmaxy},
     { NULL  ,        COORDZ, (void *)&extmaxz},
     {"$EXTMIN",      COORDX, (void *)&extminx},
     { NULL  ,        COORDY, (void *)&extminy},
     { NULL  ,        COORDZ, (void *)&extminz},
     {"$FILLETRAD",   REAL,   (void *)&filletrad},
     {"$FILLMODE",    INTEGER,(void *)&fillmode},
     {"$GRIDMODE",    INTEGER,(void *)&gridmode},
     {"$GRIDUNIT",    COORDX, (void *)&gridunitx},
     { NULL      ,    COORDY, (void *)&gridunity},
     {"$INSBASE",     COORDX, (void *)&insbasex},
     { NULL      ,    COORDY, (void *)&insbasey},
     { NULL      ,    COORDZ, (void *)&insbasez},
```

```
{"$LIMCHECK",     INTEGER,(void *)&limcheck},
{"$LIMMIN",       COORDX, (void *)&limminx},
{ NULL   ,        COORDY, (void *)&limminy},
{"$LIMMAX",       COORDX, (void *)&limmaxx},
{ NULL   ,        COORDY, (void *)&limmaxy},
{"$LTSCALE",      REAL,   (void *)&ltscale},
{"$LUNITS",       INTEGER,(void *)&lunits},
{"$LUPREC",       INTEGER,(void *)&luprec},
{"$MENU",         STRING, (void *)menu},
{"$ORTHOMODE",    INTEGER,(void *)&orthomode},
{"$OSMODE",       INTEGER,(void *)&osmode},
{"$PDMODE",       INTEGER,(void *)&pdmode},
{"$PDSIZE",       REAL,   (void *)&pdsize},
{"$PLINEWID",     REAL,   (void *)&plinewid},
{"$QTEXTMODE",    INTEGER,(void *)&qtextmode},
    double              extminx;
    double              extminy;
    double              extminz;
    double              fastzoom;
    double              filletrad;
    int                 fillmode;
    int                 gridmode;
    double              gridunitx;
    double              gridunity;
    double              insbasex;
    double              insbasey;
    double              insbasez;
    int                 limcheck;
    double              limmaxx;
    double              limmaxy;
    double              limminx;
    double              limminy;
    double              ltscale;
    int                 lunits;
    int                 luprec;
    char                menu[12];
    int                 orthomode;
    int                 osmode;
    int                 pdmode;
    double              pdsize;
    double              plinewid;
    int                 qtextmode;
    int                 regenmode;
    double              sketchinc;
    double              skpoly;
    double              snapang;
    double              snapbasex;
    double              snapbasey;
    int                 snapisopair;
    int                 snapmode;
```

```
int                        snapstyle;
double                     snapunitx;
double                     snapunity;
double                     tdcreate;
double                     tdindwg;
double                     tdupdate;
double                     tdusrtimer;
double                     textsize;
double                     textstyle;
double                     thickness;
double                     tracewid;
int                        useri1;
int                        useri2;
int                        useri3;
int                        useri4;
int                        useri5;
double                     userr1;
double                     userr2;
double                     userr3;
double                     userr4;
double                     userr5;
double                     usrtimer;
double                     viewctrx;
double                     viewctry;
double                     viewctrz;
double                     viewdirx;
double                     viewdiry;
double                     viewdirz;
double                     viewsize;
double                     zoompct;
#define STRING     1
#define INTEGER    2
#define REAL       3
#define COORDX     4
#define COORDY     5
#define COORDZ     6
#define ANGLE      7
#define LAYER      8

typedef
  struct
   {
    char        *name;
    int          type;
    void        *var;
   }            hdr_block;

char                       acadver[16];
int                        angbase;
double                     angdir;
```

```
int                     attmode;
int                     aunits;
int                     auprec;
int                     axismode;
double                  axisunitx;
double                  axisunity;
int                     blipmode;
int                     cecolor;
int                     celtype;
double                  chamfera;
double                  chamferb;
int                     clayer;
int                     coords;
double                  dimasz;
char                    dimblk[40];
double                  dimcen;
double                  dimdle;
double                  dimdli;
double                  dimexe;
double                  dimexo;
double                  dimrnd;
double                  dimscale;
double                  dimtm;
int                     dimlim;
int                     dimse1;
int                     dimse2;
int                     dimtad;
int                     dimtih;
int                     dimtoh;
int                     dimtol;
int                     dimzin;
double                  dimtp;
double                  dimtsz;
double                  dimtxt;
int                     dragmode;
double                  elevation;
double                  extmaxx;
double                  extmaxy;
double                  extmaxz;
{"$REGENMODE",   INTEGER,(void *)&regenmode},
{"$SKETCHINC",   REAL,   (void *)&sketchinc},
{"$SNAPANG",     ANGLE,  (void *)&snapang},
{"$SNAPBASE",    COORDX, (void *)&snapbasex},
{ NULL      ,    COORDY, (void *)&snapbasey},
{"$SNAPISOPAIR",INTEGER,(void *)&snapisopair},
{"$SNAPMODE",    INTEGER,(void *)&snapmode},
{"$SNAPSTYLE",   INTEGER,(void *)&snapstyle},
{"$SNAPUNIT",    COORDX, (void *)&snapunitx},
{ NULL      ,    COORDY, (void *)&snapunity},
{"$THICKNESS",   REAL,   (void *)&thickness},
```

```
{"$TEXTSIZE",    REAL,     (void *)&textsize},
{"$TRACEWID",    REAL,     (void *)&tracewid},
{"$USERI1",      INTEGER,(void *)&useri1},
{"$USERI2",      INTEGER,(void *)&useri2},
{"$USERI3",      INTEGER,(void *)&useri3},
{"$USERI4",      INTEGER,(void *)&useri4},
{"$USERI5",      INTEGER,(void *)&useri5},
{"$USERR1",      REAL,     (void *)&userr1},
{"$USERR2",      REAL,     (void *)&userr2},
{"$USERR3",      REAL,     (void *)&userr3},
{"$USERR4",      REAL,     (void *)&userr4},
{"$USERR5",      REAL,     (void *)&userr5},
{"$VIEWCTR",     COORDX,   (void *)&viewctrx},
{ NULL    ,      COORDY,   (void *)&viewctry},
{ NULL    ,      COORDZ,   (void *)&viewctrz},
{"$VIEWDIR",     COORDX,   (void *)&viewdirx},
{ NULL    ,      COORDY,   (void *)&viewdiry},
{ NULL    ,      COORDZ,   (void *)&viewdirz},
{"$VIEWSIZE",    REAL,     (void *)&viewsize},
{"$ZOOMPCT",     INTEGER,(void *)&zoompct},
{ NULL, 0,       NULL}};
```

Listing C-1. DXF header structures.

Appendix D
Working Type Definitions

THE LISTINGS IN THIS APPENDIX REPRESENT REAL TYPE DEFINITIONS THAT I EXTRACTED from working software source code. These represent the structures for AutoCAD tables, block, and entity definitions. They may differ from the examples in the body of the book, but those exist more for the sake of illustration. These are working defintions and are more thorough.

Notice that the listing for the "text_type" contains several fields that are not usually associated with the **TEXT** entity. These fields belong to the **ATTDEF** and **ATTRIB** entities. All three entities use the same structure. **TRACE** and **SOLID** use the same structure.

```
typedef
  struct dash_type
    {
    struct   dash_type *next;
    double             length;
    }                  dash_type
```

```
typedef
  struct ltype_type
    {
    struct ltype_type *next;
    char              *name;
    char              *descript;
    int                flags;
    int                alignment;
    int                dashes;
    double             length;
    struct dash_type  *dash_length;
    }                  ltype_type;
```

Listing D-1. The linetype type definition.

```
typedef
  struct layer_type
    {
    struct layer_type *next;
    char              *name;
    int                flags;
    int                color;
    int                used;
    char              *lt;
    }                  layer_type;
```

Listing D-2. The layer type definition.

```
typedef
  struct style_type
    {
    struct style_type  *next;
    char               *name;
    int                 flags;
    int                 gen_flags;
    double              txt_scale;
    double              height;
    double              oblique;
    double              last_height;
    char               *font;
    char               *big_font;
    }                   style_type;
```

Listing D-3. The style type definition.

```
typedef
  struct view_type
    {
    struct view_type   *next;
    char               *name;
    int                 flags;
    double              v_height;
    double              v_width;
    double              v_ctr_x;
    double              v_ctr_y;
    double              v_dir_x;
    double              v_dir_y;
    double              v_dir_z;
    }                   view_type;
```
Listing D-4. The view type definition.

```
typedef
  struct block_type
    {
    struct block_type  *next;
    int                 what;
    char               *name;
    int                 flags;
    layer_type         *lyr;
    ltype_type         *ltype;
    double              base_x;
    double              base_y;
    void               *ent;
    }                   block_type;
```
Listing D-5. The block type definition.

```
typedef
struct line_type
{
  struct line_type *next;
  int               what;
  char             *lyr;
  char             *lt;
  double            sx;
  double            sy;
  double            ex;
  double            ey;
  double            w1;
  double            w2;
  double            bulge;
  char              last_one;
  struct line_type  *vertex;
}                 line_type;
```
Listing D-6. The line type definition.

```
typedef
  struct point_type
    {
    struct point_type *next;
    int               what;
    char              *lyr;
    char              *lt;
    double            px;
    double            py;
    }                 point_type;
```

Listing D-7. The point type definition.

```
typedef
  struct circle_type
    {
    struct circle_type *next;
    int                what;
    char               *lyr;
    char               *lt;
    double             cx;
    double             cy;
    double             r;
    }                  circle_type;
```

Listing D-8. The circle type definition.

```
typedef
  struct arc_type
    {
    struct arc_type *next;
    int             what;
    char            *lyr;
    char            *lt;
    int             flags;
    double          acx;
    double          acy;
    double          ar;
    double          sa;
    double          ea;
    double          width;
    }               arc_type;
```

Listing D-9. The arc type definition.

```
typedef
  struct trace_type
    {
     struct trace_type    *next;
     int                   what;
     char                 *lyr;
     char                 *lt;
     double                x1;
     double                y1;
     double                x2;
     double                y2;
     double                x3;
     double                y3;
     double                x4;
     double                y4;
    }                      trace_type;
```

Listing D-10. The trace type definition.

```
typedef
  struct text_type
    {
     struct text_type     *next;
     int                   what;
     char                 *lyr;
     char                 *lt;
     double                ix;
     double                iy;
     double                height;
     char                 *text;
     char                 *prompt;
     char                 *def_value;
     char                 *tag;
     int                   field_length;
     int                   att_flags;
     double                angle;
     double                x_scale;
     double                oblique;
     style_type           *font;
     int                   gen_flags;
     int                   justify;
     double                ax;
     double                ay;
    }                      text_type;
```

Listing D-11. The text type definition.

```
typedef
  struct shape_type
    {
     struct shape_type      *next;
     int                     what;
     char                   *lyr;
     char                   *lt;
     double                  ix;
     double                  iy;
     double                  size;
     char                   *shape_name;
     double                  angle;
     double                  x_scale;
     double                  oblique;
    }                        shape_type;
```

Listing D-12. The shape type definition.

```
typedef
  struct
    {
     struct insert_type     *next;
     int                     what;
     char                   *lyr;
     char                   *lt;
     int                     att_flags;
     char                   *b;
     double                  ix;
     double                  iy;
     double                  angle;
     double                  x_scale;
     double                  y_scale;
     double                  z_scale;
     int                     rows;
     int                     columns;
     double                  r_space;
     double                  c_space;
    }                        insert_type;
```

Listing D-13. The insert type definition.

Index

273